Under Wraps

Under Wraps

A History of Menstrual Hygiene Technology

SHARRA L. VOSTRAL

LEXINGTON BOOKS

A division of
ROWMAN & LITTLEFIELD PUBLISHERS, INC.
Lanham • Boulder • New York • Toronto • Plymouth, UK

LEXINGTON BOOKS

A division of Rowman & Littlefield Publishers, Inc.
A wholly owned subsidary of The Rowman & Littlefield Publishing Group, Inc.
4501 Forbes Boulevard, Suite 200, Lanham, Maryland 20706
http://www.lexingtonbooks.com

Estover Road,
Plymouth PL6 7PY
United Kingdom

British Library Cataloguing in Publication Information Available

Library of Congress Cataloging-in-Publication Data

The hardback edition of this book was previously cataloged by the Library of Congress as
follows:

Vostral, Sharra, 1968-
  Under wraps : a history of menstrual hygiene technology / Sharra Vostral.
    p. ; cm.
  Includes bibliographical references and index.
  1. Feminine hygiene products—United States—History—20th century. 2. Women—
Health and hygiene—Equipment and supplies—United States. I. Title.
  [DNLM: 1. Menstrual Hygiene Products—history—United States. 2. Menstruation—
United States. 3. History, 19th Century—United States. 4. History, 20th Century—
United States. 5. Menstrual Hygiene Products—ethics—United States. 6. Social
Perception—United Sates. 7. Women—psychology—United States. WP 11 AA1
V971u 2008]
  RG108.V67 2008
  618.1'72—dc22   2008000180

ISBN 978-0-7391-1385-1 (cloth : alk. paper)
ISBN 978-0-7391-1386-8 (pbk. : alk. paper)

☺™ The paper used in this publication meets the minimum requirements of American
National Standard for Information Sciences—Permanence of Paper for Printed Library
Materials, ANSI/NISO Z39.48-1992.

Printed in the United States of America

For Ray & Eads
"Too"

Contents

Acknowledgments

First things first. I must thank my husband, Ray Fouché, who now knows more than any man really needs to know about menstrual hygiene. In fact, he has enough anecdotal evidence to write a piece about women who told *him* their menstrual experiences, even when I was not present. The way we both have inhabited this research for the entirety of our relationship is a testament to his goodwill, sense of humor, and belief in me. It goes without saying that this book took shape in large part because he opened a door into science and technology studies, through which I gladly leapt. Little did I know how profound this intersectional approach upon my thinking would be.

There are many people who helped me to complete this book. I would like to say thank you to those who supported my efforts during graduate school at Washington University in St. Louis. Nancy Grant provided me the tools I would need to be resourceful. I greatly appreciated the generosity, intellectual acumen and support from Jeanie Attie, Iver Bernstein, Erin Mackie, Liann Tsoukas, Christine Ruane, Andrea Friedman, Howard Brick, and Gerald Early. I would also like to thank Elaine Berland, Angela Miller, Mary Ann Dzuback, Suzanne Loui, Elizabeth Kolmer, Raye Riggins, Adele Tuchler, Bette Marbs, Sheryl Peltz, Betsy Kellerman, Ben Cawthra, Laura Westhoff, Barbara Krauthamer, Pam Sanfilippo, Linda Sturtz, and Catherine Forslund. Other folks—Steve Cline, Molly Cline, Grace Cline, John Cline, Mike Ward, Betsy Ward, Mark Hill, Kenny Blacharczyk, Lisa Conard, Chris Eckard, Glenn Yanagi, and Laura Johnson—provided me with a rich array of friendships.

Colleagues from Purdue University, Rensselaer Polytechnic Institute, the University of Illinois and beyond have contributed in multiple ways. Siobhan Somerville, Susan Curtis, Whitney Walton, Sally Hastings, Anne Fernald, Aparajita Sagar, Ron Eglash, Linnda Caporael, Nancy Campbell, Kate Boyer, Langdon Winner, Linda Layne, David Hess, Charlotte Borst, Ben Barker-Benfield, Kathy High, Alan Nadel, Katherine Isbister, Ron Kline and Marge Kline all chimed in with prescient perspectives. Antoinette Burton, Leslie Reagan, Elizabeth Pleck, Lillian Hoddeson, Gail Hawisher, Pat Gill, Cris Mayo, Sarah Projansky, Lisa Nakamura, Kirstie Dorr, Sara Clarke Kaplan, Eric McDuffie, and Paula Treichler have provided a rich environment in which to complete this book.

I also have to thank the research assistance of Kurtis Albright, Lindsey Bachman, Jordan Belen, Scott Bigler, Briana Brookes, Kevin Fodness, Aparna Kar, Stefan Melnick, Dimple Patel, Laura Szypulski and Rebecca Moore at Resselaer Polytechnic Institute. I appreciate their research forays immensely.

Skilled librarians and archivists, including Tracey MacGowan in Special Collections at Texas Woman's University Blagg-Huey Library, and Sarah Souther at the History Factory, procured items and documents for me. Lawyers Tom Riley and Sara Riley helped me sort out issues concerning the Rely tampon court case. Harry Finley, who founded the Museum of Menstruation, has single-handedly amassed the best collection of menstrual related material I have ever seen and I am indebted to him. I also relied on oral history to fill in stories that no archive houses. I thank all the many women who spoke to me and gave me their trust.

Since this book was a number of years in the making, various renditions of chapters, articles, and manuscripts were submitted to anonymous reviewers. Many of their suggestions for references, clarifications, and sources have been incorporated in this product, and I appreciate the time and energy they spent assessing the text and arguments. I also thank Sara Luttfring for copy editing the manuscript. Despite the many corrections that she suggested, any errors are mine alone.

Many thanks to my family, Henry Vostral, Lois Vostral, Mara Vostral, Chandra Vostral, Andy Schauer, Daphne Schauer, Marilynn Fouché, Chris Watkins, De Vonne Fouché, Sierra Watkins, and Francesca Watkins. And, I thank my four-year-old son Eads for his enthusiasm. Though I thought he was blissfully ignorant about the completion of this book, he has sat by me with a highlighter helping me edit, and has shared "big news" with his teacher that I am writing a book. Thank you all.

• • •

Sections of chapter 4 represent revised parts of an essay that first appeared under the title "Masking Menstruation: The Emergence of Menstrual Hygiene Products in the United States," in Andrew Shail and Gillian Howie, eds., *Menstruation: A Cultural History* (New York: Palgrave, 2005).

Chapter 1

Menstrual Hygiene:
A Techno-Social History

It seemed like the school year always began with a hot day. Wendy felt a bit nervous because tomorrow was the first day of high school, and she was part of the Croton, New York class of 1976. What would she wear: hot pants or a mini-skirt? It seemed like the mini-skirt might be cooler. After settling on the mini-skirt, things became less clear when her first period started. Would people be able to see the outline of her sanitary pad or menstrual blood seeping out underneath the skirt? She opted for the hot pants, but the pressure of going to high school and getting her period were almost unbearable. She recalled, "I didn't think anyone could see the actual napkin, but I just didn't know if going up and down stairs someone would say 'Oh, there's a spot.' I didn't know. I had never had it before."[1] Wendy still had a lot to learn about what product would work well with her body, and she had to negotiate with her mother about what she could use. Getting her period propelled her into a world not entirely of her making, filled with the politics of what it means to be a woman, as demarcated by menstruation. She also wanted to make sure her sanitary napkin would work to absorb menstrual fluid, and allow her to move throughout the day unnoticed.

Wendy's experience with menarche and menstrual hygiene technologies is not unique, but represents some important issues. The first is that the bodily event of menstruation has its own politics. Wendy knew enough that she needed to alter her behavior while at school to act like she was not menstruating. She

1

learned these cues from her friends, family, and societal reinforcement. The second issue is that menstrual hygiene technologies enabled her to pass as a nonbleeder on that first day of school. It was important to Wendy that her period be concealed under her skirt, and since this was uncertain, wearing hot pants and opting for the sanitary pad seemed to make better sense. It therefore allowed her to go about her day without teenagers taunting her about menstrual blood leaking through her clothing or showing from underneath her skirt.

This book examines menstrual politics about women's bodies and technologies of passing with menstrual hygiene products, and assumes that both political ideas and technologies are mutually constitutive and co-produced. Women's wants, uses, and desires shape the form and delivery of menstrual hygiene technologies, just as the technologies influence women's behavior and therefore societal attitudes about women and being a woman. These relationships are explored in this book by first looking at the technological history and marketing of sanitary napkins and tampons. Second, it engages women as users of technologies, citing specific examples situated within the United States at particular historical moments. Third, it argues that the practices of menstrual hygiene can be interpreted using the framework of passing to better understand how these technologies have functioned in women's daily lives.

Though much has been written about theorizing the body and this work has promoted a rethinking of the relationships between gender and power, on a utilitarian, pragmatic, and very untheoretical level, almost all women must manage visceral menstrual blood at one point or another during their lifetimes. Though this physiological process might be considered a near universal experience for women, how it is interpreted, understood, and managed varies wildly in different times, places, and cultures. For the purposes of this book, I examine developments in the United States from about 1870 to 1980, though clearly there is more work to be done in comparative and transnational frameworks. By focusing on the United States, I examine the cultural context at the moment menstrual hygiene technologies were rolled out for public purchase. Although the chapters will address specific issues, user groups, and patents, on the whole menstruation in the United States has been viewed as a problem, regardless of whether or not this is a fair assessment. Posed as a problem, it is one that technology might fix. Of course, some women do not need much technological fixing. They seem to breeze through their periods with a light flow, relatively little or no cramping, employing sanitary pads or tampons that work just as the designers intended. Other women have a heavier flow, and the technological fix only creates different problems, with blood leaking from the sanitary pad or flowing around a tampon onto undergarments. In a society that values cleanliness, stained clothing can be read as a moral, and not technological, failure. There are very real issues of bodily management that a woman participates in when using menstrual hygiene technologies. For example, the elastic belt and pad combination worn from the mid-1920s to the 1970s often caught pubic hair and tended to slip and slide between the legs; tampons introduced in the 1930s sometimes put pressure on the bladder creating the need to urinate more often; adhesive pads or those with wings available by the 1980s still often managed to wick blood onto clothing. Clearly, menstrual hygiene technologies have been no panacea. Yet despite the limitations, they do offer many women some semblance of control over their bodies.

Exploring why it is that women need this kind of bodily control and how women might use and manipulate these technologies for their own ends are questions made more visible within the framework of passing. The rhetorical use of passing can mean menstrual fluid passing out of the body, or even the idea of passage from childhood to adulthood, of which menstruation is an important marker. However, the phenomenon of passing of which I speak is traditionally associated with a person moving from one identity to another, often across lines of race, gender, or sexual orientation. For instance, there are numerous examples of individuals defined as light-skinned black people passing as white. The ability to be defined as white has historically carried opportunity and privilege not generally extended to people identified as black. Thus, passing offers a means to obtain a new political identity. In terms of gender, both men and women have dressed in drag in order to represent the other. Regardless of their reasons for donning the clothes, crossdressers alter their appearance and affectations so skillfully that many people believe the representation and the performance, and thus the practice of passing is convincing.

Passing need not be so dramatic, however, and can be thought of as much more subtle and common. Hair coloring enables a brown-haired person to pass as blonde, for example, and this passage might allow a person to fulfill the misguided stereotype that "blondes have more fun." The concept of passing is not new, but thinking about the relationship of passing to technology provides a different lens with which to view the use of menstrual hygiene products. Linking the ideas of passing with the artifacts, practice, and knowledge associated with technology comprises what I call the *technological politics of passing*. This concept offers a means to interpret the use of artifacts, and how these artifacts can be understood as affecting a person's identity. In this regard, menstrual hygiene products can be interpreted as technologies of passing. The technologies help to hide female bodies viewed as dysfunctional, thus assisting women in passing as healthy. They allow women to present themselves as non-menstruants. The framework of the technological politics of passing is one means of explaining the practices and behaviors connected with women's use of menstrual hygiene products.

To appreciate why this is a compelling argument, it is necessary to understand the historical context in which passing would benefit women. The best place to begin is with the exploration of menstruation by late nineteenth-century physicians, and the creation of a mode of thinking that I have termed *scientific menstruation*. In the late nineteenth century, views about menstrual blood as a plethora or surplus of blood, followed by a natural monthly purging to keep the body's humors in balance, were replaced with evidence-based models of menstruation. Much like scientific motherhood, in which experts in psychology, sociology, and medicine sublimated women's agency and authority as mothers by doling out advice concerning the best ways to rear children, scientific menstruation dictated menstrual practices supported by evidence-based medicine and in effect stripped women of control over their bodies. Scientific menstruation is extremely important because it marks a shift away from women as the arbiters of their bodies, replacing women's knowledge with the knowledge of experts whose power is derived through professionalization and the "truth" of scientifically derived facts. Scientific menstruation also became a legitimate field of inquiry concerning women's bodies. The expertise touted by these physicians had the power to influence policies at both the individual as well as national levels.

The contesting views of scientific menstruation fell at opposite ends of the spectrum during the 1870s and 1880s. On one side were ideas about women's biological weakness due to menstrual incapacity, and the other side held that menstruation was perfectly normal. Edward Clarke, an ear doctor practicing in Boston with aspirations of presiding over Harvard's burgeoning medical school, provided a strong and conservative voice popularizing the advice that women, especially adolescents, take a mandatory rest from school and activities during their periods. Enforced by parents, educators, and physicians, the reasoning held that excessive energy expended during studies robbed vital force from the reproductive organs, thus creating weak, feeble, and often infertile women. Other physicians like Dr. A. F. A. King argued that menstruation was a disease. Whether it was a disease, plethora, condition, or debility, it resulted in a belief system that judged menstruation and its effects on the body as unnatural and problematic, and helped create a systematic approach to menstrual prejudice. These pejorative readings of the female body troubled many women's activists and female physicians. By the 1910s, physicians like Clelia Mosher who promoted feminist agendas argued for the normalcy of monthly periods and for women to carry on as if nothing at all were different. The arguments within scientific menstruation set the context for political debates, in which menstruation provided a means to question women's reliability as paid workers and general fitness as political beings.

Women could not of course hide all indicators of their female bodies to be like men, nor would they necessarily want to. Since the problematic bodily event was the menses, if women could act like they were not menstruating or at least convincingly hide their bleeding bodies, they might be spared the unsavory opinion that they were unstable and unfit as political beings and workers during their periods. The need for women to efficiently manage their own menstrual flow grew as corporations relied on women laborers. Yet, their choice of menstrual hygiene was rudimentary at best. Women washed and reused pieces of soft flannel, worn broadcloth, and even rags to trap their menstrual flow. For those women ordered to remain in bed, menstrual blood most certainly stained nightshirts and sheets. During the 1890s, menstrual hygiene products began appearing in catalogs such as Sears and Roebuck. Lister's Towels, as well as rubber aprons and pants, were alternatives to the commonly referred to "homespun" napkins that most women folded and fashioned for themselves from flannel or birdseye cloth. Thus, the sale of new menstrual hygiene products might not only offer a technological fix to the problem of menstruation, it might also provide a technological means of passing as normal and healthy.

During the late nineteenth and early twentieth centuries, the rise of technology as a means of creating a modern society became paramount. Industry, mass production, and engineering seemed to offer never-before-heard-of solutions to life's daily struggles. This opened space for the technological management of menstrual blood, and women's adoption of manufactured menstrual hygiene products to do so. Kotex sanitary napkins introduced for sale in 1921 were the first products to be successfully marketed and sold, with many others soon to follow. The technological management of menses became so popular and profitable that Johnson & Johnson hired efficiency expert Lillian Gilbreth to study the existing market in order to create the best new sanitary napkin. Gilbreth delivered her detailed findings to the company, which then incorporated suggestions and launched an improved product called Modess. The seriousness with which Johnson & Johnson took women's suggestions and remarks heralded a new era in menstrual hygiene. The ubiquity and preponderance of the products caused William Faulkner to deem the 1930s "the Kotex Age." Bombarded with advertisements convincing them to buy the new products to get on with their lives, women were now encouraged to manage menstruation through the modern technology of sanitary napkins.

How women used the technologies of sanitary napkins and tampons, and the practices and knowledge surrounding the artifacts, can be more easily seen in the interwar years and the employment of women during World War II. Common knowledge about menstruation as a temporary debility, a condition, and a potential infirmity still influenced many women. They often called in sick with cramps, or rested at home when possible. Menstrual education campaigns became a new approach to manage female workers. Armed with data from medical and psychological studies, wartime managers began to enlist experts to promote attendance and reduce absenteeism at work, in part due to the temporary pathological state of menstruation. Encouragement to stop feeling sick and go to work came from wartime posters, newly hired occupational counselors, and even the design and furnishings of women's restrooms. Though women in the factories were urged to abandon habits of menstrual weakness, female pilots were warned to heed their menstrual-induced instability and remain grounded during their periods. However, female pilots often ignored direct orders and maintained their personal agency and control over their own bodies by using menstrual hygiene products to hide their periods from officers. Women had come to rely on menstrual hygiene technologies and the products became mandatory to a woman's health, mobility, and bodily maintenance. The technologies helped to regiment women's bodies, conform to industrial work schedules, and lessen the importance of menstrual debility.

However, the technologies, practices, and knowledge meant something different to and for adolescent girls and young women presumed to be virgins. The introduction and sale of menstrual hygiene products to pre-pubescent and teen-aged girls during the 1930s, 1940s, and 1950s exemplifies the complications of unintended users appropriating technologies. Adolescent girls proved to be a lucrative consumer group after World War II, but the business of menstrual hygiene raised the unsettling subject of teen sexuality. As a general practice, the use of menstrual hygiene products implies fertility, as evidenced by menstruation. As a bodily process, menses also indicates the physiological maturity of a sexual persona. Advertisements, education films, and medical brochures downplayed this connection between menstrual hygiene and sexuality by systematically suppressing it, employing the rhetoric of freedom only to present confined stereotypes of women and their appropriate behaviors. This was important, for menstruation now merely previewed womanhood and the use of menstrual technologies served as a passage only to adolescence and not into mature adulthood. The technologies functioned as a compromise, for it was easier to discuss the artifacts of menstrual hygiene rather than sex in many sex education classes. Ironically, the technologies helped teenagers pass as happy-go-lucky girls and hedge their representation as sexualized adolescents.

What price women had to pay for maintaining these menstrual practices, and what place the technologies had in women's lives, were questions raised by the women's movement. By the early 1970s, it became clear to feminists in the women's health movement that women needed more control over their own bodies concerning medical decisions. From the reduction of radical mastectomies, to the way vaginal exams were conducted, to demands for legal abortion, the shortcomings of gynecology mounted. The lingering haze of menstrual prejudice and the way that menstruation continued to be viewed as a liability contributed to the devaluation of women's biological identity. Feminism raised the troubling question of how to celebrate a uniquely female bodily process while not being simultaneously defined by it. Companies for menstrual hygiene products caught on to this sentiment, capitalizing on cultural feminism and the ways it might be packaged and sold. Menstrual hygiene advertisements purported that newly designed pads freed the body, and New Freedom sanitary napkins sought this market niche. New designs in tampons emerged as well, with the emphasis on improved absorption capabilities. Ironically, the "improved" technologies exposed women as the menstruants that they were. The public health scare in 1980 involving Rely tampons, linked to the deaths of thirty-eight women due to Toxic Shock Syndrome, revealed how the technological fix, meant to free women by hiding menstruation, failed. This technological failure resulted in a new public health campaign, with warnings about TSS in each package of tampons. This safety concern did not, however, diminish women's reliance upon the technologies. In effect, a newly revealed cost to women of using menstrual hygiene technologies was the understanding that they were linked with health risks.

Some feminists began asking why women needed these kinds of products at all. For some this meant boycotting manufactured, disposable products that contributed waste to landfills every year. Some embraced the old idea of reuse, making their own washable flannel pads. Others purchased reusable menstrual cups such as the Keeper or the Diva Cup, which many testified prevented leaking and were more comfortable than tampons or pads. The more radical option of free bleeding which abandoned menstrual hygiene altogether proved too far-flung for most women. Caught between suggestions to return to the menstrual hut as a way of celebrating menstruation, and guerilla attacks upon tampon dispensers warning women of dioxins in the products, women were not left with many good options. While many could see the benefits of interpreting menstruation more positively, most women still purchased manufactured menstrual hygiene products. The technologies of menstrual hygiene still mediate the vagaries of an uncontrollable leaking body, and are chosen by women for the practical reason of convenience. This social change surrounding menstrual hygiene technologies indicates the partial reception of feminism and its incomplete revolution. How to empower women through the strength of their bodies without being compromised as an essentialized woman is an elusive middle ground. Even the importance of cyclical and recurrent periods is at question with hormonal birth control such as Seasonale, whose major selling point is that women need not menstruate but four times per year.[2] Contemporary physicians such as Elsimar M. Coutinho have asked the question "is menstruation obsolete?" The contradictory advice to eliminate menstruation through a drug regime or celebrate it by saving it and using it as plant fertilizer is the consequence of complicated identities between which women negotiate.

This examination of the social history of menstrual hygiene technologies stems from a variety of sources and an array of evidence, including historical documentation such as marketing reports, articles in medical and popular journals, and court transcripts. I also use periodicals and advertisements, which according to Susan Speaker "provide an index to the culturally resonant themes and images of the period."[3] In addition, I have compiled a limited set of oral histories of self-selected women. I have chosen to use only first names to indicate the speaker as a means of protecting anonymity. These interviews are by no means comprehensive or representative, but they do exemplify specific experiences at certain points in time. In total, the archival sources, material artifacts, and accounts by women comprise the techo-social history of menstrual hygiene technologies in the United States that I present.

The interpretive framework of the technological politics of passing provides a means to understand women's relationship to menstrual hygiene products and their bodies. How these technologies contribute to women's identity shaping and the notions of what is female, as well as how the technologies can be used as tools of control or liberation, emerges from menstrual stories which have remained under wraps.

Notes

1. Interview with Wendy, with Rebecca Moore (August 13, 2005).

2. Jennifer Aengst, "A Need to Bleed? Nature, Necessity, and Menstruation," (paper presented at the annual meeting of the Society for Social Studies of Science, Pasadena, CA, October 22, 2005).

3. Susan Speaker, "From 'Happiness Pills' to 'National Nightmare': Changing Cultural Assessment of Minor Tranquilizers in America, 1955–1980," *Journal of the History of Medicine and Allied Sciences* 52 (July 1997): 342.

Chapter 2

Technology and Passing

In the futuristic film *Gattaca* (1997), Vincent Freeman (Ethan Hawke) dreams of traveling to outer space, but his DNA prevents this. Since genetic determinism dictates his place in the social order, he is doomed. Born with congenital heart defects and severe myopia, he was marked by his genes and tagged as imperfect, only able to live as a second-class citizen. Yet, Vincent's dream propels him to fight the system. To do this, he needs a new bio-identity, and uses the genetic materials of the now handicapped super athlete Jerome Morrow (Jude Law) to do so. Jerome provides Vincent hair, skin, urine, and blood samples, which Vincent must use to maintain his identity at each bio checkpoint in the Gattaca Corporation. Trouble ensues when one of his own eyelashes is discovered at the sight of the murder of his mission director, and this person with the genetically imperfect eyelash is the main suspect. In this story, Vincent passes as genetically fit by using technologies to attain goals only offered to those of the genetically superior gene pool. The complicated rituals of bathing, sloughing the skin, and ridding his body of stray hair, as well as the complex system of extracting, preserving, and depositing bodily fluids all rely on technologies. Without the technologies, Vincent cannot perform his successful pass, and his identity is powerfully shaped by his skill in using and manipulating available technologies.

In some ways, this film employs the time worn plot of progressive, futuristic technologies. It also exemplifies traditional motifs of linking technology with manliness. As a genetically defunct second-class citizen, he is emasculated and

9

reclaims masculinity by becoming an astronaut, a sure occupation of male pres-
tige. However, he can only accomplish this by passing, and the plot hinges on
the authenticity of his pass. I suggest that gender, technology, and politics must
be included in an analysis of the film to better understand the dynamics of the
story, and that an additional framework be used to engage analysis about those
artifacts that alter and shape personal identities: technological politics of passing. By contributing the idea of the technological politics of passing, I hope to
open up critical inquiry into passing by including technological experiences.
Often, credit is not attributed to the technology through which an act of passing
might be rendered successful. It is important to include technology within the
critical lens of passing, and take seriously the practices, skills, and artifacts—the
technologies—that often produce the effects. There is no doubt that the act of
passing carries political consequences, but credit must be given to the ways in
which it is often technologically mediated or produced. The field of Science and
Technology Studies provides insights into the politics embedded in technologies, but feminized technologies are generally under-theorized or over-
generalized. The fields of literary analysis and film studies are saturated with
examples of passing, but as a practice passing has not been examined through
the lens of technology studies. Technological politics of passing might breathe
fresh air into passing scholarship while bringing significant insight to Science
and Technology Studies. It opens terrain by which to learn about lived technological experiences.

It is clear that the technological should be considered along with the practices of passing, for often artifacts and technics allow for a successful pass.[1] The
preponderance of passing, and the success by which people do so, sheds interesting light on the ways that technologies contribute to its practices. Passing can be
a useful tool in negotiating and challenging social systems that deny individuals'
very existences, and technologies often provide the props to pass. We need to
engage the multiple ways that women have practiced passing, because these
actions are often normalized and rendered invisible by their very ubiquity. This
is why an examination of the history of menstrual hygiene technologies provides
a provocative means to view this relationship of gender identity, technology, and
passing in recent United States history. Menstrual hygiene technologies are hidden artifacts that have enabled women to pass, to overcome prejudice leveled
against a bleeding body. At certain moments the technologies helped women
pass as healthy. In others, they helped them to pass as non-bleeders. Because
women have relied on the pass, their exposure is felt more keenly in moments in
which menstrual blood seeps through clothing, for instance. Though menstrual
hygiene technologies have been used and construed as personal and private, and
even at times secretive, these hidden artifacts function in a similar way as visible
artifacts because they help to represent the body as something else: not bleeding.
The importance of this is that the representation is both outward and inward. The
act of technological passing presents an altered external identity, but also re-

quires the technological user to agree to a sort of temporary amnesia. In the example of plastic surgery, many profess to feel happier, their identity ultimately changed by the nose job, face lift, etc. One might actually believe the visible truth of the transformed body, though noses, poor eyesight, and wide hips cannot be genetically masked so easily. Menstrual hygiene technologies allow for a temporary passage, to "forget 'time of the month'" as one ad claimed, and get on with life as if menstruation were not occurring.[2]

This chapter establishes the conceptual groundwork for linking technology together with passing. First, it addresses the issue of gendered technologies, and why menstrual hygiene technologies are unique, in part due to the female-specific bodily event of menstruation. Second, the chapter presents passing as a category of analysis, and how it functions as a motif. Third, I weave together the notion of passing with technology to argue for the technological politics of passing, in which I suggest four components that comprise its definition. The first is the narrative act of the pass. The second is an examination of the pragmatics and efficacy of passing while using the technology. The third is the agency engendered by the technological pass, co-produced by both the user and the artifact. Fourth is the limitation of the pass, as determined by the technology. These four elements shape the contours of technological politics of passing, and will anchor the historically situated examples in the following chapters.

The Unique Case of Menstruation and Technology

There is a long-standing tradition of defining males as the universal human.[3] As such, men do not menstruate, and women do, thus marking women as different and menstruation as unique to a sex. In addition, though menstruation is a natural bodily fluid like a lot of other lubricants and excrements produced by both men and women, it is not viewed like all the rest.[4] For example, though earwax oozing from the ear is unattractive, it has not garnered medical study concerning its production as an impediment to brain function like menstruation has. Furthermore, women were not politically disfranchised by scientific arguments about earwax, but they were by menstruation. Many bodily functions, including perspiration, post-nasal drip, and even defecation can be embarrassing, shameful, and downright nasty, but they do not engender the same politics that menstruation does. No matter how hard women work to gain equal rights as measured next to male citizenship, menstruation seems to betray them. Menstruation represents a fluctuating body, and therefore a seeming loss of sovereignty that places women in a precarious political place. As philosopher Denise Riley has so aptly noted, "being a woman" is fraught with politics, and significantly, menstruation summons one back to her female body.[5] In this regard, when gender awareness and sex are presumed to be the dominant forms of a woman's essence, menstruation is a sure sign of that being. It therefore can be viewed as a liability, and even at times a debility, for women. Menstruation as a bodily fluid carries meaning about fertility, sexuality, and womanhood that other functions simply do not. There is not a legacy of a man getting fired for pulling a hanky out to blow his nose. Yet, most women dare not leave a box of tampons in plain sight at a workspace without some sort of repercussion.

Of course, one might argue that plenty of technologies have been designed to extract earwax, eliminate body odor, wipe bottoms, and the like. But these technologies again are different because they do not implicate a politically inferior body and citizen, namely *woman*. Using a menstrual hygiene technology implicates the body as female, and as a fertile, potentially sexual woman. That is why a teenage girl using a sanitary napkin or tampon represents a significant cultural marker of maturity, and even a change in political status. In addition, since these technologies are so loaded with meaning, when they are appropriated for other ends it makes the technologies more visible because they seem uncomfortably out of place. It is the odd story that emerges about the man with a profuse sweating problem who puts sanitary pads in his armpits to absorb the sweat, his embarrassment redoubled not only by his physiological aberration but also by his remedy for it.[6] In eastern Washington after the 1980 Mount St. Helens explosion, residents found humor in using sanitary pads in their lawnmowers to filter out the ash, and I am sure that paper towels or furnace filters would have gone unnoticed if used for similar ends.[7] These alternative uses of menstrual hygiene products demonstrate ingenuity, but also elicit a joke, snicker, or a raised eyebrow of disapproval. It is from the disapproval that it is clear that menstrual hygiene technologies are somehow different. They are associated with uniquely female bodily processes, and must be examined in the context of a society that privileges "man made" technologies for men. It is in this context of male privilege and the contradictory act of women's use of technologies that women are caught. In this scenario, women are inferior to men as bleeders, yet empowered through technology.[8]

Menstrual Hygiene Artifacts as Technologies

Engaging sanitary napkins and tampons as technologies allows for broader contours of interpretation and analysis about their function and use. Defined as a technology, the physical artifact, knowledge about its function, and how people use it can all be analyzed. Though artifacts are commonly understood to be free of power politics, and merely the "stuff" of our environment, this is very shortsighted. Langdon Winner makes this point clear in his essay, "Do Artifacts Have Politics?"[9] Winner contributes to a tradition of the philosophy of technology, concerned about the political implications of technologies.[10] He engages the notion that "technical things have political qualities."[11] Of course, it seems counterintuitive that things or objects themselves might possess political meaning outside of the people who created them or use them. Certainly, it makes sense that the "social or economic system in which it is embedded" creates the meaning, not the object itself.[12] Yet, according to Winner, "the theory of technological politics suggests that we pay attention to the characteristics of the technical objects and the meaning of those characteristics." In this way we might see how "artifacts can contain political properties."[13] The importance of this mode of thinking is that it allows a means to understand the unexpected consequences resulting from the technologies, and also the consequences built into the design before the artifacts are even used. This kind of thinking about technologies is different than a more traditional reading or a determinist argument, "the idea that technology develops as the sole result of internal dynamic and then, unmediated by any other influence, molds society to fit its patterns."[14] In terms of menstrual hygiene technologies, the logic would follow that manufactured cellucotton napkins displaced homemade pads and dictated women's behavior and affected cultural change. Although one of my contentions is that social change resulted from the use of manufactured menstrual hygiene products, this explanation cedes all power to the technology. It removes women's wants, beliefs, and desires, and does not fully explain how the technologies became accepted or what kinds of change emerged. Therefore, Winner's notion that artifacts have politics recognizes the technologies as participants in change, and the process by which technology and culture inform one another.

Part of the difficulty in conceptualizing the artifacts of menstrual hygiene as technologies is that they are not usually viewed as such. R. L. Rutsky has argued that the ways we have framed technologies is problematic, most notably because the "definition of technology is taken for granted."[15] Generally viewed as functional or instrumental, this conception of technology is limited. He calls for a view that encompasses the aesthetics of technology, but also engages technologies as "emergent" in which "a complex interaction of factors leads to a major change."[16] This, he claims, removes us from the binds of calling something revolutionary or evolutionary, and also rescues us from the unproductive argument of whether or not a technology is beneficial or detrimental. Engaging technologies as emergent allows for multiple interpretations and meanings, and understands that the process is mutable. It also recognizes the place of technology in participating, but not necessarily dictating, social change.

A shortcoming in this approach is that the technological is often gendered masculine. Judy Wajcman has noted how "little attention has been paid to the way in which technological objects may be shaped by the operation of gender interests."[17] Wajcman examines how gender neutrality has been assumed when designing, using, and even critiquing technology. She also argues that technofeminism can help us to understand how gender identities and technologies are shaped together, in which women transform technologies and technologies are also the result of socio-technical systems.[18] However, in the case of women Anne Balsamo has noted the importance of examining the relationship of technologies to the body. She describes how "reproductive technologies also reinscribe dominant narratives of gender identity on the material body by providing the means for exercising power relations on the flesh of the female body."[19] In terms of technologies of menstrual hygiene, it is fruitful to think about how these artifacts have contributed to the formation of women's identity, and what notions about women are reproduced through the use of the technologies.

The case of menstrual hygiene technologies is fairly unique as a female-specific and female-centered technology. Judith McGaw defines "feminine technologies" as "those technologies associated with women by virtue of their biology" or "by virtue of their social roles."[20] By looking at feminine technologies and women's "selection and use of products, the study of women's technologies reveals technological choice and technological knowledge to be pervasive, not confined to a corps of experts." Importantly she notes, "because feminist technologies are often the technologies of the private sphere, bringing them to light exposes how interwoven with modern technologies are novel conceptions of privacy, conceptions very much at issue in current political debates."[21] While her work is useful in validating the technological experiences and knowledge of women, the term feminine technology is not specific enough. Do the technologies make one feminine, or does a woman's use of an object, by virtue of her social role, feminize an artifact? A "feminist technology," in turn, promotes women's best interests, and, I would suggest, does so politically and consciously.[22] I employ the term "female-specific technology" to address those technologies associated with women's biological, which often equates to reproductive, attributes. Accordingly, technologies associated with female biological functions render them less visible, and therefore they are naturalized.

Thus, menstrual hygiene technologies embody a very specific set of attributes and contradictions. Sanitary pads and tampons are not usually considered technologies. Since technology is presumably gendered masculine, they are further made invisible. As such, women are usually not thought of as technological users. It is from this trap that the technological politics of passing can be framed. In simplistic terms, the biological act of menstruating differentiates bleeders from non-bleeders, and a menstruant needs a menstrual hygiene technology to pass and maintain cultural norms of a female body in modern American society. It is often useful to transcend this designation as a bleeder, and menstrual hygiene technologies can help to do so.

Passing as a Category of Analysis

The lens of passing offers a fresh perspective to engage in the knowledge, practices, and artifacts that provide the artifice for a new personal identity. In the most basic terms, passing constitutes the ability to represent to the world and oneself a different identity, to forego a prior self, and be perceived as other than formerly identified. There is a strong critical literature that has engaged the historical acts as well as literary motifs of passing. This theoretical framework is most clearly developed within race and gender studies, and these analyses often rely on fictional accounts of protagonists passing from one group to another. Examples of this include James Weldon Johnson's *Autobiography of an Ex-Colored Man* (1912) or the 1934 film *Imitation of Life*. Both grapple with questions of racial identity, and what it means to slip into dominant white culture with inside knowledge about being a black person living in the segregated United States. This type of passing most often relies upon sight, and reading or visually assessing the outward appearance of an individual. Amy Robinson discusses the complications of a simplistic "reading" of the individual, and suggests that passing needs more than one actor and one viewer, and should be "regarded as a triangular theater of identity."[23] She offers three terms to describe the points of the triangle: *passer*, the person passing from one identity to another; *dupe*, the hegemonic spectator who reads the pass as authentic and not as a performance; and *in-group*, a term used "to designate the group *from which* one has passed."[24] She argues that the pass should not just be read in terms of the dupe, by which a successful pass might be measured. It also includes the recognition of the pass from the inside group, so that a pass may be interpreted, or read, two ways—from the inside or the outside. The successful pass means to be accepted as a "natural" member of the group, but within the mechanism of the passing narrative spectators from the in-group know the real, or pre-passing, identity and must be present to witness the duping. In addition, this creates a narrative structure of suspense, because there is always a threat of exposure.

The following examples are not meant to be instructive, but point out themes that are already familiar, because outside of fiction and film, passing has real consequences. For instance, in modern U.S. society, passing for many black people, who transcend a racial category into whiteness, can bring with it white privilege. For example, at the turn of the twentieth century civil rights activists often spoke about the phenomena of passing, as they were intentionally exposing the problematic interpretations of race—based on visual cues of hair texture or skin tone—that rationalized a bifurcated system of treatment. Purposely unveiling the passer to white people was meant to underscore the hypocrisy, and ultimate illogic, of such a racialized social system. The act of unveiling often had profound effects. The 1896 Supreme Court case of *Plessy v. Ferguson* dealt with the codification of segregation based upon racial distinctions. Homer Plessy, who was one-eighth black by standards of the time, could pass as white, and agreed to test the case of intrastate railway transit in the state of Louisiana. Though he was read as being white and directed to sit in the white section of the rail car, he told the conductor that he was seven-eighths white and refused to sit in second-class accommodations. Consequently, he was detained as a black person violating segregation ordinances. The inherent argument was that conductors were ill equipped to follow the law if they could not accurately tell who was white and who was black.[25] Plessy's lawyer, Albion Tourgée, argued that the state denied Plessy his rights of equal protection, and that segregated cars were inherently unequal. He eventually lost, ushering in "separate but equal" until the 1954 *Brown v. Board of Education* case. In terms of rail cars, the system was not willing to budge, though the case did elucidate the arbitrary and often conflicting readings along the race continuum.

A now famous example of racial passing is the case of John Howard Griffin who sought to use his white privilege to expose racism by attempting to pass as black. As a white man he manipulated perceptions of race and created the biological illusion of being black with skin darkening creams and pharmaceuticals in order to go undercover as a Negro. In his popularly received *Black Like Me* (1961), an autobiographical exposé of the pass, Griffin expressed the depths and extent of racism, as he could sense it, from his position of a white black man. One of the ironies of *Black Like Me* is that Griffin's description of racism was received as credible. Undoubtedly as a white man, his perceptions could be believed as truths and were more reliable than those of a black person. What is less well recognized is that his pass as a black man was dependent upon technological origins, which need to be addressed in informing his temporary identity. Importantly, the technologies afforded him the opportunity to return to whiteness at the end of his experiment. In fact it is easy to become so occupied with the believability of his black identity that the technologies are forgotten. They are merely a means to an end. This diminishes their significance, for technology is the very crux of his pass. The technology produces dupes, in this case of both black people and white people. The role that technology plays in creating his racial identity carries both social and political consequences.

The concept that artifacts have politics makes visible the stakes of employing technologies of passing. For instance, it is easy to see how clothing as technology can provide a vehicle for a successful pass. In the slave narrative and autobiography by William Craft, *Running a Thousand Miles for Freedom* (1860), he and his wife avoid capture by cross-dressing, and each represent a different gender. Craft hit upon the idea that if his light-skinned wife, Ellen, could dress and pass as a white gentleman slave owner, she could act as his slave master, and thereby both might secure freedom. Though Craft carefully argued that he was still a man, and that donning women's clothing was an act of desperation, other people more contemporarily incorporate cross-dressing into their lives as part of their identities. Transgender generally describes those individuals living with more fluid materializations of sex and gender. Some transgender individuals may also be transvestites, who appropriate the manners, clothing, and affectations of gender in an effort to pass in public. And, there are many transvestite entertainers whose over-the-top, stylized costumes are consciously represented and read as part of a performance. Eddie Izzard, an entertainer and comedian, delivers stand-up comedy routines as a cross-dresser.[26] He jokes that he is a "corporate transvestite," in part by way of his upscale dress. Importantly, the technological artifact of clothing creates a crucial element of the pass. This type of passing is temporary, dependent upon technologies that can be easily changed or removed from the body, while being situated within particular historical and political circumstances.

Technological Politics of Passing

Scholars have put together the ideas of technologies and passing, but have not interrogated that relationship in a systematic manner. In Sander Gilman's book, *Making the Body Beautiful*, an overriding theme is that plastic, reconstructive, or aesthetic surgery has allowed individuals to pass by permanently remaking the body as healthy, acceptable, and even beautiful. In Gilman's examples, the participants/patients usually seek surgery in order to transcend some category: sickness to health, Jewish to gentile, deformed to normal. By altering the physical they seek to be read through their visual representation as a new identity. Of course, the definition of normal changes at different historical moments, and submitting to plastic surgery reifies that normal ideal by which they were formerly excluded. In these accounts, medicine abets passing, and I would argue that technology is also an actor in the creation, though Gilman rarely gives acknowledgment to the technics.

David Serlin comes close to an analysis linking passing and technology when he examines the ways that masculinity, conformity, and patriotism influence definitions of "normal" in *Replaceable You*. He argues that these ideas shaped the acceptability of prosthetics in the mid-twentieth century, and that these medical technologies made it unnecessary and unfashionable to suffer with an abnormal body, deformity, or mutilation after World War II. This example seems rife for analysis through the lens of the technological politics of passing, for using an artifact to mimic human bodily performance would enhance the chances of passing as a normal, physically functioning person. In terms of permanent medical transformations, Carolyn de la Peña describes "technological passing" which used X-rays and radium in a 1903 experiment to lighten and whiten Negro skin. These "technological passers," as she calls them, posed questions about authenticity for both white and black people and raised a great degree of concern over boundaries and racial hierarchies.[27] This work foreshadows the technological politics of passing which I take further by examining the gendered components of a ubiquitous, female-specific technology.

The aforementioned examples of passing are rather dramatic, transgressing fairly clear boundaries, involving bold acts in which people subvert dimorphic systems, ironically mimicking that very system which disfranchised them in the first place. However, I contend that passing can be much more subtle, and can occur not only between these dimorphic categories but also within a category. Technological politics of passing allows for a subtle reading of normality within a category, and in this case the category of women's identity. The use of a tampon technology by a woman does not transgress gender or even racial boundaries, but reinforces what it means to be female by representing a healthy woman as not visibly menstruating. A woman can convincingly cover her identity as someone who possesses a fluctuating, leaky body and present a controlled, orderly, and contained "normal" female body with her pass.

The technological politics of passing contains four elements. The first component is the narrative act of passing. This narrative may be delivered in many forms, and in the case of menstrual hygiene, it is evident in advertisements, menstrual education materials, and even fictional novels. The repeated stories about menstrual passing provide a prescriptive account of how it can be done; the stories assure women that they need only follow the example of the protagonists to have similar successes. The second component is the very efficacy of passing by means of the technology. How well does the artifact work in any given situation, and how convincing is it? How much strain will the technology shoulder before it undermines a pass? For example, physical activity, especially swimming, tests the value of tampon technology and how well it performs under less than ideal circumstances. The third strand of technological passing includes how a user might manipulate the technology, and how identity can be co-produced with the technology, to provide personal agency. In the film *Boys Don't Cry* (1999), based on a true story, Brandon Teena, a biological female who passes as a young man, is cyclically reminded of his biological identity. In a seemingly inconsequential scene, the camera pans to a tampon strewn under the bed. The menstrual hygiene technology is empowering in concealing his double-pass as it were, yet evidence must be hidden, further complicating the meanings of gender identity. Finally, the fourth way to assess technologies of passing is by evaluating their limits. What problems lurk beneath artifacts seamlessly integrated into personal identities of passing? What dangers are overlooked when a technology becomes ubiquitous and naturalized? For instance, some feminists and political ecologists have implicated tampon use, and in particular the bleaching process of cotton that creates the by-product of dioxin, as the source of increased endometriosis. Though this claim has yet to be scientifically validated, common knowledge circulates that women are not as highly valued as men, thus there is little urgency to confirm such health suspicions. Tampons are construed as invisible, thus their potential danger might not be recognized. These four components of technologies of passing will be evident through the myriad stories presented in the following chapters. The nuances of technologies of passing change in different time periods, yet this practice remains surprisingly persistent in the United States during the twentieth century.

As a personal example, the importance of passing was delivered to me quite clearly in grade school. I remember when sex education was taught to my fifth grade class in 1979. We were divided into groups, with boys and girls viewing their respective films. After delivering her program, the public health nurse was supposed to hand out free samples of sanitary napkins, which she forgot to do. She left them for my teacher to distribute. This proved to be complicated since I was enrolled in a split class of fifth and sixth graders. She sent out the boys and the sixth graders (to do what, I'm not sure) and we girls were left to receive our packages. We gathered around a desk, collecting the mini and maxi pads. Suddenly, the class ne'er-do-well, Terry, entered, and surprised us all. "What are those? Those are napkins!" he exclaimed with a smirk. I was stricken. I threw my body over the desk and cheerily replied, "Yes, party napkins!" He added, "Then why are you hiding them?" for which I had no response. I considered saying, "Because it's a surprise . . ." but by then my teacher had escorted him out of the room, and left us alone with our sanitary pads. In this example, Terry's surprise entrance exposed the technologies and me because we were both complicitous in the idea of passing. Unwittingly, I employed double entendre to camouflage the technology and maintain the untruth of a non-menstrual body. I use Robinson's use of "untruth" here. As she puts it, "[s]een through the lens of drag, the pass violates the fundamental tenets of mimesis by insisting on the untruth of the relation between inside and outside."[28] In terms of using menstrual hygiene technologies, the practices insist on the untruth of not bleeding.

The utility of using passing is an interpretive, not necessarily descriptive, tool. In most cases, women would not use the term "passing" or consciously craft a persona to represent their new identity in a successful pass. Yet, women's actions and practices might be understood in terms of passing because their behaviors speak to historical shifts in representations of identity. Those aspects of a female body deemed unsavory and unfavorable might be erased through technologies. This imbues technologies with the power to transform but also sheds light on the political consequences of this technological transformation. Coupling the technological politics of passing with menstrual hygiene products provides a way to think about technology in relation to menstruation, and the complicated practices it provokes. Indeed, one of the results has been that the technologies help to hide menstrual blood, thus women might temporarily act like they are not menstruating. Passing is a means to examine the unintended consequences of the technologies, and the ways that they shape components of women's identities. The following stories and case studies demonstrate a variety of ways in which the technologies of menstrual hygiene have contributed to changes in women's behavior and the challenges that these technologies have provoked concerning women and their bodies.

Notes

1. I use Lewis Mumford's notion of technics here, or the practices, details, rules, and methods surrounding the artifact of interest. Lewis Mumford, *Technics and Civilization* (New York: Harcourt, Brace and Company, 1934).

2. "War Duties Lead Many Women to Use Tampax," *Parade* (1943), Ad*Access On-Line Project – Ad #BH0187, John W. Hartman Center for Sales, Advertising & Marketing History, Duke University Rare Book, Manuscript, and Special Collections Library, http://scriptorium.lib.duke.edu/adaccess (accessed October 23, 2000).

3. Carol Tavris, *Mismeasure of Women: Why Women Are Not the Better Sex, the Inferior Sex, or the Opposite Sex* (New York: Simon and Schuster, 1992).

4. Thomas Laqueur, *Making Sex: Body and Gender from the Greeks to Freud* (Cambridge: Harvard University Press, 1990).

5. Denise Riley, *Am I That Name? Feminism and the Category of "Women" in History* (Minneapolis: University of Minnesota Press, 1988), 96. See also Susan Bordo, *Unbearable Weight: Feminism, Western Culture, and the Body* (Berkeley: University of California Press, 1993).

6. Dateline NBC (week of November 9, 1998).

7. Personal correspondence, Henry Vostral, 1980.

8. Tavris, *Mismeasure of Women.*

9. Landgon Winner, *The Whale and the Reactor: A Search for Limits in an Age of High Technology* (Chicago: University of Chicago Press, 1986).

10. On the relation of culture to technology, see Lewis Mumford, *Technics and Civilization*; Carl Mitcham and Robert Mackey, eds., *Philosophy and Technology: Readings in the Philosophical Problems of Technology* (New York: Free Press, 1972), v.

11. Winner, *The Whale and the Reactor,* 19.

12. Winner, *The Whale and the Reactor,* 20.

13. Winner, *The Whale and the Reactor,* 22.

14. Winner, *The Whale and the Reactor,* 21.

15. R. L. Rutsky, *High Techne: Art and Technology from the Machine Aesthetic to the Posthuman* (Minneapolis: University of Minnesota Press, 1999), 2.

16. Rutsky, *High Techne,* 6.

17. Judy Wajcman, *Feminism Confronts Technology* (University Park: Pennsylvania State University Press, 1991), 23.

18. Judy Wajcman, *Technofeminism* (Cambridge, UK: Polity Press, 2004), 54.

19. Anne Balsamo, *Technologies of the Gendered Body: Reading Cyborg Women* (Durham: Duke Univerisity Press, 1996), 160.

20. Judith McGaw, "Why Feminine Technologies Matter," in *Gender and Technology: A Reader*, eds. Nina E. Lerman, Ruth Oldenziel, and Arwen P. Mohun (Baltimore: Johns Hopkins University Press, 2003), 15–16.

21. McGaw, "Why Feminine Technologies Matter," 16–17.

22. Linda Layne, "Feminist Technologies: The Case Study of the Home Pregnancy Test," (paper presented at the annual meeting of the Society for Social Studies of Science, Pasadena, CA, October 22, 2005).

23. Amy Robinson, "It Takes One to Know One: Passing and Communities of Common Interest," *Critical Inquiry* 20, no. 4, Symposium on "God" (Summer 1994): 715–36.

24. Robinson, "It Takes One to Know One," 715, 723, 733.

25. For a detailed study of the case, see Otto H. Olsen, ed., *The Thin Disguise: Turning Point in Negro History, Plessy v. Ferguson, A Documentary Presentation (1864–1896)* (New York: Humanities Press, 1967).

26. Eddie Izzard, "Dress to Kill," HBO, 1998.

27. Carolyn Tomas de la Peña, "'Bleaching the Ethiopian': Desegregating Race and Technology through Early X-Ray Experiments," *Technology and Culture* 47, no. 1 (January 2006): 27–55.

28. Robinson, "It Takes One to Know One," 728.

Chapter 3

Scientific Menstruation and Making Menstruation Political

The story of menstrual hygiene technologies has its roots in interpretations of and ideas about menstruation, especially during the nineteenth century when beliefs about menstruation shifted from that of healthy purging to pathology. During the eighteenth century and before, menstruation was one of many types of excrement needing to be purged and expunged to maintain good health.[1] Though menstruation carried the burden of being a curse that God leveled upon women for disobedience in the Garden of Eden, it did not necessarily signify pathology. This once healthy expulsion took on decidedly medical and political overtones by the mid- to late nineteenth century in the United States. It became symbolic of women themselves, fraught with interpretations that rendered them weak, sickly, and therefore politically disadvantaged by virtue of their sex and their bodies. No one person captured this politicization of menstruation better than Edward Clarke, who incidentally specialized in treatments of the ear. Regardless of his limited expertise, his book, *Sex in Education: or, A Fair Chance for the Girls* (1873) became wildly popular and brought attention and notoriety to menstruation in ways that others had not. The result was that theories about menstruation escaped from the domain of medicine and garnered widespread political interpretations that questioned women's fitness, capabilities, and general functionality in society. Because menstruation was now construed as a liability for women, the political stakes concerning its interpretation were great. It is no surprise then that early feminists rose up to attack Clarke's credentials and allegations, though their criticisms were not readily incorporated into more forgiving interpretations about menstruation. Without proper educational and medical pedigrees, they were easily disregarded as kooks. However, by the 1910s and 1920s, Clelia Mosher, who had acquired the proper medical training, made some inroads concerning menstrual attitudes. She promoted the idea of "functional periodicity" which did not necessarily challenge the pathology of menstruation but compromised on a middle ground by which women might regulate their own bodies and symptoms. For Mosher, if women could manage their periods to function normally, then menstruation simply could not be proof of women's inferiority.

The predominantly medical interpretations of menstruation in the late nineteenth and early twentieth centuries formed a way of knowing that I have termed *scientific menstruation.*[2] Scientific menstruation encompasses the knowledge created by professional physicians and public health officials who crafted scientific studies, determined medical procedures, and recommended policy applications of this knowledge. Some of this prescriptive advice concerning how women should act and behave during their periods was followed, and at other times it was ignored. The advice, however, was contested by both physicians and women's rights advocates, and speaks to the power that the medical recommendations had in terms of politicizing a menstruous body. By examining the conservative stance of physicians such as Edward Clarke who viewed menstruation as potentially deleterious, and the feminist position of physicians such as Mary Putnam Jacobi and Clelia Mosher who argued that menstruation was a normal bodily function, the context of menstrual politics in the late nineteenth and early twentieth centuries becomes clearer. How their ideas became embedded in practice reveals the degree to which menstruation shaped notions of women's fitness as students, employees, and citizens. It is this broader concept of scientific menstruation that frames the context for the technological politics of passing in terms of menstrual hygiene. By examining the contested meanings of menstruation and how menstruation could be used to subjugate women, it becomes far clearer why efforts to cover a menstruous body would be desirable. Therefore it is from this legacy and context that the technologies garner their earliest meanings.

Science, Medicine, and Menstruation

A by now familiar story is the reading of women's bodies as pathological and inferior to men's during the nineteenth century.[3] During this time, scientists sought to reveal "natural law" in which the methods of science marked by hypothesis, formulation, replication of results, and observations allegedly delivered pure and true data. Scientists believed laws undergird nature and simply awaited discovery and proper application. However, often unbeknownst to the scientists, natural law contained the prejudices, biases, and values of the culture in which it was produced. For example, physical anthropologists sought to gain knowledge about the body's relationship to the mind through a person's measurable anatomy. They linked anatomy to destiny, especially in terms of reproduction and intelligence, as evidenced through measurement of the skull, jaw shape, facial angle, skull volume, and weight of the brain. Since women generally had smaller heads and less cranium volume, they were deemed more childlike and not fully developed evolutionarily. This was taken as fact, not an interpretation based upon a system of economic and social privilege allotted to white, propertied males.[4]

Natural inequality, though not a new idea, garnered scientific evidence to prove the difference and inferiority of women to men. Based upon head shape and size, physiological strength, and anatomical structure including reproduction, scientists generally presumed that women were overall weaker than men. Part of the uniqueness about this interpretation was that women were generalized as a whole, so that individual difference was more of an aberration since it challenged the general assumption of women's retarded evolutionary development. Women were not the only group regaled with such reasoning. People of African descent bore the burden of such heavy-handed interpretations that rationalized their enslavement and relegated them to one small step above apes.[5] The application of this kind of science could not help but rank races and sexes, which resulted in varying degrees of paternalism at best and essentialism or downright prejudice at worst.

It is commonly understood that as women gained access to higher education in the nineteenth century, began lobbying for the right to vote, and earned wages in formerly exclusive male professions, the promotion of scientific theories to explain and justify sex inequalities proliferated. Charles Darwin, in *The Origin of Species* (1859), attempted to understand sex roles and how natural selection might cause differentiation of males and females within a species. Havelock Ellis writing *Man and Woman* (1894) believed that women were the purveyors of primitive racial elements. G. Stanley Hall, a professor of psychology at the turn of the twentieth century, characterized women's thinking processes as unconscious, therefore innate, and insurmountable. After theories such as Darwin's concerning natural selection were newly interpreted to explain patterns of society, women were so inscribed by their sexuality that their reproductive capacity became the defining factor of their overall beings, and they were viewed as evolutionary throwbacks. Deviant from male bodies, women's corporal bodies were ruled by reproductive functions including their increased menstrual activity.[6]

One of the reasons why menstruation gained medical attention was the escalation of women's menstrual activity at the turn of the nineteenth century. One theory suggests that social, economic, and ideological change in the very creation of the nation had a marked influence on fertility patterns and post-

Revolutionary-era fertility rates began to decline. Ideas of personal autonomy, as promoted by the rhetoric of liberty and freedom during the Revolution, influenced women's actions in limiting family size. Therefore, pregnancy shifted from a natural and constant state of being to an exception in the life of a rational individual.[7] Others argue that a transition to lower fertility rates began around 1840 with clear patterns of smaller families after the Civil War.[8] Pragmatics of the need for industrial labor over farm labor also leveled an influence in areas such as the Northeast. Growing emphasis on childrearing over childbearing, and the turn away from the number of children born to the value of parenting skills, also influenced decisions to limit family size. Female agency and proactive measures to control fertility partially explain declining birth rates and demographic changes during the nineteenth century.[9]

An important yet overlooked consequence of declining birthrates was increased menses.[10] If women were bearing fewer children, spending less time breast-feeding, and delaying pregnancy, then they necessarily increased the number of periods that they experienced over a lifetime. This had a profound effect upon perceptions of menstruation. Once understood as a sporadic event—happening upwards of one hundred times per lifetime—it now became an incessant reoccurrence, happening between three hundred and four hundred times during a woman's life. In fact, according the *Oxford English Dictionary*, the word *period* first appeared in the publication *Medical Journal* in 1806 to describe menstruation. This indicates that new words needed to be created for the relative changes in the occurrence of menstruation.

By the mid-nineteenth century, menstruation signified more than a purging of blood. Some physicians likened menstrual blood with estrus in animals, and hypothesized that this was a woman's fertile time. In essence, menstruation gained meaning in relation to reproduction.[11] Other physicians understood menstruation as an abnormal occurrence. Dr. A. F. A. King, professor of obstetrics at the Columbian University, Washington D.C., declared, "[i]n the strictest sense of the word, therefore, menstruation is a disease; it is not a purely physiological process, but a departure from nature."[12] He viewed women's increased menstrual activity as unnatural, and a "hemorrhage." Moreover, "[m]enstruation is the result of an interference with nature, of a thwarting of her designs, of a violation of her laws and is preventable by obedience to those laws."[13] Menstruation occurred only for the lack of conception, and was a marker of uterine atrophy since gestation was the normal state of a woman's body. With the uterus performing no useful function, it became prone to disease and decay, thus marking the epidemic of women with painful menstruation and other uterine problems due to non-pregnancy.[14] King viewed procreation as "the most natural and only strictly natural course for the female economy to pursue."[15] Through pregnancy and following this "law," women would be freed from the pernicious effects of cyclical and recurring menstruation.

His colleagues deemed King's pronouncement both "startling" and "remarkable." According to King, menstruation did not exist in prehistoric times, so to think that civilization had in essence created menstruation was indeed "startling." W. H. Studley reviewed King's article in the *American Journal of Obstetrics*, and took a different approach challenging the notion of menstrual disease. He felt that menstruation was not aberrant, and that "it is purely and simply a natural function of the organ."[16] The comparison of women of all times troubled Studley because an absolute nature of things required what he called "fixity." He employed concepts of relativism and situated knowledge to explain his critique. He argued, since "individuals and peoples will be conditioned and modified in thousands of way" it seemed impossible to define a "typical standard" of health.[17] Therefore, the logic comparing contemporary women to those from earlier epochs was flawed. As he deconstructed King's argument, he wryly noted that if King's advice were to be followed in total, then "early marriage or intercourse, in order to prevent the pathological process of menstruation, is what Dr. King argues for."[18] Studley so thoroughly dismissed King that he concluded, "the more he ponders and searches, the more he will see, I think, that he is ballooning in the mists and hazes of transcendentalism," clearly a jab to his medical pronouncements as well as the intellectual exercises of philosophers and artists of the time.[19]

While King's presuppositions may have been remarkable they nonetheless had some effect in causing physicians to reevaluate their positions on menstruation. Whether or not healthy menstruation was a disease was one matter, but linking it to health was another. Doctors adopted the attitude that women who suffered from excessive and debilitating menstrual periods, or those who did not menstruate at all, needed medical attention. In nearly all cases, this meant white middle-class women were the patients diagnosed because they were the only ones who could afford the house call and follow the doctor's prescription of bed rest during the menstrual "sicktime."[20] If a woman had the financial wherewithal, this week of rest exonerated her from her regular duties, and instead of serving others it was a time for others to serve her. Some women certainly took advantage of this small vacation from family responsibility and enjoyed the respite, thereby contributing to the understanding of menstruation as a problem. Others experienced full-blown sickness, with symptoms ranging from stomach problems, menstrual cramps, "wandering pains," and menstrual-induced neuralgia.

Some physicians questioned the mental capacity of women during their periods, with women "undoubtedly more prone than men to commit any unusual or outrageous act" during their "infirmity."[21] Dr. Horatio Storer—prominent anti-abortion activist, vice president of the American Medical Association in 1866, and founder of the Gynecological Society of Boston in 1869—distrusted female physicians and their infirmity "during which neither life nor limb submitted to them would be as safe as at other times."[22] He feared that a midwife, and worse, a female physician, who performed an abortion could "plea that the act was committed during the temporary insanity of her menstruation," in which case she could not be held fully accountable for her actions, amounting to an egregious miscarriage of justice in his opinion. Yet, because menstruation was viewed as defining women's biology and therefore their actions, it was a logical and well-grounded use of evidence by the defense to claim their innocence.[23] In a cultural environment that perceived women as hobbled by menses, it was a short step to cite menstruation as a factor contributing to their inferiority.

Dr. Edward Clarke and Menstrual Debility

Stories about women's limited abilities during their periods circulated within medical dialogue and began to be debated within medical journals. However, the question about the long-term effects of neglecting a menstruous body gained notoriety and media attention in the book *Sex in Education; or, A Fair Chance for the Girls* written by Edward Clarke in 1873. Based upon observations and case studies of a mere seven women, he concluded that "[females] must obey the law of periodicity" and that "during every fourth week, there should be a remission, and sometimes an intermission, of both study and exercise."[24] Trained as an ear specialist, respected as an administrator, and known locally as a medical historian, he had no prior experience writing about women's periods.[25] Utilizing the metaphor of the closed-economy of the body, Clarke argued that a woman's body could not function properly while expending energy toward two different biological purposes—for example using brain energy to study and reproductive energy to menstruate. Therefore, Clarke proposed a remedy: remove women from the mental strain of the classroom by requiring a mandatory rest week during menstruation, which he termed periodicity. This he claimed protected their delicate organs and offered young women a fair chance at reproductive development. Clarke's proposition reflected American society's anxiety concerning coeducation, and it helped to bar girls from the same classroom as boys.[26] His message resonated with many Americans' prevailing notions of women's political and biological weakness, and he clearly articulated a dominant belief: menstruation was an unhealthy bodily function, a problem, and in many cases a disease-producing debility, so ominous that classroom work threatened to exacerbate female invalidism. Although some criticized this recommendation, Clarke did not live long enough to fully engage their allegations (which indeed may account for his ideas' longevity). In his obituary of 1877, the *Boston Medical and Surgical Journal* reported "the rancor that still exists among radical so-called 'reformers' and advanced thinkers bears evidence to the truth and force of the book."[27]

Before he published *Sex in Education*, Clarke enjoyed a highly respected career as a physician in Boston. He was appointed the prestigious Professor of

Materia Medica at Harvard Medical School in 1855, and resigned from the faculty in 1872 to join Harvard University's board of overseers. Although he felt no compulsion to admit female students to Harvard, he admonished young male medical students at a Philadelphia training hospital who taunted female students. Although the reports vary, the women were either bodily removed from the classroom, or so harassed by the men's tobacco chewing and crude behavior that they left the program due to its hostile environment. Clarke warned that taunts only strengthened women's cause and turned them into martyrs.[28]

Because Clarke censured the male students who taunted the females, he received an invitation to address the New England Women's Club in Boston in 1872. The women undoubtedly expected a talk concerning women's advancement in the medical profession and their efforts to break down gender barriers. Instead, he argued that the medical profession should continue to allow women to enter, but proposed they be taught in segregated classrooms. To gauge the long-term feasibility of female physicians, their success should be measured in fifty years. He proclaimed that a minority would prove themselves to be capable, but the rest would be selected out of the profession due to their own inferiority. He explained that intellectual study weakened women's biological constitutions and retarded the development of reproductive organs, rendering women unfit for the profession.[29]

Clarke received criticism immediately after the meeting, and decided to hone the essay to make his point more carefully. The final product was the book *Sex in Education; or, A Fair Chance for the Girls*, and was published in 1873. Gaining wild popularity, the book sold more than 200 copies in one day according to a Boston bookseller. Even Clarke boasted that demands for a second edition appeared "a little more than a week" after the book hit newsstands and book shops.[30] It went through seventeen editions in thirteen years, and spread as far as Great Britain and the Middle East in its distribution.[31] The first president of Bryn Mawr College, M. Carey Thomas, confessed that the school was "haunted" by the book, for the instructors were unsure whether students' health could tolerate education.[32]

Clarke's pronouncement of menstrual infirmity responded to a series of challenges to separate spheres ideology and men's exclusive political rights. As an astute and political Bostonian, Clarke would have been aware of and annoyed by current events such as the protestations of Elizabeth Cady Stanton and talk of a woman's right to vote, but he took personal offense when women requested admission to Harvard Medical School. The "woman movement," as it was first referred to, threatened to infiltrate a male domain, as well as the exclusivity and reputation of the all-male medical college. Clarke invoked familiar arguments that educational standards would drop, and that women were ill prepared by ornamental finishing schools for the rigor of a medical education. Worse yet, in an attempt to expedite women's advancement, primary education for girls began to mimic the curriculum and pace set for boys. Experiments in coeducation placed boys and girls in the same classroom space at a disastrous cost. He called for "appropriate" education for boys and girls because "identical education of the two sexes is a crime before God and humanity."[33] Clarke's solution was to limit women's classroom time based upon the demands which menstruation placed upon the body. Only by enforcing rest might society offer girls a "fair chance" at their special reproductive development.

Clarke's arguments concerning periodicity were premised on the theory of vitalism—the notion that "special forces controlled living matter."[34] He viewed three major vital forces as ruling the biological processes of the body: nutritive, nervous, and reproductive. Each of these systems was in direct competition for nutrients, blood, and vital energy.[35] Clarke held that "the system never does two things well at the same time. The muscles and the brain cannot *functionate* in their best way at the same moment."[36] Therefore, a young woman taxing her brain with classroom studies while simultaneously menstruating threatened her own physiological development. Since most women over the age of twenty were physiologically mature, they could incorporate tempered sessions of study during their periods, but should still remain vigilant about the sanctity of rest. Since the economy of the body held a finite amount of "vital force," the body allotted more energy to those organs requiring immediate attention than those in a more dormant state.

Clarke argued that there was a direct relationship between periodicity and the "building of a brain" through education. He explained that the amount of "nerve-force" expended while studying directly correlated "in exact proportion to the pain endured" during menstruation. Thus, energy diverted to the brain manifested itself in menstrual cramps, for example. If proper methods were devised to minimize the pain—thus limiting study time—then education could be carefully considered with the goal of preserving "greater nerve-force at command for brain-work in adult life."[37] Thus, the results of women's education might be positive.

Clarke professed that luckily, biological rhythms helped to prevent catastrophe, because "[n]ature has reserved the catamenial week for the process of ovulation, and for the development and perfection of the reproductive system."[38] Rest was crucial during the catamenial week because Clarke believed the common medical perception that menstruation and ovulation occurred simultaneously. Thinking of the body as a machine, he warned "[k]ept within natural limits, this elimination is a source of strength, a perpetual fountain of health, a constant renewal of life. Beyond these limits it is a hemorrhage, that, by draining away the life, becomes a source of weakness and a perpetual fountain of disease."[39] How exactly anyone could maintain such a balancing act remained elusive. However, it was clear to Clarke that by not heeding the body's call for rest during this crucial time, *agenesis*, the imperfect development of the body, characterized by sterility, ensued. Although his study could in no way be called comprehensive, he nonetheless concluded "[the female organization] must obey the law of periodicity."[40] For Clarke, it was a scientific fact, devoid of bias, that "the period of female sexual development coincides with the education period."[41] However, young women paid the price for his scientific recommendation in the form of missed school days, bed rest, and possible exclusion from coeducational schools during their periods.

Edward Clarke immediately spurred debate and defined the terms of scientific menstruation for more than an entire generation. His work became the touchstone for further cultural criticism as well as medical research, and raised the stakes concerning the meaning of menstruation. Physicians, educators, and policy makers embraced Clarke's work at a particular historical moment so that menstruation became politicized. As a political topic it became the subject of debates.

Inspired by his work, Dr. George Austin agreed with Clarke's contentions concerning menstruation and education. In his book *Perils of American Women* (1883) he claimed that "overwork of the brain, and excessive development of the nervous system" acted as a detriment to women's overall health.[42] Without proper respect for the balance between menstrual rest and academic studies, there lurked the potential for menstrual induced insanity. This "special danger" triggered by menstruation he named *erotomania*. Austin claimed to have seen several of his young patients afflicted with erotomania, in which they displayed symptoms of "sexual eccentricity" at the age of puberty. Symptoms of vulgar "gestures and language" characterized this affliction, and he was dumbfounded to guess how girls so well reared might have knowledge of such things. For their sake, he argued that this "sexual eccentricity" should not be viewed as lust and treated as a moral offence, but diagnosed as insanity and medically treated.[43] Whether or not the girls deliberately displayed flirtatious gestures or were sexually active was dismissed. By medically labeling their behavior as insane, the girls were not allowed to display any sort of sexualized behavior or act outside the bounds of appropriate middle-class behavior. However, defined as illness, their behavior was easier to patrol and they were granted an honorable and acceptable retreat from society. Parents were also able to explain away their child's misbehavior as a medical problem, and therefore, not their fault.

The constructions of menstruation as a debility also veiled a much more deep-seated anxiety about the commingling of boys and girls in the classroom. Coeducational enrollment increased from 4,600 students in 1870 to 39,500 students in 1890—a marked increase duly noted by educators, and newly interpreted with anxiety by physicians.[44] Writing eighteen years after Clarke's thesis—and just five years after the last printing of *Sex in Education*—Dr. William Capp joined the battle cry of periodicity. He voiced reservations about the implications and the meaning of rest for girls in the setting of a coeducational classroom.[45] For Capp, the menstruating girl was problematic not only because of the damage she could impose upon her own reproductive development, but what damage her presence might wreak in the classroom. He warned that "[t]he recurring monthly sickness in young women, with its palpable suggestions of the function of reproduction, and accompanying nerve-excitation, have their influence upon the imagination."[46] Capp moved well beyond Clarke because he linked menstruation with sexual feelings. By banishing the menstruating student from the classroom during her period, it clearly announced her fertility, as if she were in heat, to both other girls and boys. It suggested reproduction because it was a "palpable" sign of her burgeoning sexual persona. The "nerve-excitation" influenced the "imagination" of boys and girls and acted as a catalyst for sexual feelings—feelings improper for a young woman and problematic for young men, best sidestepped until marriage.

Furthermore, Capp predicted it would be impossible to prevent that sort of sexual excitement, exacerbated by "intimate association with the other sex, in the class-room and play-ground away from parental and home constraints."[47] This breech of separate spheres ideology thrust the sexually burgeoning young woman into daily contact with boys. Neither boys nor girls could be completely trusted, because girls' reproductive capacity would be continuously dangled in front of boys, whether girls were present or absent. In a tone of resignation, Capp acknowledged that "the popular demand is now emphatic that the mental training of the sexes shall be more nearly alike, in order to insure [sic] compatible marriage unions."[48] However, he preferred this be accomplished in same-sex schools.

Azel Ames, a physician and Commissioner of Investigation for the Massachusetts Bureau of Statistics of Labor, directly credited Clarke for stimulating further study of not just the relation of women to education, but also to industry.[49] He deployed Clarke's argument to support his own political agenda. He argued that if Clarke were truly concerned about young women as a whole, he needed to evaluate their health in the mills, factories, and shops, not just the classroom. Much like Clarke, he systematically interviewed women and employers within industries such as telegraphy, typesetting, basket making, textile production, stenography, and counting (money, cane seating, etc.). His overall goal was to call attention to the working conditions of industry, and the effects of long hours, environmental conditions, and repetitive motion upon adolescents between the ages of ten to fifteen. Though there were regulations about employing children under the age of fifteen, in almost all cases Ames found that the laws were not followed. If he could show that these young working women suffered similar problems with their developing reproductive functions, he might be able to sway lawmakers to amend the current child labor practices. Indeed, Ames found that Clarke too quickly dismissed industrial workers as expendable, but upon every count Ames argued that their labor was worthwhile, and perhaps more so, than women enrolled in classes as students. Ames argued that the poor health of laboring women took a greater toll on society for a longer period of time than the poor health of educated women, who most likely had other forms of support. Like Clarke, he recommended rest. He suggested that employers allow women to take a periodic absence without losing their jobs, and saw a monthly three-day vacation as the ideal.[50] In this way the conditions of labor might be improved to prevent the "degeneracy and decay" of reproductive health likely to follow from the employment of girls in industrial settings. In many regards, he was probably right. Workers could use a day or two of rest. The problem, however, was not rest per se, but how and when it was used against women. Ames consciously chose to deploy the prescription of rest to improve women's—and therefore the nation's—reproductive health. The assertion of menstrual rest was so powerful, and resonated affirmatively with so many different groups, that Ames used it as rationalization to marshal forces against child labor practices. By relying on the politically popular notion that girls needed to safeguard their health during their periods, he hoped to influence changes in working conditions.

Besides influencing further medical research, Clarke's treatise raised the ire of many progressive thinkers and early feminists, who vocalized their disagreement quite assertively. Even before *Sex in Education* was published, they were keeping tabs on him. *The Woman's Journal*, created and edited by suffragist Lucy Stone, described his talk at the Boston Women's Club in 1872 as "valuable" since it addressed women's health. But the paper reported that the audience felt that he provided insufficient evidence to curtail "the usefulness of co-education."[51] After the publication and widespread distribution of *Sex in Education* more pointed criticism followed, especially concerning his conclusions based upon only seven case studies. Clarke catalyzed a flurry of debate, including individual tracts, essays, and books rebuking his conclusions and overturning his evidence. Overall, his critics were quick to note that he failed to include working women and the effects of menstruation upon labor. They noted his faulty logic, his social biases, and his mischaracterization of menstruation as debilitating. They criticized the impracticable system required to cater to the likes of a classroom of women menstruating at various times, and the educational tiers created by implementing his views. They provided counterpoints to challenge the assumption of debility, and exposed Clarke's supposedly unbiased scientific observations. The consequence of his assertions was a regressive model of education, which they had no intention of supporting.

George Comfort, Dean of the College of Fine Arts at Syracuse University, along with his wife, Anna Manning Comfort, a physician of homeopathy, in their book *Woman's Education, and Woman's Health: Chiefly in Reply to "Sex in Education"* (1875), charged Clarke's work "to be utterly wrong in all its essential features."[52] The Comforts assured their readers that the goals of higher education for women tended "to promote the physical health of her sex, and consequently of the human race in its entirety."[53] One of their main criticisms was Clarke's apparent shortsightedness concerning the implementation of rest on a broad-based scale and its effect on the entire labor system, especially women's household chores. They noted "he does not so much as hint at a plan by which household work, or work of any kind, can be so organized and arranged, that . . . [young women] can receive a vacation of one week during each month." It was economically impracticable, and with an ironic tone they mused, "[p]erhaps Dr. C. has a man-cook in his kitchen, or a Chinaman in his laundry; for a woman at work in those places might have to stand when she ought to sit: or to walk when she ought to be in bed."[54] That they poked fun—in gendered and racialist ways—at Clarke's domestic situation and the possibility of hiring male domestics displayed the absurdity of Clarke's proposition. They highlighted the impossibility of disrupting the labor performed by female cooks and laundresses because of menstrual "inconvenience," pointing out Clarke's short-sightedness and also his concern for upper-class white women and not those of the working class.

Another critique with a similar tone came from Maria A. Elmore, who wrote a short untitled essay in Julia Ward Howe's edited volume, *Sex and Education: A Reply to Dr. E. H. Clarke's "Sex in Education"* (1874). She asked sarcastically: "Has Dr. Clarke written a book on 'Sex in Manufacturing Establishments'? If he hasn't, he ought to."[55] Her flippant remark reflected upon Clarke's assertion that laboring women did not need the same sorts of protection as middle-class women. In a passionate voice she cried that "nobody raises an arm of opposition" when women work in the factory, at the wash tub, or sewing machine six days a week, and do work for their families that "their husbands ought to" without being given a rest for their "catamenia." As Elmore put it, it was only when "there is possibility and even a probability that in matters of education women will be as honorably treated as men, lo! Dr. Clarke comes forth and tells us it ought not to be so, because, forsooth, the periodical tides and reproductive apparatus of her organization will be ignored!"[56] Upon the cusp of equal treatment, newly invented roadblocks appeared, limiting educational advancements, chances for equality, and citizenship rights based upon women's innate biological inferiority.

Eliza Duffey, a popular author of marriage and etiquette manuals, critiqued Clarke's observations in her book, *No Sex in Education, or an Equal Chance for Both Boys and Girls* (1874).[57] She lamented that if Clarke succeeded, and "convinces the world that woman is a 'sexual' creature alone, subject to and ruled by 'periodic tides,' the battle is won for those who oppose the advancement of women."[58] The construction of menstruation as debility was problematic for Duffey, since "[n]owhere, in fact, has 'periodicity' been recognized except in the brain of our doctor, because nowhere has unperverted nature intimated any such need."[59] She viewed periodicity as the doctor's own creation, for women felt no instinctual desire to rest during their periods. Duffey believed that women's physical ills stemmed from "imagined feminine weakness and invalidism." Her use of the term "imagined feminine weakness" indicates a critical assessment of the construction of both *woman* and *disease*, both politically charged terms to benefit a system of male favoritism. The construction of assumed feminine weakness "forbids the wholesome active physical life" for a woman, which was assumed as necessary to the "normally healthful man."[60]

Duffey felt that Clarke's contentions concerning rest made little sense in light of the significant expenditure of energy women made toward housework. Since any activity allegedly diverted that vital force from the reproductive organs, should not all activities, including women's manual labor, be exempted during menstruation? She questioned "[d]oes Dr. Clarke himself insist upon his maidservants respiting their womanhood for the allotted period and forego their attention to the comforts and necessities of himself and family" including washing, ironing, baking, housecleaning, and hospitality? Furthermore, she wondered whether or not husbands would be so inclined "to be patient while their wives play the invalid for three or four days in the month, and leave dinners uncooked and children uncared for."[61] This alone, she concluded, would pressure men to argue against periodicity and rest. And, if husbands were unwilling to grant a vacation from housework, they would be hypocrites by promoting rest from schoolroom learning based upon similar grounds.

If, as Clarke argued, strenuous exertion caused health problems, why then did his claim that German women, "yoked with a donkey and dragging a cart," were less likely to experience menstrual problems than the American girl? If this were true, Duffey contended, shouldn't women's biological similarities outweigh differences in nationality? Therefore, the conclusion to be drawn was that more exercise and work, not less, prevented complications. In a scathing tone, Duffey charged "[i]t seems to have escaped Dr. Clarke's observation that in all ages and in all nations, except the most civilized (and even these latter are not entirely exempt for the rule), all the most irksome and degrading labor has been imposed upon woman, without any thought of providing for her 'periodicity.'"[62] Clarke's new call for rest during menstruation seemed a particularly weak argument due to its omission of working-class women throughout time. Clarke responded that because laborers "work their brain less," little energy was expended and virtually no energy diverted from the reproductive organs to the brain.[63]

Duffey also took Clarke to task due to his omission of housework as labor intensive.[64] Although the call for rest during menstruation attended an imagined state of debility, Duffey pointed out that a more immediate danger loomed, as Clarke nowhere acknowledged, "women can be in any way sexually injured by the wear and tear of housewiferey." By saying women were "sexually injured," Duffey referred to the damage heavy housework could cause to reproductive organs. For instance, the repetitive lifting of heavy objects while wearing a corset often predisposed a woman to a prolapsed uterus.[65] For Duffey, this well-recognized health hazard held more immediacy than the questionable premise of imposed rest during menstruation.

Furthermore, Duffey believed the most dangerous effect of housework to be mental, not physical, as "lunatic asylums show a frightful record of the evil effects of this kind of labor upon them." Lunacy, allegedly due to the lack of meaning women gleaned from inane housework, further supported Duffey's point that housewifery was more deleterious to women and their bodies than education was in stunting reproductive development. Duffey's critique helped expose Clarke's pastoralization of housework. Under this premise, if housework were leisure, then there was no real need to rest from mere entertainment.[66] Clarke's construction of housework as leisure was significant, for it was not housework which required stamina, but the exercise of the mind. Education taxed both physical and mental vigor.

In fact, Duffey was quite astute about the ramifications, calling Clarke's tract "a covert blow against the desire and ambition of woman in every direction except a strictly domestic one." Another critic, only known as "C," added: "[c]an any woman read this book without feeling depressed,—crushed by this cosmic law of periodicity which is to exempt her from nothing, but only debar her from a higher education?"[67] Educational opportunities would diminish because of the difficulty in offering a two-tier system, in which periodicity commanded curriculum and forced girls to continuously play "catch up" each month. Additionally, any sort of labor advances were stymied, because "[Clarke] knows that labor is valued only as it is continuous and reliable, and that if women can be persuaded to become unreliable on principle, there is an end to the competition between the sexes in every department of employment."[68] Therefore, the promotion of periodicity and the limiting of both education and job opportunity were used as justification to exclude women on multiple levels. Ideas about menstruation held serious ramifications in terms of viewing women as equal to men, and menstruation therefore helped to reinforce sex difference.

With so much attention paid to women's reproductive functions including menstruation, Duffey believed it narrowly defined womanhood and exaggerated this one biological event out of women's many facets. Duffey claimed that a woman's reproductive system already monopolized too much of a doctor's attention, and that if Clarke's advice were to be followed, "woman will be woman no longer, but an exaggerated female, weak and wanting in all other functions and faculties, and abnormally developed in the peculiarly feminine parts of her organization."[69] For Duffey, Clarke's arguments contributed to the hyperfeminization of *woman*, with disproportionate attention given to the meaning of menstruation.

Duffey proclaimed, "I have called this book an attack, but it is rather the last, the most desperate struggle of the advocates of fogyism against the incoming new order of things."[70] She identified the fear concerning this "new order," which included not only female physicians and the rise of coeducation, but also the growing woman suffrage movement. With the demand for universal suffrage, the tenets of limited democracy no longer held together. Yet, with suffrage looming large, a treatise such as Clarke's worked to entrench women's biological and sexual differences as inferior, and reify white male hegemony.

As rational as the arguments of the woman's rights advocates were, they had little impact on the medical profession. Physicians did not respect their qualifications as lay critics, and Clarke held power as a highly esteemed physician who boasted the largest private practice in Boston.[71] Despite these essayists' efforts to contest menstrual limitations, menstrual debility gained currency to become the dominant understanding through the remainder of the century.

Redefining Scientific Menstruation

Unwilling to accept such a profoundly regressive interpretation of menstruation, Dr. Mary C. Putnam Jacobi served a crucial role in redirecting the discourse and the construction of scientific menstruation (Figure 1). She crafted a career first as a physician, and then as a feminist. She received her training in 1863 from the Female Medical College of Pennsylvania, one of few schools where a woman could go to study medicine in the United States. Seeking a medical degree equivalent to that of other male practitioners, Jacobi moved to Paris in 1868 to attend École de Médicine, where she was the first woman to be admitted to the school. After completing her degree amidst the siege of Paris during the Franco-Prussian War, she returned to her home in New York, and became bored with routine medical practice. She quickly agreed to an offer made by the Drs. Emily and Elizabeth Blackwell to join their staff at the Woman's Medical College of New York. No woman, and few other men, could boast her medical pedigree, and she was a legitimating force at the hospital.[72]

While at Woman's Medical College, she pursued a career as a researcher and medical school instructor, holding the Professor of Materia Medica and Therapeutics from 1872–1889. She established a clinic at Mount Sinai Hospital devoted to the diseases of children, and often lectured about her clinical work. In her quest for professional status and recognition from an exclusively male-dominated medical field, she commented widely upon subjects of disease processes, medical education, medical associations, and women's health.[73] True to her feminist sensibilities, Jacobi founded the Association for the Advancement of the Medical Education of Women in 1872, serving as its president from 1874–1903. The association sought to elevate the standard of medical training for women and raised money to promote this goal. With help from the association, the Woman's Medical College of New York lengthened the program of study, expanded the medical practicum, instituted preliminary exams, and boasted that with the exception of Harvard, it was the only school that exacted such standards. In addition, she actively promoted woman suffrage, and wrote a scathing book concerning women's natural rights modeled upon Thomas Paine's work, even borrowing his title for her own: *"Common Sense" Applied to Woman Suffrage* (1894).[74] The depth of her knowledge, breadth of scholarship, and activism within the medical community made Jacobi a preeminent female physician during the nineteenth century.[75]

Jacobi made a splash in the American medical community with her 1877 book, *The Question of Rest for Women During Menstruation*, which began as a prize-winning essay. Prompted by the Harvard Medical School annual Boylston Medical Prize essay competition of 1874, Jacobi decided to submit a paper and compete for the chance of publication and prize money. It proved to be the perfect vehicle to offer legitimization and notoriety within the field. The topic under consideration was "Do women require mental rest and bodily rest during menstruation and to what extent?" and was a subject on which she had completed some preliminary work. The topic immediately responded to Dr. Edward Clarke's book and his lack of statistical evidence and narrow case studies. The competition was meant to prompt objective and rigorous study of the question, and conclusive evidence toward recommendation of rest. Jacobi decided to conduct research and submit a paper.

Since contestants submitted articles under anonymous cover, the selection committee did not disqualify Jacobi's essay based on her authorship as a woman. She had previous experience submitting articles under a pseudonym. While studying in Paris, she sent articles to the *Medical Record* which readily published her letters, editorials, and papers. She penned them with the initials P. C. M., her initials from Mary Corinna Putnam, listed backwards, which masked her identity as a woman and helped her to get paid as an author. Submitting the anonymous essay to Harvard was just one more exercise in necessary maneuvering to prove her abilities to a dubious audience. Thoroughly researched, well written, and firmly grounded in the latest medical scholarship, her essay was selected for the coveted Boylston Medical Prize in 1876. To the disgust of the Harvard selection committee, they grudgingly awarded a woman the two hundred dollar premium. That they unknowingly selected the essay of a female physician proved the committee's worst fears. Women could equally compete with, and defeat, their male counterparts. They could learn, assimilate facts, and worse yet, produce knowledge desired by the profession as a whole. Jacobi addressed one of the most profound questions of the medical community during the 1870s, and to Harvard's chagrin, better than any of its own male physicians.

Unwilling to promote either Jacobi as a prize-winning physician or her findings, the committee refused to fulfill the terms of the prize by publishing her essay. Her conclusion that healthy women did not require rest proved to be a radical assessment coming from a female physician, and disruptive to the status quo of the white male-dominated medical profession. The silencing of her work attempted to deny the application of her data and her success challenged the decision to uphold male exclusivity at the university. However, the rejection did not inhibit her from getting her work into print. Her father, George Palmer Putnam, the founder of G. P. Putnam's Sons publishing, facilitated the quick production of her research as a monograph in 1877, followed by two more reprints.

As a result, it reached a broader audience than if published in a medical journal.[76]

In her book *The Question of Rest for Women During Menstruation,* Jacobi tested the hypothesis of whether or not women required rest by applying rigorous scientific method to the study of women's bodies. No one had undertaken such a comprehensive study, yet with policy decisions being based upon the assumption of debility, her findings held broad applications to women's work patterns in society. She believed that if the recommendations spelled out by Clarke were true, "the practical consequences are at once so important and so inconvenient, that they should only be accepted after the strictest scrutiny."[77] Part of this scrutiny meant collecting evidence from more than just a few unhealthy patients. In her survey, Jacobi sent out 1000 questionnaires, of which 268 were returned. She asked a series of questions about educational background, medical health during college years, and experiences of menstruation.[78] To her surprise, she found that more than half of the women surveyed experienced no problems whatsoever. This finding struck her as significant, for it established that menstruation and the reproductive functions themselves did not cause inherent debility in all women.

Importantly, she concluded that rest could not be shown to prevent menstrual pain, and as long as women felt well it was unnecessary to stop work for days at a time. In fact, "nothing would be gained, but much lost, by a single intermittence of work during the few days of the menstrual hemorrhage."[79] She did however promote the idea that frequent breaks in the workplace helped improve concentration and general performance whether or not women were menstruating. Therefore, "[t]here is nothing in the nature of menstruation to imply the necessity, or even the desirability, of rest, for women whose nutrition is really normal."[80]

As with many of the criticisms espoused by Anna Comfort and Eliza Duffey, Jacobi found a menstrual respite to be entirely disruptive to women's paid labor. This construct of menstrual debility served as a rationale preventing women's employment and advancement in the workplace. Capitalist expansion, the rise of the male wage earner, and the ideology of female domesticity shaped the concept that women possessed the luxury to rest. Naturalized menstrual debility offered the excuse for this romanticized notion of labor. As Jacobi observed, "this ideal society where the man might suffice for the necessities of the family, and the woman only be obliged to look after the house and the education of the children, has never existed in the past."[81] Its promotion idealized sex differences and inequality in a rapidly changing society.

Even though women's unpaid labor remained unaccounted for in the official U.S. census records, Jacobi included both paid and unpaid women in her statistics. Since these unpaid white women carried out the bulk of the nation's work, she decided to include them in her study group. Jacobi based her study entirely upon experiences of white women, not, for example, black agricultural laborers or sharecroppers. She systemically denied their presence, and stated "negroes, who for our purposes may be excluded from the reckoning" were unnecessary to complete her statistics. Of course, field workers experienced an equal share of pain, and probably took advantage of menstrual debility to assert small work slowdowns and gain a break from the watchful eyes of white landlords.[82] Though evidence about black women and their menstrual cycles is scanty, there was apparently some acknowledgement about slave laborers and menstrual invalidism. In his discussions with slaveholders, Frederick Law Olmstead, celebrated as a landscape architect yet working as a journalist during the 1850s, recorded frustrations with female slaves. Slaveholders called them a liability to productivity due to "disorders and irregularities which cannot be detected by exterior symptoms." One Virginia slave owner commented that women "will hardly earn their salt, after they come to the breeding age," meaning once they started their periods. He continued, "they don't come to the field, and you go to the quarters and ask the old nurse what's the matter, and she says, 'Oh she's not well, master; she's not fit to work sir;' and what can you do?" He lamented, "You have to take her word for it that something or other is the matter with her, and you dare not set her to work." The result was that "she lay up till she feels like taking the air again, and play the lady at your expense."[83] "Playing the lady" meant donning the behaviors of menstrual respite from work. Jacobi, however, was not interested in black women because ideologically it was impossible for them to be ladies and suffer from diseases of "civilization," including menstrual debility. Gender differentiation required delicacy of sex, and a gendered division of labor that Jacobi did not observe in black women.[84] Jacobi expressed racism in her medicalized discourse and couched this exclusion in her perspective as a white, economically elite, feminist. Since she did not view black women as part of a civilized race, Jacobi saw no reason to include them in a subject group or study about menstruation. Black women's advocates such as Anna Julia Cooper and Mary Church Terrell constantly harped on such acts and the racist white women who excluded them from the whole of a truly universal woman movement.[85]

Jacobi thoroughly dismissed black female laborers, and instead formulated her argument around white women, and the fact that "marriage and domestic service constitute the only natural equivalent for the paid industry of women." Therefore, all (white) women must be included to create a clear picture of menstrual health in America. Thus, by accounting for these women, it became clear to her that housewives neither exercised a mandatory rest during their periods, nor did husbands promote it. Jacobi concluded that regulated rest periods were unnecessary to healthy women, unproductive to the economy if broadly applied, and meant to bolster a false domestic ideology in which women's work was devalued, and women had the leisure time to rest.[86] Even if women were allowed to rest, as promoted by Azel Ames, Jacobi believed the social consequences of mandatory rest were far more disruptive to women's political standing.

Her political beliefs also influenced medical interpretations of menstruation. She asserted a bold point concerning menstruation in relation to the vital forces. Edward Clarke explained menstruation in terms of vital force, interpreting it through the idea of limited economy. Due to competition of the vital forces, the nervous force required by the brain siphoned energy from the reproductive organs, causing developmental problems and diseases of the uterus. Even though both men and women possessed the same sum total of vital force, since it was "distributed over a greater multiplicity of organs and directed to the development and support of special reproductive energies" it was weakened in women.[87] In addition, Clarke believed menstruation and ovulation occurred simultaneously, thus heavily taxing the body's resources. Jacobi viewed things differently, and harkened back to an earlier interpretation of menstruation that was not pathological. Jacobi termed this the "Plethoric Theory of Menstruation"— meaning the superabundance of blood—whose premise dated back to Galen's theory of bodily humors.[88] Her interest in revitalizing this plethora model demonstrated scientific menstruation was contested by some physicians and within the medical community itself. In her plethoric theory, women produced more blood than they could use. The excess blood was purged monthly, and indicated the healthful excretion of a potentially dangerous substance. The excess blood was important because the fetus used it for nourishment during gestation. Without pregnancy, it was "thrown away as superfluous during non-pregnant states, but retained as soon as the embryo began to develop."[89]

Jacobi extended this Plethoric Theory of Menstruation to re-interpret the role of the vital forces. She believed that nervous force—and its association with sexual arousal in women—had been given too much attention, to the extent that it obscured understandings of other vital forces.[90] Instead, it was the nutritive force that prevailed upon reproductive development, not the nervous force. "An excess in women of nutritive force and material," she argued, "when not utilized in reproduction, is expended in menstruation."[91] Food provided the necessary energy for the body—including the reproductive organs—to develop. Assuming a woman maintained good health and nutrition, her uterus and ovaries also developed from nutritive force.[92] The nutritive force exerted extensive control over the woman's body, so that the "formation of ova is a nutritive phenomenon that exists throughout childhood, and therefore before the acquisition of reproductive powers, or the exercise of sexual functions."[93] Therefore, as nutritive phenomena, the production of ovum remained *separate* from sexual behavior or sexual development. She argued that there was "widespread, though unconscious perversion of the view" which associated "menstruation with the sexual instead of the reproductive functions of women." The conflation of menstrual, sexual, and nervous force led physicians to believe that the sexual component of menstruation "must necessarily hold in abeyance all other activity of the central nervous organs."[94] This relegated far too much power to menstruation and its hold on a woman's body.

Jacobi conceded that the production of egg cells and uterine activity by women required a certain expenditure of vital force, and more so than a man "having no corresponding organs." However, after a woman had matured, the body produced enough vital force to accommodate its own needs, and was never drained of energy by the reproductive organs. Some viewed the demand for vital force as occurring in intervals, like Clarke who believed in simultaneous menstruation and ovulation. In this case, menstruation was a "nervous crisis" which demanded high amounts of energy, leaving the body listless after it exhausted all its fuel.[95] Another theory termed "spontaneous ovulation" explained that nervous force triggered ovulation, in which ovulation might occur at any moment. Both menstruation and ovulation were related to sexual force, but the relationship remained unclear. Jacobi presented a different theory called the "supplemental wave of nutrition." Nutritive force provided for the energy output of a woman and built up during childhood and puberty. She viewed energy requirements of menstruation as "continuous" so that the body made "a permanent provision" for the existence of menstruation. Therefore, she found rest to be an unnecessary prescription during menstruation.[96]

Unlike Clarke, Jacobi hypothesized from observations of some of her patients that "the period of menstruation may be one of increased vital energy and especially of increased mental force."[97] She attributed this to surplus nutritive activity reserved for the menstrual period. Jacobi more clearly defined this idea in a letter to Dr. Robert T. Edes in 1895, in which she suggested that woman's brain activity was at an all-time high in the course of human history. In fact, women's brains demanded exercise, and eagerly responded to systematic education. This was not surprising, since educational opportunities were offered more liberally to women by the 1890s than at any previous time in American history. The second reason that women's brains were more active was in compensation for the "imperfect development of the reproductive organs" so that the brain made up for reproductive short falls. She departed from Clarke in that education did not cause reproductive problems, but only revealed those women predisposed to them by childhood disease, harsh climate, or weakened constitutions.[98] She warned that "mental work exacted *in excess of the capacity of the individual*, may seriously derange the nutrition," not the sexual development, of an adolescent girl.[99]

This difference of opinion between Clarke and Jacobi concerning the vital forces seems obscure, confusing, and just plain wrong in light of modern understandings of hormones. But it demonstrates the precarious knowledge which physicians possessed in the 1870s and 1880s, and that this knowledge remained contested. Nineteenth-century medical science reinforced women's biological inferiority, but Jacobi appropriated the same tools, language, and discourse of male physicians to level legitimate criticism against her colleagues. For Jacobi, her point that nutritive energy promoted reproductive development was key to her entire argument. Because she divorced menstruation from the nervous force of sexuality, women had a better chance of becoming autonomous beings freed from the biological grasp of the uterus upon the body.

Arguments about menstruation, including sexuality, provided evidence to anti-feminists that women were ruled by their sex. Jacobi upheld the notion of vital force and the importance of reproduction for women, but only as it made up part of a woman's definition, not her whole being. Jacobi charged that men were "accustomed to think of women as having sex, and nothing else" yet thought of themselves "as possessing sex attributes and other things besides."[100] She sought this similar evaluation for women. The double standard "foisted upon that sex condition," meaning woman, was "the condition of political non-existence."[101] Emphasis upon nutritive force directed attention away from "the sex condition" and menstruation, and offered biological grounding for examining woman as a whole. She also concluded that women's bodies were well equipped for menstruation and accustomed to producing and excreting excess blood each month. According to her findings, the majority of women remained untroubled by menstruation, and there was no evidence to enforce rest from school or work. She found that over-prescribed rest promoted weakness and hindered women's quest for social and political equality. Jacobi provided sufficient scientific evidence to question the validity of mandatory rest during menstruation.

Although Dr. Mary Putnam Jacobi presented scientifically sound evidence for her day and refuted Clarke's notion of rest, she had success only in small feminist circles. Doctors still adopted the attitude that women suffered from menstrual debility. In an effort to reinforce and revive Jacobi's findings, the Association of Collegiate Alumnae—composed of female graduates—published their 1885 report, *Health Statistics of Women College Graduates*. They surveyed alumnae from ten universities—ranging from Smith College, to Cornell University, to the University of Michigan—to better assess what the so-called average woman considered to be "healthful." Of particular interest was the report quantifying disorders during menstruation. Among 705 graduates, 288 reported no complications, while 417 expressed experiencing some sort of problem during menstruation. However, among the 417 women, nearly three-fourths reported two or fewer problems during their entire lifetimes. The report interpreted these isolated incidents not to be a sign of permanent debility, but rather relative health.[102] Using statistics and the tools of scientific inquiry, their conclusions challenged Clarke's ubiquitous argument. The Committee found that "the seeking of a college education on the part of women does not in itself necessarily entail a loss of health or serious impairments of the vital forces." Ultimately they concluded that "female graduates of our colleges and universities do not seem to show, as the result of their college studies and duties, a marked difference in general health from the average health likely to be reported by an equal number of women engaged in other kinds of work, or in fact, of women generally without regard to occupation followed."[103] Moreover, the evidence pointed toward the "healthful tendencies of mental work."[104] Their findings bolstered the notion that menstruation was not deleterious, and the construction of menstruation as disease producing was poor evidence to limit educational pursuits and the pursuit of equality.

Regardless of their efforts, models of menstrual debility and rest still circulated. In a society where woman suffrage and co-education challenged separate spheres ideology, the scientific evidence of women's biological inferiority persisted. Frustrated by this problematic scientific tradition, and what she believed to be a misdiagnosed epidemic of menstrual sickness, Dr. Clelia Duel Mosher worked to reform the dominant perception of menstruation. Although she disagreed with Jacobi and her "supplemental wave of nutrition" theory, Mosher followed in Jacobi's path to overturn notions of menstrual debility.[105] Mosher gained notoriety as well as success by not just refuting claims, but in many ways by conceding to them. In doing so, she developed a comprehensive exercise plan for women to follow to overcome their periods, with the ultimate goal of eliminating them altogether. With the idea of the eventual elimination of menstruation, women's periods could not be used against them as a pejorative marker of sex differentiation.

Graduating from Wellesley College in 1891, Mosher received an A.B. degree in zoology and an A.M. degree in physiology from Stanford University. She later graduated in 1900 with her M.D. from Johns Hopkins University (Figure 2). After completing her medical training, she practiced as a physician and taught at Stanford from 1910 to 1929 as a professor of personal hygiene, and became emeritus from 1929 to 1940.[106] The field of personal hygiene included physical education, posture and poise, health education, and nutrition. Mosher wrote twenty-one books and numerous articles that spanned topics of personal hygiene, exercise, and preventative medicine.[107] More recently celebrated by historians for her twenty-eight-year study of women's sexual attitudes—detailed in *The Mosher Survey*—she dismissed the notion of Victorian women's sexual prudery.[108]

As an early feminist within a male-dominated society, Mosher's research, medical practice, and goals aimed to improve women's lives. She sought legitimacy by gaining recognition through traditionally male measures of success, as in her university appointment and the publication of her numerous articles. By the 1910s she had moved beyond Jacobi's work on menstrual health and developed proactive measures to break the cycle of menstrual illness. Though she conceded somewhat to Clarke's notion of periodicity, she offered a feasible alternative for women: "functional periodicity." Mosher described this as a sensible remedy to the "monthly sicktime." Mosher proposed that women should manage their periods and regulate the physical symptoms of menstruation through her plan of physical education.[109] She developed an exercise regime— counter-intuitive to all contemporary medical prescriptions—to achieve this new model of functional periodicity. Functional periodicity allowed women's continuous participation in societal activities without dropping out during menstruation. She called her plan "a new method of dealing with this problem of the functional health of women."[110]

Reflecting prevailing trends that focused on public health at the turn to the twentieth century, Mosher invested in exercise, physical education, proper hygiene, and germ theory to improve the overall quality of daily life. Within her immediate influence, she sought to alleviate the symptoms of dysmennorhea, or painful periods, in her college students. On a broader level, Mosher recognized-her students as the future mothers of American citizens, and proposed that "[p]hysical fitness is not only an individual, a national, but a racial obligation."[111] Through exercise and muscle building, women—not just men—needed to prepare for the demands of civilized society.[112]

Mosher promoted and utilized the discourse of civilization—which relied upon notions of white racial progress and white superiority—to strengthen women's bodies and redefine the terms of womanhood. She recognized that perceptions of female infirmity, as signified through menstruation and menstrual sickness, rationalized women's weakened physical and political status in society. The discourse of civilization, which favored manliness, pointed toward increasing sex differentiation as proof of progress—the ideal woman was delicate, domestic, and homebound, while men were strong, economically independent, and worldly. Mosher believed the opposite to be true. Delicacy, most notably distinguished by a medical diagnosis of neurasthenia—an ailment unique to highly "civilized" women (and men)—indicated regression of bodily development, not progress. Instead, women needed physical exercise and a regime of fitness to improve the course of the "race." The term "race" implicitly meant white Anglo-Saxon Americans, and was understood as such by her predominantly white readers.[113] Mosher's ideas about white superiority were not unique at the turn of the century, in an age of racial segregation, but they were problematic. Mosher maintained membership with the Daughters of the American Revolution, infamous for its celebration of white elitism. As a long-time resident of the San Francisco Bay area, she would have witnessed the influx of European immigrants, but also Chinese and Japanese laborers, Latino migrant workers, and black people moving from the South. The preponderance of brown skin must have unnerved her, and their seeming fertility exacerbated her concerns about white people—"the race"—losing ground. Besides just harboring such feelings, Mosher actually promoted them programmatically in the classroom, in her writings, and when she spoke. She sought to ensure against the decreasing future birthrate of white Americans by celebrating reproductive health among young white women.

In order to carry out this campaign, she first needed evidence and scientific findings concerning menstruation. She began by examining past studies conducted by male and female physicians to assess the state of gynecology and its position on menstruation. She found the methods and underlying assumptions of earlier gynecological studies to be flawed, inaccurate, and misleading for a variety of reasons. Mosher contended, "[t]he greater part of the observations on which the current view of menstruation is based were made by men and are therefore less accurate than those made by women."[114] Men's perceptions tended to reinforce pathology to bolster constructs of female inferiority, and women were supposedly more innately understanding as medical practitioners. Furthermore she believed that men's lack of rigor or adherence to procedure resulted in misleading data. Mosher herself noticed "the degree of suffering and incapacity described by different authorities has varied from disease to mere nervous instability."[115] Mosher accused male physicians of viewing menstruation pejoratively and using questionable terms to make diagnoses. However, she acknowledged that the female patients could be just as compliant in contributing to the language of menstrual disease since they often misrepresented the severity of their periods or felt uncomfortable speaking frankly with their male physicians.

Mosher concluded that in most cases, women were not to blame for their painful periods or their sense of dread about menstruating. If children were taught that indigestion was a "sick time," Mosher believed that "[a]fter each meal every sensation would be exaggerated and nervous dread would presently result in a real condition of nervous indigestion," so that in essence it was a psychological problem.[116] Mosher accused male physicians of being the culprits who naturalized menstrual sickness by the very same method. She believed the terms "sicktime" and "being unwell" held a psychological influence on girls and women, thus entrenching menstruation as an illness by exaggerating the slightest symptom, so much so that even unrelated stomach problems were linked with menstruation.[117] Psychological forces influenced young women to perceive menstruation as a painful illness, thus demonstrating the idea that menstruation promoted those very behaviors. This compelled her to banish the terms, calling for a "universal crusade" against such language to reduce the number of patients with these symptoms.[118]

Mosher called for a "more limited view of menstruation," and one that saw it as neither responsible for every imagined ailment nor the origin of larger disease processes. She noted that if doctors and patients evaluated menstruation with as much regard as a sneeze, it would result in fewer cases of imagined menstrual "sickness" and more healthy American women. She limited menstruation to be "but one small part of the activity of the reproductive machinery."[119] She continued "[b]ecause it is an obvious function, everything occurring at or near the time of this periodic flow of blood from the uterus of the woman has been referred to this function."[120] Overall, this exaggerated the effects of menstruation, and helped to reduce women to one biological process. She asked, "do we not tend to translate too much of the whole of a woman's life into terms of menstruation?"[121] Mosher's response to this question was to diminish the role of menstruation, and follow a more well-rounded approach to health, without "undue emphasis" on "sexual characters" and reproductive mechanisms.[122] She tentatively asserted that "we might almost look for a revolution in the physical life of women" by positively understanding menstruation.[123]

To promote the revolution of women's physical lives, Mosher decided to conduct further research to more clearly understand dysmenorrhea and promote functional periodicity. In her study, she interviewed 400 women at the time of their periods and collected data which extended over "more than 3350 menstrual periods."[124] In 1911, she published her findings in the *California State Journal of Medicine*, in an article entitled "Functional Periodicity in Women and Some of the Modifying Factors."[125] Her position as medical advisor to women and director of Roble Gymnasium at Leland Stanford Junior College offered her access to test subjects: captive members of her health and hygiene classes.[126] Interacting daily with her students, she collected data over a number of months and created a serial menstrual record for each woman. The record included length of period, the amount of flow, and complications, if any. She found that data taken at the time of the period, compared to data collected based upon a woman's memory of her last period, varied tremendously from the serial menstrual record. In fact, very few women could accurately recount their past menstrual periods. This finding provided sufficient evidence to question the accuracy and applicability of earlier menstruation studies that were based upon women's recollections. Moreover, Mosher argued that questionable statistics from previous surveys "set down 30 to 95 per cent. of all women as having some sort of dysmenorrhea," which "grossly" exaggerated widespread debility.[127] These findings indicated there was a need for long-term studies conducted on menstruating women. Furthermore, it reinforced her contention that "women will speak more freely to one of their own sex than to a man, even though he is a physician."[128] The potential study of menstruating women provided her with a professional niche and helped to establish her career in a male-dominated environment.

Mosher's work departed from other studies by offering concrete suggestions and a set of exercises to counteract physical weakness and promote functional periodicity. She developed a yoga-like form of deep breathing exercises to work the lungs and diaphragm, which she believed "massaged" the internal organs and toned the abdominal muscles. These torso-strengthening exercises were to abate severe dysmennorhea. She published her findings in the *Journal of the American Medical Association* and the *California State Journal of Medicine* with the goal that other physicians would pass along her methods to their patients. She also implemented her breathing exercises through a carefully crafted physical education course that monitored the students' progress, and more importantly, their periods.

Called "Physical Training and Personal Hygiene," the course focused on gym exercises during the first three weeks of the menstrual cycle, and "laboratory work in personal hygiene" during a student's period. While menstruating, each student filled out a form, noting the day and time her period began and

ended, whether or not she experienced any pain, and if she had faithfully practiced her breathing exercises. After completing the appropriate paper work, the
woman met with Mosher and the other menstruating students for a lesson in
personal hygiene. Although her data gathering served a larger purpose, it is
ironic that her method of congregating and segregating the menstrual women
mirrored that very same practice promoted by Clarke. Like many other educators, she removed students from heavy physical exertion in class, and perhaps
worse, made their private bodily functions openly studied in public by an expert,
reifying the abnormal menstrual state.[129]

After segregating the menstruants from the non-menstruants, Mosher purposely infused her students with a sense of both responsibility for their menstrual health and their obligation to "the race." After students finished a set of
breathing exercises, "[t]he remainder of the hour is devoted to an informal talk
on some hygienic subject, eugenics, vocational opportunities, dress or kindred
topics which have some vital interest and relation to the woman's every-day
life."[130] Mosher intended for these discussions to redefine a woman's conceptu-
alization of her period from that of a sickness to a normal process of a healthful
body. With the dual approach of physical and mental training, women might
"disregard" menstruation as a debilitating interference of daily activity.

Topics of dress centered on the loosening of the corset in daily fashion and
wearing clothes which freed rather than constricted the body. She noted that
tight clothing and corsets impaired normal respiration and were responsible for
many menstrual disturbances. Poor posture and a lack of muscular development
also contributed to dysmennorhea.[131] Defining the origins of menstrual pain
meant that preventative and interventionist methods could be utilized to reduce
it. In this regard, she practiced what she preached. Unaffected by fashion dictates, Mosher dressed pragmatically and comfortably. A former student admitted
that Mosher was "quite a sight" marching across campus, shoulders back and
breathing "diaphragmatically"—a cornerstone to her exercise regime. She wore
a "shirtwaist dress, starched collar, four-in-hand tie, and untrimmed round hat"
and abandoned the obsolete corset. She provided a functional example of healthful dress, and not surprisingly, her style never wavered.[132]

Although Mosher mentioned the subject of eugenics in a rather casual manner, her writings reinforced the need for healthy, strong, fertile, and implicitly
white women to be an "advantage to the race." She believed that educated, white
middle- to upper-class women held the key to diminishing birthrates (it is ironic,
however, that she had no children). Mosher poised herself at an interesting junc-
ture, for she believed that she could positively affect white women's fertility,
thereby producing strong bodies as a national resource. Additionally, an appeal
to national urgency located menstruation within a discourse of motherhood and
progress toward a perfected civilization, which other physicians may have
grasped more readily than mere "functional periodicity" to redefine women's
periods.

Mosher's rhetoric only became more direct and pointed by the 1920s. She declared that there was "no advantage to the race to have one-half of it incapacitated one week out of four." Understood pragmatically and in terms of productivity, for the public to cling to the ideology of menstrual debility reflected poorly on the nation. In fact, obtaining "relief from whatever incapacity may be associated with this physiological function is important, not only to woman as an individual, but to her as the mother of the race."[133] Linking individual health with a strong democracy, Mosher stated that "[h]ealth is the birthright of every woman as well as every man." However, until the old views of weakness and menstrual debility were shed, "the average woman will not attain this birthright, and not only the individual and the nation, but the race will be robbed of its due."[134] Mosher politicized menstruation in new terms, equating menstrual blood not with disease processes but white racial vigor. In a prophetic warning, she declared that women were responsible for their own health. "It rests alone with her, whether she rejects it, clinging to the old ideal of physical weakness and dependence, or with open mind takes the opportunity of tasting the richness of physical perfection and the fullness of life which comes in its train, making of herself a better citizen, a better wife, a better mother."[135] Mosher used a heavy-handed approach to link race preservation, motherhood, and national duty to demonstrate woman's necessity in the building of American citizenry.

She believed this new perception of menstruation and women's health benefited the woman movement as well. In 1915 she addressed a national convention of YWCA members and officers, and her talk formed the seeds of her book *Health and the Woman Movement*, which she later revised into her well-regarded 1923 work, *Women's Physical Freedom*.[136] She repeated many of her beliefs concerning fashion, breathing exercises, and a positive attitude toward health. She also stressed that women themselves had the means to end systematic physiological inferiority by caring for their bodies and changing their mindsets. Furthermore, as modern women it was their duty and responsibility to seize the opportunities afforded by this health and ensure the progress of civilization. She took proactive measures to change women's attitudes by linking healthful menstruation and popular concerns about race preservation at the beginning of the twentieth century.

As an early feminist physician, Mosher upheld equal pay for equal work as a vital element to achieve equal rights. Economic parity with men leveled the playing field and offered women leverage. However, many women argued for the politics of difference rather than the politics of equality; as biological, menstruating women, they deserved special treatment because they were not men. She criticized those who dismissed her exercises and her message while preferring special privileges afforded to sex difference. She found that many women claimed to have cramps and exaggerated the severity of their periods "for the sake of special privileges which custom has decreed that it bring."[137] Certainly many women enjoyed the freedom from work that their menstrual periods brought, and welcomed a respite from work without reporting to bosses. Yet, this notion helped to reinforce women as inconsistent workers, and men as the reliable family wage earners. Mosher remained unsympathetic to women who claimed menstrual debility as a crutch to avoid work, for it only encouraged substandard treatment and expectations of lowered job performance. This resulted in pay disparity and job discrimination. Mosher argued that women's absences from work "would be greatly decreased if women realized the economic handicap they are helping to perpetuate. Equal pay for women means equal work; unnecessary menstrual absences mean less than full work."[138]

Mosher's reform of menstruation extended to attitudes about menopause as well. She viewed woman suffrage as particularly urgent in altering negative attitudes about menopausal and post-menopausal women. Mosher declared, "[w]hatever may be one's personal opinion of the advantages or disadvantages of woman's suffrage, it may be said that equal suffrage, like many of the economic and philanthropic opportunities now open to women, helps to meet the problem of the hygiene of middle life." This mid-life hygienic problem Mosher described caused a psychological crisis in some women, usually because it correlated with children maturing and moving away. This symbolized an end to a woman's career as a mother, and indicated that she had outworn her biological value to society. Having invested so much time in mothering, "her intellectual occupations and interest outside of the home are laid aside."

However, "[w]here equal suffrage exists, civic matters become a topic of home discussion; they concern the mother and daughters as well as the father and sons." Women remained attuned to community and national politics because as citizens it was their duty to vote. In addition to useful, meaningful roles outside of motherhood—a central and defining role for most women—they would make a better transition into their non-menstruating bodies. "Thus," Mosher concluded, "'votes for women' becomes not only a safeguard to the woman of middle age, a help in preserving the integrity of the family, but a protection to the community from the menace of the unoccupied middle-aged woman." Using similar rationale for menstrual health, Mosher referred to suffrage as a "protection to the community" from menopausal woman. No longer employed in her job as mother, a post-menopausal woman possessed abundant time. Mosher claimed that unoccupied time, if not properly channeled, led to sanitarium treatments, doctor's bills, and indulgence in dangerous fads.[139]

With Mosher's attention to menopause, attitudes about menstrual health came full circle. Thus she sought to use politics to change menstrual attitudes and use menstruation to change politics. Changing attitudes about menstruation for all stages of women's development contributed to a civil society. Regulated rather than over-exerted physical exercise yielded positive results in menstruating women, just as civic activity and full citizenship served to keep older women mentally stable and involved in their communities.[140]

It is difficult to determine whether or not Mosher immediately succeeded in convincing women to exercise and practice menstrual health. Ruth Lyons, Stanford Class of 1917, recalled doing her "Moshers" and swore by them, whereas her roommate found "Moshering" to be a waste of time.[141] By the 1920s, the New York City chapter of the YWCA recommended her book *Women's Physical Freedom* as an important source on menstruation. Physical education instructors in Detroit reported that young women given the "special Mosher exercises" felt better by the end of gym class.[142] And when Mosher proposed the provocative notion that functional periodicity could diminish menstruation to a mere "internal secretion," many health practitioners seemed to agree. Miss Brightey, Head of Health Department for Women at the International House, New York City, noted that "[I] delivered a baby from a woman who had practically no flow, to substantiate Dr. Mosher's theory that menstruation may not be necessary for child bearing."[143] That Dr. Elizabeth Kenyon of Teachers College Columbia frowned upon the concept because she herself "had no grounds on which to base such a theory," demonstrated that Mosher's more radical views were indeed discussed within the medical profession, or at least among female physicians.[144]

For the most part, women did not rally around "Moshering." The exercises required medical supervision, time, and attention. Some women thought them to be fruitless, and many physicians agreed. In reality, the average woman without access to a Stanford education was more likely to find everyday advice in popular books such as *The People's Home Library*.[145] Dispensing household tips about subjects from washing clothes to baking biscuits, the guidebook also walked women through the process of birthing a baby and managing menstruation. The dominant view cautioned women against strenuous physical and mental exertion, and warned against the danger of cold baths that would hemorrhage the flow. Though menstruation was starting to be viewed as normal, women were still treated differently because of it.

This could be seen in the application of scientific menstruation to issues of public policy. Lawyers drew upon the tenets of scientific menstruation concerning issues of women's paid labor. The persuasive arguments of defense lawyer Louis Brandeis, arguing for the defendant in the Supreme Court case *Muller v. Oregon* (1908), demonstrated the legal codification of scientific menstruation in relation to women's labor. Curt Muller, an owner of a laundry, appealed the legality of protective legislation that limited women's work to ten hours per day. He wanted to employ them for longer hours, and claimed the washerwomen wanted the extra hours, too. The question before the court was whether or not a woman's right to contract, as protected by the Fourteenth Amendment, was violated. The court found that though the general right to contract is protected by the Constitution, a state also has the ability to restrict that right. The premise used to rationalize this restriction, and thus limit a woman's ability to contract for a longer workday, was that "woman's physical structure" and the "burdens of motherhood" needed to be protected as a matter of public interest.[146] Instead of merely relying on legal precedent, Brandeis took the unusual step of supporting his defense with expert-based evidence provided by the likes of industrialists, physicians, professors, and government bureaucrats. Significantly, Brandeis quoted a physician who believed that factory labor was detrimental to women based upon "the periodical semi-pathological state of health of women."[147] In other words, menstruation provided the foundation for women's weakness and inequality in the workplace. For women whose health was already undermined by their own female bodies, the factory sealed their fate. Becoming invalids or rendered sterile due to both toil and the factory environs, women became a burden to the nation. Thus, limits on the workday protected "the strength and vigor of the race."[148] This court case solidified differences and inequality of the sexes based upon female biology, citing menstruation as a significant detriment and burden to women.

The late nineteenth and early twentieth centuries marked a new political discourse about menstruation. The effects of menstruation became political after Edward Clarke's popular publication, and the ideas that he promoted prompted dialogue amongst physicians, educators, and early feminists and produced a movement called scientific menstruation. However, the differing prescriptions concerning how a woman should work, act, and behave during her period defied a single meaning of menstruation, though debility came to dominate the discourse. The scope of scientific menstruation demonstrates the stakes of body politics and who had power to control women's bodies. It points to the larger question of women's citizenship in the United States, and how challenges to expand democracy were met with reasons to limit it, often predicated upon women's naturally inferior status. The cyclical and recurring menstrual infirmity justified women's unfit biology and their inability to handle the rigors required of full participatory citizenship. A 1912 article in the *New York Times* charged that the woman's movement was filled with militant suffragists whose minds suffered from "the reverberations of her physiological emergencies."[149] These physiological emergencies—menstrual periods—explained the cause of their mental disorder, because as the logic followed, only unfit women would demand the right to vote. It is because of this overwhelming preponderance of menstruation as negative, deleterious, and an all-encompassing bodily event that technology, and specifically menstrual hygiene products, might provide a solution.

Notes

1. Thomas Laqueur discusses understandings of anatomy and the construction of sexual difference. See *Making Sex: Body and Gender from the Greeks to Freud* (Cambridge: Harvard University Press, 1990).

2. I have taken this concept from the notion of scientific motherhood, in which successful mothers required the professional guidance and advice of a scientifically trained elite to accomplish the rearing of children. See Rima Apple, "Constructing Mothers: Scientific Motherhood in the Nineteenth and Twentieth Centuries," *Social History of Medicine* 8, no. 2 (August 1995): 161–78; Barbara Ehrenreich and Deirdre English, *For Her Own Good: 150 Years of the Experts' Advice to Women* (New York: Anchor Books, 1978).

3. Cynthia Russett, *Sexual Science: The Victorian Construction of Womanhood* (Cambridge: Harvard University Press, 1989); Carol Tavris, *The Mismeasure of Woman* (New York: Simon and Schuster, 1992); Anne Fausto-Sterling, *Myths of Gender: Biological Theories About Women and Men* (New York: Basic Books, Inc., 1985); Caroll Smith-Rosenberg, *Disorderly Conduct: Visions of Gender in Victorian America* (New York: Oxford University Press, 1986); G. J. Barker-Benfield, *The Horrors of the Half-Known Life: Male Attitudes Toward Women and Sexuality in 19th Century America* (New York: Routledge, 2nd ed., 1999); Rima Apple, *Mothers and Medicine: A Social History of Infant Feeding, 1890–1950* (Madison: University of Wisconsin Press, 1987); Judith Walzer Leavitt, *Brought to Bed: Childbearing in America, 1750 to 1950* (New York: Oxford University Press, 1986); Judith Walzer Leavitt, ed., *Women and Health in America: Historical Readings* (Madison: University of Wisconsin Press, 2nd ed., 1999).

4. Londa Schiebinger, *Nature's Body: Gender in the Making of Modern Science* (Boston: Beacon Press, 1993).

5. Winthrop Jordan, *White Over Black: American Attitudes Toward the Negro, 1550–1812* (Chapel Hill: University of North Carolina Press, 1968).

6. Emily Martin analyzes how metaphors of production inform medical descriptions of female bodies. See *The Woman in the Body: A Cultural Analysis of Reproduction* (Boston: The Beacon Press, 1992). See also Catherine Gallagher and Thomas Laqueur, eds., *The Making of the Modern Body: Sexuality and Society in the Nineteenth Century* (Berkeley: University of California Press, 1987).

7. Susan E. Klepp, "Revolutionary Bodies: Women and the Fertility Transition in the Mid-Atlantic Region, 1760–1820," *Journal of American History* (December 1998): 910–45; Sylvia Hoffert, *Private Matters: American Attitudes Toward Childbearing and Infant Nurture in the Urban North, 1800-1860* (Urbana: University of Illinois Press, 1989); Catherine Scholten, *Childbearing in America Society: 1650-1850* (New York: New York University Press, 1985).

8. J. David Hacker, "Rethinking the 'Early' Decline of Marital Fertility in the United States," *Demography* 40, no. 4 (November 2003): 605–20.

9. Linda Kerber discusses how sexual autonomy preceded political autonomy in the early nineteenth century, with declining birth rates attributable to this growing control. See Linda Kerber, "Separate Spheres, Female Worlds, Woman's Place," *Journal of American History* 75, no. 1 (June 1988): 9–39; Carl Degler, *At Odds: Women and the Family in America from the Revolution to the Present* (New York: Oxford University Press, 1980). Demographers have long been interested in the lowered birthrate in the nineteenth century. See Daniel Scott Smith, "Family Limitation, Sexual Control, and Domestic Feminism in Victorian America," in *A Heritage of Her Own*, eds. Nancy Cott and Elizabeth Pleck (New York: Simon and Schuster, 1979), 222–45; Linda Gordon, *Woman's Body, Woman's Right: Birth Control in America* (New York: Penguin Books, 1990).

10. Joan Jacobs Brumberg mentions this and calls it an "ovulatory revolution." See Brumberg, *The Body Project: An Intimate History of American Girls* (New York: Random House, 1997), 6.

11. Laqueur, *Making Sex*, 213.

12. A. F. A. King, "A New Basis for Uterine Pathology," *American Journal of Obstetrics and Diseases of Women and Children* 8 (May–February 1875–76): 237–56.

13. King, "A New Basis for Uterine Pathology," 242.

14. Mary Putnam Jacobi, *The Question of Rest for Women During Menstruation* (Farmingdale, NY: Dabor Social Science Publications, 1978), 6–7, reprint of the 1886 ed. published by G. P. Putnam's Sons, New York.

15. W. H. Studley, "Is Menstruation a Disease? A Review of Professor King's Article Entitled 'A New Basis for Uterine Pathology,'" *American Journal of Obstetrics* 8 (May–February 1875–1876): 487–512, quoted on 487. Dr. Mary Putnam Jacobi quoted King as recommending "girls be encouraged to marry immediately upon arriving at the age of puberty, so that menstruation may be at once interrupted by a pregnancy which should be repeated so frequently as to entirely exclude its pathological substitute from the existence of the woman" (*The Question of Rest*, 7).

16. Studley, "Is Menstruation a Disease?" 489.

17. Studley, "Is Menstruation a Disease?" 489.

18. Studley, "Is Menstruation a Disease?" 498.

19. Studley, "Is Menstruation a Disease?" 512.

20. For an excellent discussion of race, class, citizenship, and medicine see Laura Briggs, "The Race of Hysteria: 'Overcivilization' and the 'Savage' Woman in Late Nineteenth-Century Obstetrics and Gynecology," *American Quarterly* 52 (June 2000): 246–73.

21. Horatio R. Storer, *Criminal Abortion; Its Nature, Its Evidence, and Its Law* (Boston: Little, Brown, and Company, 1868), 98–101, as referenced in Jacobi, *The Question of Rest*, 4–5. See also Vern Bullough and Martha Voght, "Women, Menstruation, and Nineteenth-Century Medicine," in *Women and Health in America*, 28–37; Carroll Smith-Rosenberg and Charles Rosenberg, "The Female Animal: Medical and Biological Views of Woman and Her Role in Nineteenth-Century America," *Women and Health in America*, 12–27.

22. Storer, *Criminal Abortion*, 101.

23. Storer, *Criminal Abortion*, 98–101. On the use of menstruation to establish constructions of gender, see Julie-Marie Strange, "Menstrual Fictions: Languages of Medicine and Menstruation, c. 1850–1930," *Women's History Review* 9, no. 3 (2000): 607–28.

24. Edward H. Clarke, *Sex in Education; or, A Fair Chance for the Girls* (Boston: J. R. Osgood & Co., 1873), 55–56, 157. See also Janice Delaney, Mary Jane Lupton, and Emily Toth, *The Curse: A Cultural History of Menstruation* (Urbana: University of Illinois Press, 1988); Joan Jacobs Brumberg, *The Body Project: An Intimate History of American Girls* (New York: Random House, 1997).

25. Edward H. Clarke, *Observation on the Nature and Treatment of Polypus of the Ear* (Boston: Ticknor and Fields, 1867); *A Century of American Medicine, 1776–1876* (Philadelphia: H. C. Lea, 1876).

26. Mabel Newcomer, *A Century of Higher Education for American Women* (New York: Harper and Row, 1959), in *Liberty, Equality, Power: A History of the American People*, John Murrin, et al. (Fort Worth: Harcourt Brace, 1999), 700. Menstruation also

proved to be a problem of virgins, thus Clarke's emphasis on school-aged girls. See Helen King, *The Disease of Virgins: Green Sickness, Chlorosis and the Problems of Puberty* (New York: Routledge, 2003). On the creation of girls, and the place of monthly periods, see Jane H. Hunter, *How Young Ladies Became Girls: The Victorian Origins of American Girlhood* (New Haven: Yale University Press, 2002).

27. "The Death of Dr. Clarke," *Boston Medical and Surgical Journal* 97 (1877): 657–59.

28. Mary Roth Walsh, *Doctors Wanted: No Women Need Apply* (New Haven: Yale University Press, 1977), 120; Edward H. Clarke, M.D., "Sex in Education" in *Images of Women in American Popular Culture*, ed. Angela Dorenkamp, et al. (New York: Harcourt Brace Jovanovich Publishers, 1985), 43–45.

29. The contents of the speech were reported in "Sex in Education," *The Woman's Journal* (December 21, 1872).

30. Edward H. Clarke, *Sex in Education; or, A Fair Chance for the Girls* (Boston: J. R. Osgood & Co., 1874, 2nd ed.), preface.

31. *Sex in Education* went through five editions within the first year, with the last edition published in 1886. See *Sex in Education; or, A Fair Chance for the Girls*, 17th ed. (Boston: Houghton, Mifflin, 1886). See also Walsh, *Doctors Wanted*, 124; Bullough and Voght, "Women, Menstruation, and Nineteenth-Century Medicine," 31. Clarke's name appeared in the table of contents of the Egyptian journal, *al-Muqtataf. Monthly Scientific Journal*, eds. Faris Nimr and Ya'qub Sarruf (Alexandria, 1877–1976).

32. Walsh, *Doctors Wanted*, 124.

33. Clarke, *Sex in Education*, 126.

34. Henry M. Leicester, *The Historical Background of Chemistry* (New York: Dover Publications, Inc., 1956), 231. Vital force was rather amorphous, "peculiar," and represented all kinds of organic functions and activities. Early scientists described vital force as sustaining life itself. See William Coleman, *Biology in the Nineteenth Century: Problems of Form, Function, and Transformation* (New York: John Wiley and Sons, Inc., 1971). Clarke's suppositions also relied upon ideas about body constitution and temperament, which characterized patients as sanguine or choleric, and for women most often nervous. See John Haller, *American Medicine in Transition: 1840–1910* (Urbana: University of Illinois Press, 1981), 17–29.

35. Clarke, *Sex in Education*, 32. Although the closed-economy model applied to both men and women, women's systems were characterized as being more sensitive to changes in energy allocation. See Regina Morantz-Sanchez, *Conduct Unbecoming a Woman: Medicine on Trial in Turn-of-the-Century Brooklyn* (New York: Oxford University Press, 1999), 114–37.

36. Clarke, *Sex in Education*, 40.

37. Edward H. Clarke, *The Building of a Brain* (Boston: James R. Osgood and Co., 1874), 60.

38. Clarke, *Sex in Education*, 41–42. The new interpretation of menstruation compared women to mammals, who have an estrus cycle and come into "heat" during which time they are fertile. Scientists hypothesized that women were therefore fertile during their own estrus, signified by menstrual blood. The knowledge of mid-cycle ovulation did not occur until the 1920s. See Brumberg, *The Body Project*, 7–8.

39. Clarke, *Sex in Education*, 64–65.

40. Clarke, *Sex in Education*, 53–56. Clarke argued that among males and females, the nutritive and nervous systems were identical, however reproductive systems set them apart. In men, the results of over-taxation of the brain resulted in "adipose effeminancy" with the "element of masculineness" taken out of them.

41. Clarke, *Sex in Education*, 132–33.

42. George Lowell Austin, *Perils of American Women: Or, A Doctor's Talk with Maiden, Wife, and Mother* (Boston: Lee and Shepard, 1883).

43. Austin, *Perils,* 150–51.

44. Mabel Newcomer, *A Century of Higher Education for American Women,* 700.

45. William Capp, *The Daughter; Her Health, Education, and Wedlock* (Philadelphia: F. A. Davis, 1891), 57.

46. Capp, *The Daughter*, 77.

47. Capp, *The Daughter*, 77.

48. Capp, *The Daughter*, 77.

49. Azel Ames, Jr., *Sex in Industry: A Plea for the Working Girl* (New York: Garland Publishing, Inc., 1986 [reprint]; Boston: James R. Osgood and Company, 1875).

50. Ames, 142–44.

51. "Sex in Education," *The Woman's Journal* (December 21, 1872). *The Woman's Journal* proved to be a strong advocate of female physicians. A watchdog publication, it reported limitations placed on women's practice of medicine, and other barriers toward full citizenry. See Walsh, *Doctors Wanted*, 89–91.

52. George Fisk Comfort, *Woman's Education, and Woman's Health: Chiefly in Reply to "Sex in Education"* (Syracuse: T. W. Durston & Co., 1874), ix.

53. Comfort, *Woman's Education*, 155.

54. Comfort, *Woman's Education*, 20.

55. Maria A. Elmore, untitled, in *Sex and Education: A Reply to Dr. E. H. Clarke's "Sex in Education,* ed. Julia Ward Howe (Boston: Roberts Brothers: 1874), 175.

56. Elmore, untitled, 180.

57. This was not her most popular book. Duffey's most widely read book, *What Women Should Know; A Woman's Book about Women* (Philadelphia: J. M. Stoddard & Co., 1873), went through four additional printings (1879, 1881, 1882, 1895), and her advice provided her notoriety.

58. Eliza Brisbee Duffey, *No Sex in Education, or An Equal Chance for Both Boys and Girls. Being a Review of Dr. E. H. Clarke's "Sex in Education"* (Philadelphia: J. M. Stoddard and Co., 1874), 117.

59. Duffey, *No Sex,* 96.

60. Duffey, *No Sex,* 7.

61. Duffey, *No Sex,* 96.

62. Duffey, *No Sex,* 96–98.

63. Clarke, *Sex in Education*, 132–33.

64. Duffey, *No Sex,* 96. Here, she refers to Clarke as "the chivalrous doctor," clearly a reference meant to jab at his self-proclaimed masculinist role. The reference also implied that his help was both unsolicited and unwanted.

65. Catharine Beecher blamed tightly laced corsets as the culprit for displaced internal organs. See *Letters to the People on Health and Happiness* (New York: Harper and Brothers, 1855), and Kathryn Kish Sklar, *Catharine Beecher: A Study in American Domesticity* (New York: W.W. Norton & Company Inc., 1973).

66. Jeanne Boydston, *Home and Work: Housework, Wages, and the Ideology of Labor in the Early Republic* (New York: Oxford University Press, 1990), chapter 5.

67. "C," in Howe, *Sex in Education*, 123.

68. Duffey, *No Sex*, 117–18.

69. Duffey, *No Sex*, 56.

70. Duffey, *No Sex*, 118.

71. Charles W. Carey, "Edward Hammond Clarke," *American National Biography* (New York: Oxford University Press, 1999), 961–62.

72. Apparently French people were no more magnanimous than the Americans in admitting women to the university, just more open to payment. Later in her life Jacobi remarked, "It is astonishing how many invincible objections on the score of feasibility, modesty, propriety, and prejudice will melt away before the charmed touch of a few thousand dollars." Dr. Mary E. Putnam Jacobi, "Social Aspects of the Readmission of Women into the Medical Profession," *Papers and Letters Presented at the First Woman's Congress of the Association for the Advancement of Woman, October, 1873* (New York: Mrs. William Ballard, Printer, 1874), 177.

73. Jacobi left much commentary in the form of letters to *The Medical Record*, lectures and addresses made to various associations and societies, political treatises, short stories, and compiled works published by her father's press, G. P. Putnam's Sons.

74. Mary Putnam Jacobi, *"Common Sense" Applied to Woman Suffrage* (New York: G. P. Putnam's Sons, 1894). See also Carla Bittel, "The Science of Women's Rights: The Medical and Political Worlds of Mary Putnam Jacobi," Ph.D. Dissertation (Cornell University, January 2003).

75. The Women's Medical Association, ed., *Mary Putnam Jacobi*, xxii–xxiii, and Walsh, *Doctors Wanted*, 60.

76. The book went through at least three editions: 1877, 1878, and 1886. See Walsh, *Doctors Wanted*, 99, 130–31, and Sheila M. Rothman, "Introduction," from Mary Putnam Jacobi, *The Question of Rest for Women During Menstruation* (Farmingdale, NY: Dabor Social Science Publications, 1978), reprint of the 1886 ed. published by G. P. Putnam's Sons, NY.

77. Jacobi, *The Question of Rest*, 17.

78. Jacobi, *The Question of Rest*, 26–27.

79. Jacobi, *The Question of Rest*, 205.

80. Jacobi, *The Question of Rest*, 227.

81. Jacobi, *The Question of Rest*, 17–20.

82. Todd L. Savitt, "Black Health on the Plantation: Masters, Slaves, and Physicians," in *Science and Medicine in the Old South*, eds. Ronald L. Numbers and Todd L. Savitt (Baton Rouge: Louisiana State University Press, 1989), 327–55.

83. Frederick Law Olmstead, *A Journey in the Seaboard Slave States* (New York: Dix and Edwards, 1856), 190.

84. Jacobi, *The Question of Rest*, 17–20. See also Gail Bederman, *Manliness and Civilization: A Cultural History of Gender and Race in the United States, 1880–1917* (Chicago: University of Chicago Press, 1995); Briggs, "The Race of Hysteria."

85. Paula Giddings, *When and Where I Enter: The Impact of Black Women on Race and Sex in America* (New York: Bantam Books, 1984).

86. Jacobi, *The Question of Rest*, 17–20.

87. Jacobi, *The Question of Rest*, 4. She cited Dr. Hutchins's 1875 New York State Medical Association prize essay.

88. Jacobi, *The Question of Rest*, 8–9, 64.

89. Jacobi, *The Question of Rest*, 7–8.

90. Thomas Laqueur, *Making Sex*, 184, 222. Laqueur states that until the 1840s scientists understood that "coitally induced ovulation in humans as well as in other mammals was the norm." Thus, both men and women contributed generative "seed" during orgasm. After the 1840s physicians believed the seed could be produced in women without the sensation of orgasm. This accounts for explanations of nervous force, instead of generative force, triggering ovulation.

91. Jacobi, *The Question of Rest*, 111.

92. Vern Bullough and Martha Voght, "Women, Menstruation, and Nineteenth-Century Medicine," 28–29.

93. Jacobi, *The Question of Rest*, 79.

94. Jacobi, *The Question of Rest*, 166.

95. Jacobi, *The Question of Rest*, 108.

96. Jacobi, *The Question of Rest*, 231–32.

97. Jacobi, *The Question of Rest*, 109.

98. Mary Putnam Jacobi, "On Female Invalidism," in *Mary Putnam Jacobi, M.D., A Pathfinder in Medicine* (New York: G. P. Putnam's Sons, 1925), 478.

99. Jacobi, *The Question of Rest*, 231.

100. Mary Putnam Jacobi, M.D., *"Common Sense" Applied to Woman Suffrage* (New York: G. P. Putnam's Sons, 1894), 99.

101. Jacobi, *"Common Sense,"* 99–101.

102. Association of Collegiate Alumnae, Special Committee, *Health Statistics of Women College Graduates* (Boston: Wright and Potter, 1885), 65.

103. *Health Statistics*, 77–78.

104. *Health Statistics*, 10.

105. Mosher outlines her disagreement in *Women's Physical Freedom* (New York: The Woman's Press, 1923).

106. Elizabeth Brownlee Griego, "A Part and Yet Apart: Clelia Duel Mosher and Professional Women at the Turn-of-the-Century" (Ph.D. diss., University of California, Berkeley, 1983).

107. Mosher's writings appeared in journals such as *The Medical Women's Journal, The California State Journal of Medicine, The American Physical Education Review,* and *Journal of the American Medical Association.*

108. Clelia Duel Mosher, *The Mosher Survey: Sexual Attitudes of 45 Victorian Women,* eds. James MaHood and Kristine Wenburg (New York: Arno Press, 1980); John D'Emilio and Estelle B. Freedman, *Intimate Matters: A History of Sexuality in America* (Chicago: University of Chicago Press, 1997).

109. Martha H. Verbrugge, "Recreating the Body: Women's Physical Education and the Science of Sex Differences in America, 1900–1940," *Bulletin of the History of Medicine* 71 (1997): 273–304.

110. Clelia Duel Mosher, *Personal Hygiene for Women* (Stanford: Stanford University Press, 1927), 77.

111. Mosher, *Personal Hygiene*, 77.

112. Janet L. Kreger, "A Gymnasium of Their Own," *LSA Magazine-The University of Michigan* (Fall 1995): 10–16.

113. Bederman, *Manliness and Civilization,* 123–24, 145.

114. Mosher, "Functional Periodicity in Women and Some of the Modifying Factors," *California State Journal of Medicine* IX, no. 1–2 (January-February 1911): 6.

115. Mosher, "Functional Periodicity," 5.

116. Mosher, "Functional Periodicity," 7.

117. Mosher, "Functional Periodicity," 7.

118. Mosher, "Functional Periodicity," 8. In England, a similar campaign was underway to promote a model of menstrual discretion rather than menstrual pathology. See Julie-Marie Strange, "The Assault on Ignorance: Teaching Menstrual Etiquette in England, c. 1920s to 1960s," *Social History of Medicine* 14, no. 2 (2001): 247–65.

119. Mosher, "Functional Periodicity," 57–58.

120. Mosher, "Functional Periodicity," 57–58.

121. Clelia Duel Mosher, "A Physiologic Treatment of Congestive Dysmenorrhea and Kindred Disorders Associated with the Menstrual Function," *Journal of the American Medical Association* (April 25, 1914): 1300–301.

122. Mosher, "Functional Periodicity," 58.

123. Mosher, "Physiologic Treatment," 1301.

124. Mosher, "Functional Periodicity," 4.

125. Mosher, "Functional Periodicity," 4–8, 55–58.

126. Clelia Dual Mosher, "The Physical Training of Women in Relation to Functional Periodicity," *The Woman's Medical Journal* 25 (April 1915): 71. Mosher's course, "Physical Training and Personal Hygiene," was not mandatory, but by the fall of 1917 the class split into both "Personal Hygiene" and "Physical Training." Undergraduates were required to enroll in physical training for two years. Margaret Kimball, University Archivist, Stanford University, "Clelia Mosher," e-mail to the author (June 23, 2000).

127. Mosher, "Functional Periodicity," 6.

128. Mosher, "Functional Periodicity," 6.

129. Elinor Accampo, comment to panel "Women's Minds, Women's Bodies: Construction of Female Medical Expertise in Early Twentieth Century Japan, the Ottoman Empire and the United States," 114th Meeting of the American Historical Association, Chicago, January 7, 2000. See also, Regina Markell Morantz and Sue Zschoche, "Professionalism, Feminism, and Gender Roles: A Comparative Study of Nineteenth-Century Medical Therapeutics," *Journal of American History* 67 (1980): 568–88.

130. Mosher, "Physical Training," 71–74.

131. Mosher, "Functional Periodicity," 56.

132. Her students came from white upper-class homes, and Lou Henry Hoover was one of the more famous. See Griego, "A Part and Yet Apart," 265. See also Kathryn Allen Jacob, "Clelia Duel Mosher," *Johns Hopkins Magazine* (June 1979): 8–16.

133. Mosher, "Functional Periodicity," 4.

134. Mosher, "Personal Hygiene," 77. Mosher attributed the falling birthrate of white, upper-class, educated women to three main reasons: "contraception, selfishness in men and physical maladjustment of which menstruation played a part" (underline hers). See *The Mosher Survey,* 5.

135. Mosher, "Personal Hygiene," 86.

136. Clelia Duel Mosher, *Health and the Woman Movement* (New York: Young Women's Christian Association, 1916); *Women's Physical Freedom* (New York: The Woman's Press, 1923), entered into six printings.

137. Mosher, "Personal Hygiene," 35.

138. Mosher, "Personal Hygiene," 35.

139. Mosher, "Personal Hygiene," 45–46.

140. Mosher, "Personal Hygiene," 46.

141. Jacob, "Clelia Duel Mosher," 11.

142. Lillian Gilbreth, "Report of Gilbreth, Inc." to Johnson and Johnson, 1927, 100–108. Papers of Frank and Lillian Gilbreth, Special Collections, Purdue University.

143. Gilbreth, "Report of Gilbreth, Inc.," 102–108.

144. Gilbreth, "Report of Gilbreth, Inc.," 102.

145. R. C. Barnum, ed., *The People's Home Library* (Cleveland: The R. C. Barnum Co., 1914).

146. *Muller v. Oregon*, 208 U.S. 412 (1908). Justice Brewer delivered the opinion.

147. *Muller v. Oregon*, 208 U.S. 412 (1908), 22.

148. *Muller v. Oregon*, 208 U.S. 412 (1908).

149. *New York Times,* March 28, 1912, in Leta Hollingworth, *Functional Periodicity: An Experimental Study of the Mental and Motor Abilities of Women during Menstruation* (New York: Teachers College, Columbia University, 1914), 97.

Chapter 4

"The Kotex Age": Consumerism, Technology, and Menstruation

"What most of them wish, (and as yet they have not had this wish granted)," noted researcher and efficiency expert Lillian Gilbreth, "is for a new product which will be completely invisible no matter how tight or thin their clothes are."[1] By the 1920s and 1930s women wanted manufactured menstrual hygiene products that would be imperceptible to the eye. This was a new technological turn from the late nineteenth century. Scientific menstruation did not disappear, but added to this was a predominantly technical discussion about how to manage menstrual flow. The problem of menstruation, characterized in part as a "hygienic handicap," was one that could be addressed through modern technology.[2] Furthermore, if this technology could be rendered invisible, it would be all the more appealing to women. One advertisement for Meds tampons, so certain of this possibility, claimed, "You don't know you're wearing one, *and neither does anyone else.*"[3] Since euphemisms for menstruation still circulated, including calling it a condition, ailment, disability, and "the sicktime," the new technologies might help to manage and therefore mask menstruation. In essence, the technologies allowed women to forget about their periods, and in a manner of speaking, temporarily deceive themselves. It provided a means for a double pass: passing as a healthy non-menstruant to oneself and to others.

59

The major way that sanitary napkin manufacturers enticed women consumers and drew attention to their products was through advertisements in women's magazines.[4] In 1929, home economist Christine Frederick wrote *Selling Mrs. Consumer* to teach advertisers in the marketing industry how to more skillfully entice women to purchase their products. Frederick argued that products were no longer simply bought; they had to be sold, and sold skillfully, because women made decisions about purchases and wanted items that appealed to their preferences.[5] That companies should then focus more of their attention and resources on women was not unusual. However, Kimberly-Clark Corporation gave women a different kind of attention with a preponderance of Kotex ads characterized by cryptic script, and a deluge of concealed boxes. Some men felt slighted by all this attention toward women. Arnold Gingrich, a copywriter and editor of *Esquire* magazine, lamented that "[t]he general magazines, in the mad scramble to increase the woman readership that seems to be so highly prized by national advertisers, have bent over backwards in catering to the special interests and tastes of the feminine audience." This attention to women was so onerous that it "has reached the point where the male reader is made to feel like an intruder on gynaecic mysteries."[6] These "gynaecic mysteries" included such practices as douching with Lysol as a form of contraception and then using Modess, Kotex, or Meds for soaking up menstrual blood. William Faulkner, generally known for his masculinist prose, seemed flustered by these same mysteries. Deeply in debt and allured by quick money, Faulkner assured his literary agent that he would "try to cook up something for *Cosmopolitan*." Accustomed to working on novels, film scripts, and short stories, he felt "out of the habit of writing trash" for serials, but the quick acceptance and publication of a formulaic romance would still stroke his ego. Uninspired, he speculated about copying one of *Cosmopolitan's* stories, changing the locale and names, and offering it to the editors as a new piece. On second thought, he believed that sort of revision was "probably hard work too and requires skill." Frustrated by his flirtation with plagiarism, he lamented, "I seem to be so out of touch with the Kotex Age here that I can't seem to think of anything myself."[7]

Faulkner merely may have been complaining about writer's block, the popularity of pulp fiction, or the influence of women's romance novels on the literary market in the 1930s.[8] Nonetheless, he chose to express his frustration in terms of a female-specific technology used to mask menstrual blood: Kotex sanitary napkins. He could have couched this frustration in terms of newly marketed cosmetics—the Maybelline Age or the Pond's Cold Cream Era. Surely he understood no more about these things than he did Kotex. However, Kotex represented the tension about women's biological nature, appropriate roles, and proper place. Women had gained the right to vote; spearheaded reform of child labor, health, and working conditions in the progressive movement; and were economically supporting families when men were stripped of their jobs during the Great Depression. They enrolled in college in unprecedented numbers, and in essence, were acting more like *men*. To top it off, they now had a powerful technology at their fingertips that fostered newfound agency over their formerly unruly bodies by masking menstruation, one of their distinct biological differences with men.

The transition from homemade pads to manufactured pads emerged at a specific cultural moment. Faith in technological progress, attention to practices of sanitation and hygiene, and women's changing roles and circumstances due to woman suffrage and women's rights between the 1910s and 1920s contributed to the purchase and use of sanitary napkins. In addition, the explosion of national advertising of nonessential items in newspapers, billboards, and in particular, women's magazines, created representations of idealized lifestyles through the purchase of products. Since more sophisticated forms of advertising emerged during this time, advertisements educated consumers both about how to read the messages in the advertisements as well as about the attributes of the product.[9] However, sanitary napkins proved to be fairly unique in their representation as female-specific technologies. Advertisers were hesitant about how to sell a hidden and potentially embarrassing technology without mentioning its explicit use or showing an image of a product. Advertisers perceived this to be a great challenge and underestimated women's savvy and their ability to articulate preferences. With so little information about women purchasers, the results of Lillian Gilbreth's 1927 survey concerning products and practices of menstrual hygiene offers a bevy of information about numerous technologies and women's overall dissatisfaction with the technologies. Results from her research indicated that better products would lead to more sales, and accordingly, higher profits. She discovered that women already possessed sophisticated knowledge about the complicated processes necessary to tailor-fit sanitary pads. As technologies of passing, store-bought menstrual hygiene products offered women the technological means to leave home, go to school, work at the office, and travel in cars without the hassle of washing used pads. Using disposable sanitary pads, and the presumption of activity that went along with their use, meant that women were not tethered to the bed for days in a row, swaddled in rags to catch their menstrual flow. The technologies of menstrual hygiene offered women powerful tools to create new practices around their monthly periods, and often defy recommendations about rest and curtailment of activities during their menses.

Modernity, Technology, and Hygiene

The turn to the twentieth century marked a moment of intense interest in technology. Ruth Schwartz Cowan has examined how technological development and social change during this time period influenced one another, and how the United States has often been defined through its technological character.[10] However, it is not so easy to separate technology from science. She argues that technoscience, the intertwining and interdependency of technology in the development of scientific research, and the technological developments stemming from scientific research, has influenced society.[11] She examines how automobiles, aircraft, electronic communication devices, and biotechnology, and the corresponding technological systems in which they are imbedded, have shaped social change, but also how social needs have molded technologies and their systems as well. Cowan warns not to dismiss earlier colonial technologies, claiming that Americans have always been technological. What made the late nineteenth and early twentieth centuries different was the rate of change, and the accompanying national systems that allowed the technological distribution to the many, for example railways, automobiles, or the telephone. For instance, my grandmother, Helen Matter, who was born in 1915, grew up on a farm in the panhandle of Oklahoma, where she remained for most of her life. She tells the story that transportation changed so quickly, she was convinced that since she rode a horse to grade school, and then owned a car by her early 20s, her own personal helicopter was the next progressive step. These seemingly stunning leaps in locomotion and the wonder of technological innovation shaped her perception of changes in transportation.

With this fascination with technoscience and technological progress, it is not surprising that all sorts of technologies, contraptions, and household devices emerged. However, these technologies became products by means of organized distribution and consumption.[12] Although manufactured products were not new, the infrastructure to deliver them was. New technologies of refrigeration, mechanization for cardboard boxes and canning, and transportation systems provided the means for new products to be mass distributed quickly. Local grocers easily purchased wholesale goods manufactured in states thousands of miles away. Companies promoted their brand names through advertising, and relied on the hope that consumers would choose neatly packaged Quaker oats, for instance, over bulk stock sold in one hundred pound burlap bags.[13] Companies discovered that consumers who trusted a product, relied upon a standard delivery and quality, and believed in its usefulness over another similar product were willing to pay a bit more for it. In turn, once consumers knew to shop for and purchase more expensive brand name products, advertisers warned them to "accept no substitutes."[14] Cheap price did not necessarily constitute value.

As food production and sales increased, items once considered non-essential such as soap and other personal hygiene products also found lucrative markets. The success of the products also stemmed from attention to cleanliness, and an obsession about living in a germ-free environment.[15] Bathroom and kitchen design reflected the growing paranoia that all germs spread disease; easily disinfected white ceramic tile, enamel tabletops, and porcelain sinks became immediate necessities. In fact, hygiene was linked to civilization itself. In 1917, *House and Garden* claimed that "[t]he bathroom is an index to civilization. Time was when it sufficed for a man to be civilized in his mind. We now require a civilization of the body. And in no line of house building has there been so great progress in recent years as in bathroom civilization."[16] Medical practitioners, social reformers, home economists, and female consumers promoted the idea that cleanliness indicated advanced civilization. A clean, well-managed home signified a high quality of life and a successful, prosperous family. The environment of a clean home promoted the ideal of individual vigor and health, and in a time when typhoid, dysentery, and cholera might be held at bay with better sanitation, it made sense to remain vigilant about the spread of germs.

Not just the home, but also the body required attention to hygiene in order to maintain vitality. Specifically, control and regulation of bodily by-products helped to civilize the body and elevate it from its most banal processes. The Prophylactic Toothbrush Company, through its ad campaigns, educated the public about benefits of maintaining oral health.[17] Colgate published pamphlets about dental hygiene and shaving techniques, linking better hygiene with personal success. Gillette claimed that its razors provided a public service. A liberal gargling with Listerine mouthwash tackled the annoyance of bad breath and killed bad germs. Regular bathing and lathering with Ivory soap conquered body odor and washed it down the drain. Less savory products, such as toilet paper and laxatives, emerged to manage the vagaries of a messy human body. However, the fixation on cleanliness embodied elements of racial hierarchy and rationalization of white, upper-class superiority; a clean, fresh smelling, perfectly coifed upper-middle-class body looked and smelled very different from an unbathed, unkempt, and working-class body. Within the model of perfectible civilization, cleanliness represented human progress, and indicated a level of personal control and bodily efficiency.[18]

This demand for clean and hygienic bodies raised an uncomfortable contradiction between public and private. Intimate matters of hygiene affected outcomes of public health and companies quickly capitalized on these fears.[19] Deodorant, talcum powder, toothpaste, laxatives, pomades, and breath fresheners were unabashedly promoted by advertising. The most seemingly private moments of bathroom routine were broadcast for the entire world to observe, with national advertising helping to change the relationship between person and body.[20] Menstrual hygiene technologies provide one of the best examples of the way women construed their physical experiences through public discourse about private bodily functions. The discourse was so significant that the process of menstruation became primarily understood as a matter of civilization and a modern hygienic problem managed by means of technology.[21]

The Technology of Sanitary Napkins

Part of the uniqueness about manufactured sanitary napkins was that they were a female-specific technology. However, women had employed menstrual technologies prior to purchasing them from corporations, and were intimately familiar with their construction, routine washing, and wear. Throughout the nineteenth century, American women hand-produced their own napkins, folding and sewing cotton, gauze, flannel, or rags into pads to be pinned into their undergarments. These were hand-laundered, wrung out, hung out to dry, folded, stored away, and then reused each month. The practice of layering petticoats and the use of devices such as rubber aprons and bloomers helped to protect the outer garment from stains.[22] In 1896 Johnson & Johnson manufactured the first mass-produced sanitary napkins—Lister's Towels—that were disposable, gauze-covered cotton pads.[23] Sold directly through the Sears and Roebuck catalog, the towels were listed alongside other household sundries. For the most part, women simply constructed better pads than could be purchased. However, by the end of World War I medical practitioners frowned upon women's home production of their own menstrual hygiene products. Not only did they catch blood, they trapped the "decidedly offensive odor" of its decomposition.[24] Dr. William Robinson, author of *Sex Knowledge for Women and Girls* (1917), warned women about the dangers of menstrual rags. He believed that they should not be used unless they were "recently washed and kept wrapped up and protected from dust." Unclean rags led to infection, and he had "no doubt that many cases of leucorrhea [white discharge from the vagina] date back their origin to unwashed rags."[25] In order to reassert this point, he believed that "hygiene of menstruation can be expressed in two words: cleanliness and rest."[26]

Interestingly by the 1920s though the theme of cleanliness and hygiene dominated the representation of manufactured sanitary napkins, the advice for women to rest was downplayed. In part, the woman's movement had left a mark. The need and ability to rest no longer seemed to fit the representation of what women wanted to be, since it was based on a sexual system of dependency, which contradicted the very essence of equality. The passage of the Nineteenth Amendment in 1920 giving women the constitutional right to vote permanently altered the political relationship of men to women, and the suffrage movement inspired forms of cultural change. Furthermore, women's increased presence in the workplace, enrollment in college, and unabashed public personae led the media to dub them the "New Woman."[27] The New Woman represented a variety of culture shifts that followed the burgeoning of a distinctly modern, and decidedly un-Victorian, United States. This included women working in offices, as stenographers and typists for example, and their subsequent economic mobility gained by earning an income. Some young women remained single for longer than their parents might have liked, and part of the appeal was often an expanded sense of sexuality. This, in turn, held consequences for the idea of companionship, intimacy, and pleasure, for both heterosexual and homosexual relationships. Politically, many women sought full equality with men, yet remained loyal to women as a sex through political solidarity. Many women questioned the politics of marriage, sought professions based upon their inclinations and skills, and began appreciating the pleasure of leisure and consumption of new products.

In essence, the promise of technology, the fixation on hygiene, and the cultural context of New Woman created the environment for the introduction of the first successfully marketed sanitary napkin, Kotex, manufactured by Kimberly-Clark Corporation.[28] The company repackaged one of its wartime products—cellucotton—a new bandage material manufactured from cellulose wood pulp and used as surgical dressing for wounded soldiers. An unintended consequence of the bandages was that battlefield nurses used them during their periods, and Kimberly-Clark began product development based upon their responses. In 1920 Kimberly-Clark formed the Cellucotton Products Company as a separate division to sell the brand name Kotex (*CO*tton-like *TEX*ture) as a new name in feminine hygiene.[29] The design of the pad was not revolutionary, though the composition of the cellucotton wadding covered with gauze was slightly different. Its most original attribute was the successful national advertising campaign placed in *Ladies' Home Journal* in 1921. Kimberly-Clark credited the success of Kotex in large part to the willingness of editors at the journal to run the carefully designed ads that they deemed elegant, discrete, and tasteful. Wallace Meyer, hired to create these advertisements, drafted an entire set of ads for the first year to convince editors that they would remain aesthetically pleasing.[30]

Coordinated with advertising, distributors delivered products to merchants—most of whom were druggists—where women could purchase sanitary napkins from their local drugstore. Since menstruation was still considered a "condition" at best, it made sense that pharmacists sold sanitary pads along with other products to remedy sicknesses. Women either phoned in an order for pick up, or approached the clerk and asked for it by name. Similar to the purchase of Preparation-H to treat hemorrhoids, there was no need to announce that ailment to the world for all to witness and judge.

Like Colgate toothpaste, early sanitary napkin advertisements used the rhetoric of science and hygiene to appeal to customers (Figure 3). One ad stated, "Kotex are hygienic, convenient, and so low in cost that they form a new sanitary habit."[31] Like the Gillette razor and Prophylactic toothbrush, Kotex was meant to be used and discarded. Ads announced, "Kotex is cheap enough to throw away and easy to dispose of by following simple directions in every box."[32] Additionally, women did not have to deal with the dirty rag afterward.[33] Once used, Kotex could be burned or trashed, without guilt or the hassle of laundering. This fulfilled the quest for a germ-free environment and clean body through proper hygiene.

The early ads employed medical authority to create the presentation of a legitimate, salubrious, and hygienic product. A fictitious character, graduate Nurse Ellen Buckland instilled fears that "60% of many ills, according to many leading medical authorities, are traced to the use of unsafe and unsanitary makeshift methods."[34] Her one-on-one conversational tone encouraged a more personal relationship to the product. She made general references to medical claims, which created the tone of expertise. Advertisers believed that the ad copy educated consumers and the empathetic yet stern female "graduate" nurse urged women to heed her advice. Nurse Buckland represented the expertise of the medical profession and gave the product clout.

Use of menstrual hygiene products supposedly created a sanitary habit that translated into a civilized body.[35] The products helped to transform vile bodily excretions into an appropriate behavior, all by linking hygiene to upward white mobility. Kotex ads projected refined images of socially mobile and financially secure women. One ad read, "[l]ow price sometimes causes people of means and refinement to hesitate in buying a new article. Kotex is inexpensive, yet women who can afford the best were first to accept Kotex."[36] Yet Kotex were hardly inexpensive; five cents per pad was equivalent to a loaf of bread. This point was made quite clear to a classmate of mine. She retold the story of her grandmother, who was a young woman during the Great Depression. The family held a meeting to decide how the last dollar should be spent. The choice fell between the purchase of bread and the purchase of a box of Kotex. Kotex prevailed.[37] The success of the sales relied upon women open to learning about and experimenting with a new technological product, and then constructing it as a necessity.

Mindful of changing roles and requirements for bodily freedom, Kimberly-Clark advertisers appropriated aspects of feminism and reinterpreted them through Kotex ads. The products claimed to offer to women a realm of wholly unknown freedoms—of movement and travel, and from leakage and laundry—available only by using Kotex: "[t]hey are unsurpassed in business, when traveling, or at home."[38] As historian Nancy Cott argues, advertisers reworked feminist agendas and translated them so that women's purchases exerted the appearance of choice and control. In effect, this collapsed woman's demand for economic, marital, and educational choice into consumerism. Possessing the power to choose a product supposedly led to personal fulfillment.[39] By exercising their right to choose Kotex, women appeared to liberate and modernize their bodies from the restraints of old-fashioned ideas—and menstrual rags. Menstrual hygiene ads cleverly appropriated this technique to turn the purchase of sanitary napkins into an act of personal fulfillment and emancipation. One ad claimed that "the comforts of Kotex" played a vital part "in new-found feminine freedom and peace-of-mind."[40]

Part of this peace of mind for women came from the ability to hide menstruation and in effect pass as normal. The use of menstrual hygiene products meant a woman could hide her menstrual blood, thus remaking and cloaking her "true" self. This allowed her to transgress boundaries from being perceived as debilitated to appearing healthy, normal, and operative. It allowed a degree of control in a world still willing to judge menstruation as a liability. Kimberly-Clark Company participated in this masking, with ads assuring women that sanitary napkins could be purchased hassle-free: "Kotex saves embarrassment in many ways: It is easy to buy without counter conversation by asking not for 'sanitary pads' but 'Kotex.'" Kotex brand name signified sanitary napkins, without referring to name or function. Of course, the name became nationally recognized, but the system of masking persisted. Kotex boxes sported special blue camouflage as well. Kotex ads claimed to hedge embarrassing situations because of its simple packaging: "a plain blue box free from descriptive matter, the name the only printing."[41] Though consumers knew exactly what was in the sanitary napkin box, ads implied that a woman could purchase needed supplies while maintaining the better part of discretion. Eventually, the simple blue box readily symbolized Kotex, and required further masking to assure propriety. Many local grocers took the extra step to wrap Kotex boxes in newspaper to quell fears of embarrassment.[42] Yet, "Kotex blue" was still discernable through the single sheet of newsprint. Johnson & Johnson participated in this same cover up as well by promoting the Modess sanitary napkin box as indistinguishable from other gift boxes filled with bath salts or candies, pleasantries that surely carried no references to menstruation.

Complaining that the size and shape of the box were too obvious, Mrs. V. V. Davidson of Charleston, West Virginia wrote to Johnson & Johnson about her grievances and offered ideas for a new product. As she viewed it, a competitor to Kotex might do better. The problem with Kotex was that it was "so well advertised that to see a woman carrying the package is to know what it contains and, logically, the condition she is in."[43] In essence, the efforts to conceal the box ironically undermined a woman's successful pass. Clearly, she wanted the benefits of Kotex to mask her period, but the box betrayed to all her "condition"—a polite code word for sickness. "Despite the fact we are getting over a lot of our modesty," Davidson continued, "that is one condition we do not like to have exposed to the public in general as we do when we walk down the street carrying your well known package."[44] Advertisements that too highly touted products undermined women's efforts to pass.

The box and "telltale outlines" signified menstruation and revealed the unsavory personality-altering changes associated with it—nervous instability, depression, and tension.[45] If women could thoroughly hide the blood and the visual representations of menstruation, they could feasibly deceive others by masking it, and thereby present their non-menstruating selves to society. Seventy-five-year-old Laverne, who attended high school in the 1930s, remembered her anxiety about such unveiling. She recalled, "it was custom for the Seniors to wear all white every Friday. When I was a Junior, I happened to notice that one of the Seniors was wearing a thin white skirt which showed the outline of her sanitary pad so when I had my Senior skirt made I bought rather heavy material and had a double panel put in the back."[46] When Laverne became a senior, she decided to modify her white skirt, thereby protecting herself by hiding her menstruating body. In this way, she solicited neither teasing nor responses of sympathy due her menstruating body. At Smith College one observer noted that students "chastely" hid Kotex, but "the size and shape are so well known that anyone carrying a box frequently comes in for much humor and taunting and this is accordingly not a pleasant feature of the napkin."[47] These instances demonstrate the practice and use of technologies of passing, and what happens when these technologies are accidentally exposed.

Perhaps taking a bit of advice from dissatisfied customer Mrs. V. V. Davidson, Johnson & Johnson addressed this problem of a public purchase that exposed a private bodily function. In 1928, advertisers devised the "silent purchase coupon" for Modess sanitary napkins. Created so that "Modess may be obtained in a crowded store without embarrassment or discussion," a woman simply handed over a coupon which requested "one box of Modess, please."[48] In order to demonstrate control over her body and representation, she needed to relinquish it ever so briefly to purchase the necessary technologies of passing.

Passing was only as successful as the products, which still left much to be desired, but Johnson & Johnson heeded the call for improved sanitary napkins. Cautious to re-enter the market due to the past poor performance with Lister's Towels (1896) and abysmal sales of a second sanitary pad—Nupak—Johnson & Johnson chose to approach the menstrual hygiene arena armed with data. According to its market research, Kotex cornered at least 75% of all sanitary napkin sales; Nupak held less that 2% of the market, and Lister's Towels a measly fraction of one percent.[49] Johnson & Johnson usually relied upon customers' letters and the experiences of its female employees for comments, but the company needed better marketing data.[50] Comprehensive market research was not the standard, but Johnson & Johnson was anxious to tap into the wealth of female consumers. R. W. Johnson hired efficiency expert Lillian Gilbreth as a consultant for its new product, Modess sanitary napkins. Newly widowed with few clients interested in her as a lone female researcher, she redefined her services to study women's consumer behavior.[51]

Johnson & Johnson chose Gilbreth because she had established herself as a preeminent expert in time-motion studies. Lillian Gilbreth gained fame with her husband Frank, and together they formed "Gilbreth, Inc.," a management-consulting firm. They primarily analyzed repetitive motions within the workplace and ascertained the most efficient procedures for management to implement in their industrial factories.[52] Lillian Gilbreth's educational background and Ph.D. in psychology from Brown University aided the pair by incorporating human behavior—along with mechanical engineering—to study "motion psychology." Although Frank died in 1924, Lillian continued with the company well into the 1960s. She served on special committees during the Hoover, Roosevelt, Eisenhower, Kennedy, and Johnson administrations, providing advice on issues such as civil defense, war production, aging, and rehabilitation of physically disabled people. She was the first woman to gain membership in the American Society of Mechanical Engineers in 1926, and was the first female professor in the engineering school at Purdue University in 1935 (Figure 4). She considered herself an expert in human psychology, industrial management, efficiency models, business consultation, and home economics (her personal expertise earned by rearing twelve children).[53]

As a proponent of scientific management, Gilbreth believed that there was indeed one superior method to accomplish any given task. The techniques that she applied to time-motion studies at the factory she believed were easily applicable to the home as well. Gilbreth argued that if educated women applied scientific management to the home and made use of manufactured items, they would gain more time for leisure and "mental life." Through home economics and the systematic application of efficiency, women could more professionally manage their homes. Part of being most efficient meant purchasing manufactured goods.

When R. W. Johnson presented her the opportunity to design, produce, and market "a new type of sanitary napkin to supplement those already made by Johnson and Johnson," she approached the project with keen interest and vigor.[54] For a one-time fee of $6,000 she conducted the most thorough marketing research on sanitary napkins up to that time, submitted in 1927 simply as "Report of Gilbreth, Inc."[55] Gilbreth's interest in efficiency models easily translated onto women's bodies. If manufacturing processes could be streamlined, so too could elimination of waste from the body. Gilbreth used her perspective as an engineer to approach menstruation as a hydraulic problem, and evaluate the "equipment" to meet the needs of the period.[56] "Equipment" takes on a decidedly mechanical as well as technological feel to fix the hygienic problem. In this regard, the first goal she had for the project was to apply social engineering and "determine what types of napkins would be most serviceable."[57] Her second objective was to study "the period during which sanitary napkins are used with the hope of making a contribution to the health problem."[58] By defining menstruation as a problem, it could therefore be solved by engineering. From the data collected, Gilbreth sought to deliver specifications for the "One Best" sanitary napkin.[59]

Gilbreth held preconceived notions about what a sanitary napkin should be, and developed assessment criteria based upon aesthetics of the five senses. The napkin needed to look both "attractive" and "sanitary," as well as appeal to a sense of touch. It should be compatible with "kinaesthesia, or muscle sensations" and be tested under all types of bodily motion and strain. It should also "be made of material which will not crackle or make any kind of noise," including "opening the package, unwrapping the napkin, adjusting, and so forth through to the final disposal."[60] This attention to noise reveals the importance of creating useful technologies of passing to mask menstruation without being exposed, even by the sound of wrappers. Developing a new and efficient sanitary napkin had the potential to offer women control and agency through better body mechanics during menstruation, and a tool to manage debility and facilitate passing as normal. By purchasing sanitary pads, women could maximize efficiency of the body and minimize menstrual angst.

First, Gilbreth justified the need for a systematic study of menstruation. Gilbreth estimated that in 1926 there were "approximately 30,000,000 women between the ages of 13 and 45" who menstruated. She assumed that the average woman menstruated 13 times per year, and that her menstrual life extended 32 years, amounting to 416 periods during a lifetime. She calculated that a woman used eleven pads each period, equating to 4,576 napkins during a woman's menstrual life. She figured that if even one-third of the market were saturated, which it was not, that numbered to over 45 billion napkins to produce.[61] This indicated a potentially lucrative market.

Gilbreth and her staff members evaluated fifty-three different sanitary napkins, including those marketed in the United States, Canada, and England. They also evaluated menstrual accessories such as belts, pins, clasps, rubber aprons, and "step-ins"—waterproof panties worn between the sanitary pad and a woman's clothing.[62] From the examination, they hoped to determine "what type of equipment is ideal to meet the needs of the period." Gilbreth began with the assumption that "all existing equipment is probably wrong" because they either "have been copied from a home made product," which she viewed was composed of an unacceptable material, or from a "hospital pad designed for obstetrical use," which was long and unwieldy. In either case, they were "not designed to meet the actual needs" of menstruating women.[63] The problems with sanitary pads and their accompanying elastic belts were endless, and ranged from the wide elastic belt disintegrating with frequent laundering, narrow belts curling or cutting, and safety pins rusting and tearing holes in fabrics. In addition, "the present sanitary napkin is too long as to front tab and too short as to back tab," and lastly, "the containers are conspicuous and ugly, and therefore it is unpleasant to purchase napkins or carry packages or have them about one's room."[64] Gilbreth drew a fairly bleak picture concerning the efficacy of the available menstrual products on the market.

Besides the physical attributes, the names of products needed evaluation as well, and Gilbreth provided her characteristic blunt opinion of them all. Brand names needed to invoke a positive, or at worst neutral, association in women's minds with their periods, and many seemed downright stupid. Gilbreth summarily dismissed most of them. "Bev–Dot #19: This is a strange name. We have no use for it; L. B. Sanitary #24: If you have to say *sanitary*, you may as well add napkin; Eagle Brand #25: A buyer would be lucky if she got what she asked for under this name instead of cheese or baby's milk; A. R. Williams #48: Why give an article like this a man's name!"[65] Gilbreth was particularly attuned to the growing sophistication of female consumers and their ability to decipher messages implied and embedded in product names and marketing. With names like "Flush Down Ideal," which was "most offensive and we can't imagine anyone asking for it," or "S. S. Napkin," which sounded like a ship, companies pandered to women rather than respecting their purchasing skills.[66] Gilbreth thought that the name Kotex proved to be a great advantage for the product because it signified sanitary napkins without actually using those words in the description. However, with the first advertisements the name meant nothing, and "men as well as women read about it and there was much embarrassment and confusion." Gilbreth reported that "one young man at a mixed dinner party said, 'I wish someone would tell me what Kotex is.'"[67] This, of course, was the point. Kotex was a code word, and the technological pass had duped him.

The size of the box proved significant as well. Gilbreth suggested in order to be inconspicuous it should resemble other kinds of containers and not be distinctive because of a unique size. "The containers measuring 3 3/4" x 9" x 3 3/4", for example, look like graham cracker boxes, and there is nothing objectionable about carrying them." By mimicking other product shapes, the products might be better hidden. Furthermore, "the boxes measuring around 6 1/2" x 9" x 3 1/2" are distinctive in shape. We know of no other container on the market like them. They are awkward to carry and conspicuous, and many girls are embarrassed to be seen carrying them."[68] Gilbreth advised Johnson & Johnson to stop worrying about decorator colors, and noted with exasperation, "No one would want to keep the container no matter how attractive it was."[69] Later, when Gilbreth surveyed women concerning whether or not they kept the boxes, women's replies ranged from a "disgusted 'Hell, no!' to the comedic, 'I use them for sending Christmas presents.'"[70] These types of responses create a picture of sophisticated, savvy, and smart female consumers.

Although the detailed examination of products and correlative menstrual equipment provided useful data concerning product shortcomings, the report to Johnson & Johnson also incorporated a revealing field survey. Gilbreth and her staff contacted more than twenty groups to partake in the survey, including college instructors at the "Big Four" (Smith, Radcliffe, Vassar, Wellesley), the Women's Bureau Department of Labor, the National Committee for Prison Work, Winchester Laundries, public schools, normal schools for teacher training, and medical schools, to mention just a few. Gilbreth limited the study to young women and the "college girl," although they represented the minority of menstruating women. She admitted "[w]hile it may seem that the home making women are still in the majority, her needs are not typical of the most difficult needs to meet." The college student proved to be more challenging because she "sets the styles in clothing" and demands the most from sanitary napkins due to her activities.[71] Of course, it is ironic that she did not include women like herself who reared and cared for numerous children.

The survey that Gilbreth conducted sought "to secure a comprehensive opinion on the requirements of an ideal sanitary napkin." She and her staff obtained data through three methods. First, they sent out 3,000 questionnaires, of which 1,037 were returned (1,000 college and business women, 37 high school students). Next, they held conferences at different colleges with specific target groups, in which they discussed current products on the market and their shortcomings. Finally, they interviewed college presidents, deans, and faculty mem-

bers of hygiene departments to ascertain their views concerning sanitary napkins. Although many of the test groups she targeted chose not to participate,
those that did displayed "great interest . . . in the possibility of a new sanitary
napkin, and questions were frequent as to when it would appear, what name it
would bear, and who was manufacturing it." If nothing else, it proved to the
Johnson & Johnson Company "the friendly interest and the potential market it
has developed for their napkin."[72]

The survey asked questions such as "What type of napkin do you use? How
many each period? Per year?" They became increasingly detailed. "Where do
you buy your supplies? Why?" and "Do you alter the napkin before you use
it?"[73] Of the 1,000 college and businesswomen surveyed, only 91, or 9%, still
used homemade napkins. Those who continued to make their own believed they
could make them more comfortably and of a better size than those found on the
market. Gilbreth reasoned that girls living at home with mothers who had materials on hand usually constructed their own sanitary napkins. "But the college
and business woman, the majority of whom live in single rooms or small apartments have little space for materials that have to be kept about" and had little
time to make them.[74] Of all the 1,037 women, only 16% indicated that they were
satisfied with either homemade or manufactured products. Gilbreth called this
number "significant" because it "would seem to indicate to us something lacking
in the commercial napkins now available."[75]

Of the women surveyed, "244 of these same users considered the package
conspicuous, 207 that it is inconvenient to carry, 175 that it is too large, 115 that
the napkin is uncomfortable, 108 that it is the wrong size."[76] Gilbreth also
learned that women spent a good degree of time modifying, or hacking, the sanitary napkins, fashioning them to fit their own bodies. At least half of the women
altered the napkins by either shortening the tabs, cutting the corners, or thinning
the filler.[77] They also often softened the edges of the gauze with cold cream or
Vaseline.[78] Women chiefly altered Kotex more than other brands by matter of
course, as its somewhat malleable form was what supposedly made it flushable.
Instructions in the package directed women to disassemble the pad, soak the
parts, and then flush gauze and filler piecemeal down the toilet. Gilbreth received reports that "few of the girls would read the complete instructions, and
fewer would take the time to follow them."[79] Inevitably, trying to flush sanitary
napkins led to plugged drains and plumbing problems. Gilbreth included one
story in which a woman recounted learning that Kotex was not flushable. "I
went to visit after a football game at the home of a young man. I had heard that
Kotex was easily disposed of and when I dressed for dinner, threw one into the
toilet. Halfway through the dinner, the corner of the dining room ceiling developed a large wet spot. Everyone jumped up from the table and the father of the
house went up to investigate. It ended by a plumber being called to fish out the
napkin. I nearly died of embarrassment."[80] Kotex advertisements continued to
claim that the napkins were both disposable and flushable, to the chagrin of

many health and hygiene instructors. Gilbreth also discovered that when women attended proms at men's colleges, "they are forced to wrap them and conceal them until they can leave the houseparty. As a result many are forgotten, and there is embarrassment for both the men and the women."[81] In her practical tone, she noted if simple garbage cans were always available, women would not have to worry about what to do. Of course, people did not need garbage cans if there was nothing to throw away, and since Kotex was one of the first disposable hygiene products, with Kleenex tissue following in 1927, practices and behaviors concerning trash continued to evolve.[82]

Women had a lot to say about the different brands. One woman complained about Kotex. "Kotex are always too big and they are so stiff and square. I hate them, but always seem to get them—since they're cheapest I suppose." Another woman, influenced by the group discussions prompted by Gilbreth's research assistant, stated, "I think the Modesses are good, but everyone seemed to think that the gauze was awfully harsh. Most of them use napkins whose containers are soft like a union suit." A union suit was full body long underwear, made of cotton, which presumably would be softer than gauze. She added with a bit more conviction, "I think the ends could be more rounded although I suppose that is a small point. Otherwise, these are fine. I do wish the gauze could be changed because it is apt to be irritating."[83] The issue of the fabric of the pad covering was serious, because it chafed skin on the thigh, and worse, the tender skin rubbed raw and sometimes bled.

In addition to Modess and Kotex, Gilbreth also asked about a sanitary napkin with a "rubber holder and special filler." Not surprisingly, Gilbreth reported "[t]his type of napkin met with absolutely no approval in any of its forms. Neither the design nor the underlying idea received approbation from one person."[84] Gilbreth also condensed women's reactions concerning accessories of sanitary napkins. Rubber aprons, sported by 162 of the women, were worn between the undergarments and the skirt and were unpopular. They slipped, twisted, faded, and smelled of rubber. Rubber bloomers were equally problematic, and Gilbreth thought them to be unhealthy, as they did not breathe whatsoever. She approved the majority view of 879 women, that safety pins were better than clasps, as they could be easily adjusted and tended to lie flat.[85]

Within her questionnaire, Gilbreth assumed that women felt entirely embarrassed to articulate the need for and purchase of sanitary napkins from male clerks. She believed that women preferred female sales clerks and would seek out their assistance regardless of price of product or location. To her surprise, this was not the case. She found in a margin of two to one that women favored low price, location of store, and the convenience of calling in an order and charging it to an account over the service of a woman. Armed with this evidence, Gilbreth concluded "[i]t seems reasonable to suppose then from these general returns that if the desirable napkin is placed upon the market, women will have no hesitation in buying it."[86] Since many products were of such poor quality, even the slightest improvement would boost sales.

Gilbreth suggested youthful women were the consumers who would most likely experiment with and purchase new products. She drafted a mock-up of a new product for "college girls" that she called "Invisos."[87] That the product should be invisible, and therefore render menstruation invisible, showed how the technology held transformative power to offer women a means of passing. She advised the marketing department "to advertise to the girls themselves" in lieu of the older generation since "in most families the daughters are the ones who undertake to do the telling" to their mothers.[88] Sanitary napkins were poignant artifacts representing the gulf between old-fashioned mothers and modern daughters.

Upon Gilbreth's recommendation, a new series of ads emerged from Johnson & Johnson in 1929 called "Modernizing Mother," installed in episodes as if it were a radio show. In episode number three, Mother learns from Daughter how to do stretching exercises. She also discovers Modess. "Millions of mothers whose girlhood was repressed are being trained by daughters to be young again—to know freedom—to grasp the idea that drudgery and useless labor are a sinful waste of life."[89] In episode number five, Mother learns to golf. This time, the "game" is not only golf, but also the "game of escaping the bondage of old-fashioned ideas and being happily young again."[90] These ads demonstrate how feminism, stripped of its more radical overtones, became laced throughout the ads to promote Modess. The ads lauded the efficiency of the home and body, disparaged former methods of housework in favor of household mechanization (which ironically increased attention to housework), and valued youthfulness as a worthy characteristic.[91] Older women, by using Modess, could become modern Americans; younger women could gain freedom. The ads highlighted generational differences between mother and daughter, represented by managing the body with manufactured sanitary napkins.

A librarian at Columbia College, who wore Modess at work and at "dancing parties," liked their smaller size so much that she attested that for the first time in her life she had "not been uncomfortable through fear of conspicuousness."[92] Modess had not betrayed her body for the entire world to inspect, and she could mask her real body and pass as healthy and free of menstrual burdens. This librarian characterized the kind of person that Gilbreth recommended Johnson & Johnson identify in its marketing: the modern woman who bathed regularly, washed her clothes more often, purchased ready-made garments, and paid attention to hygiene in all its forms. Along with this attention to cleanliness, "[a] sanitary napkin made to fit her needs will be an important factor enabling her to attain her two aims,—'to be good looking and to have a good time.'"[93] The attitude of the New Woman, coupled with the intense marketing of new products in women's magazines, irrevocably changed the way that women managed their periods and constructed their identities with technologies of menstrual hygiene.

Advertisements, though, were careful not to promote overly radical interpretations of women's behavior, but to present ways that manufactured sanitary napkins would improve women's traditional and daily activities. The rhetoric surrounding deodorant sanitary pads is one such example. The advertisements tapped into the common notion that women should meet the needs of others and be self-sacrificing. This could be accomplished by using deodorant pads to ensure a fresh smelling body not just for oneself but also for the benefit of others. The ad began, "Since the comfort of sanitary protection is as much mental as physical, Kotex scientists have sought and found the way to end two important feminine fears."[94] The first fear was offending others, and the second was being conspicuous. Scientists, viewed as the purveyors of progress, supposedly solved such problems with technological breakthroughs to eliminate such fears. Although unnamed in the advertisement, the scientist referenced, Ernst Mahler, created a technique to apply a chemical deodorant to the sanitary napkin. The deodorant itself was a disinfectant powder, but Mahler patented a device to dust the powder onto the layers of cellucotton in the sanitary napkin, which ended up being a matter of paper science engineering.[95] The Kotex ads celebrated the patented process and the scientific means of ending menstrual odor so that "No longer does this oppressive thought of offending others interfere with the day's activities, at any time."[96] Another ad announced, "[t]he embarrassment that comes with knowledge of this grave social offense is finally ended, an important phase of women's oldest hygienic problem solved."[97] These technologies of passing were so effective, that "when they learn of this new process which neutralizes all odor in sanitary pads, they no longer fear offending others—self-consciousness disappears entirely."[98] Deodorant may have helped, but the new technological means of tampons proved to be more successful, and more problematic, than sanitary pads.

Technology and the Tampon

Because menstruation proved to be a problem which technological innovation could address, inventors responded by developing and selling through corporations a new "internal sanitary napkin": the tampon.[99] Inserted in the vagina and held in place by the vaginal walls, tampons proved to be an entirely different means to technologically manage menses. Tampons avoided the shortcomings of pads: they concealed menstrual blood and menstrual scents, left no outlines, required no belts or harnesses, and promoted mobility. On a pragmatic level, the technological fix offered an immediate physical freedom during menstruation previously unavailable by using rags or even pads. Tampons also hid the evidence of blood inconspicuously, thereby protecting a menstruating woman from the judgments of other men and women. Kimberly-Clark Corporation named its ill-fated tampon "Fibs," shorthand for "fiber." However, it was understood as a synonym for lying, and may have been an appropriate name considering its purpose. The name indicated the extent to which tampons could hide menstruation and allow a woman to lie about her "condition."[100] One ad suggested, "Next time try fibs," which meant purchasing both the product and acting deceitful to hide menstruation.[101] In addition, "with Fibs you can change to shorts, play suit or even swim suit with nobody the wiser!"[102] Tampons, and presumably Fibs, helped transform the appearance of the body to that of a non-menstruant.

Manufactured tampons had a different origin than sanitary napkins. Physicians first used tampons as medical devices to stop up large, bleeding wounds. Gynecologists often administered tampons, soaked in calomel, to treat vaginal discharge and brace the vaginal walls. Of the patents granted for tampons between 1890 and 1921, all referred to surgical or medical applications.[103] Additionally, tampons served contraceptive purposes when soaked with the appropriate compounds and inserted into the vagina. Because distribution and use of contraception was often interpreted as illegal activity, tampons gained notoriety as illicit.[104] Since doctors often inserted tampons or pessaries—doughnut shaped rings constructed of painted wood, ivory, bone, or metal—into women's vaginas, and even used electrical vibrators to relieve "pelvic congestion," and women themselves inserted and removed pessaries and vaginal packs, it seems a short step to use tampons for absorbing menstrual blood.[105]

A few different people got this idea at the same time. In 1927, Ives Marie Paul Jean Burill filed an application for a "catamenial appliance" which he claimed was a new means of absorbing menstrual flow. Because sanitary pads could aggravate lesions and irritate skin leading to possible infection, Burill argued that his appliance would stop blood without these kinds of effects. His design called for a core of touchwood to absorb most of the fluid, though it would be covered with cotton, cellulose, and gauze. A piece of colored silk string to tie off the gauze would be used to remove the plug once it was full.[106] Marie Huebsch also filed her patent for a hygienic device in 1927. She stated that hers was a device "directed to an improved simplified non-washable, pack-plug for absorbing the catamenial flow or other discharges from the vagina."[107] The composition of the absorbent material could be cellulose derived from linen, or cotton, wool, flax, or even wood fiber. The importance of her patent was not in materials but design. She proposed rolling the filler and coiling the external gauze to keep the filler tightly in place. By winding the gauze and extending it past the filler, it also served "to form a projecting handling end" in order to remove it from the vagina. Though both patents claimed similar results, neither emerged as successfully mass-produced items.

Another claim appeared in 1931. It belonged to Frederick S. Richardson, who purported to be "the first to have provided any practicable form of catamenial device intended and adapted for use inside the vagina."[108] The difference with Richardson's design was in the wrapping of the string. The plug itself, composed of cotton or cellulose, measured two and a half inches wide and three-fourths inches in diameter. The moisture pervious "slipper" of perforated cellophane wrapped the plug, held the material in place, and eased insertion into the vaginal canal. The pull string, though, was threaded through the coiled layers of absorbent material and then laced out of the end of the plug. Because the products would be made in different sizes, women could choose the size to match their flow. Richardson managed to market his new product as Wix tampons, advertised as "sanitary protection." According to its ads, Wix eliminated "the embarrassment of protruding pads" and gave "complete, healthful protection *internally, invisibly.*"[109] Advertisements for Wix appeared in the 1934 Sears Fall/Winter catalog, making it arguably the first tampon to be advertised.[110]

The Wix Company was short lived, however. It competed with another brand, whose patent was filed the same year as that of Wix in 1931. This patent grew into the product name Tampax, manufactured by Tambrands, Inc., and was the very same corporation to purchase Wix on March 1, 1939, and eventually phase the tampons out of production. Tambrands may have needed to acquire the company to add more to its product line, but more likely it needed to buy out its competitor. Since tampons held less than five percent of total feminine hygiene sales, the stakes for gaining market shares were high.[111] Despite the small toehold, it was enough to build a clientele. The acceptance and reliance upon menstrual hygiene indicated that women not only used the products to increase their bodily efficiency, but that they would purchase a product that offered comfort, concealment, and ease of passing. The inventor of Tampax tampons, Earle Cleveland Haas, an osteopath by training, banked on this notion and filed his tampon patent in 1931. In an interview with a company historian, he admitted that he conceived of the design because he "just got tired of women wearing those damned old rags."[112] He also pitied women during their menses. In an interview during a court deposition, he spoke freely about how he developed the tampon, and how he became interested in designing them. He replied, "Well, I suppose I thought of the poor women that got in that mess every month, you know. It was very disagreeable to them and I thought, well, surely there is a better way to take care of that."[113] In Haas's design, cotton was first stitched together then compressed. The "longitudinal stitching of the cotton" allowed for expansion lengthwise in which "the expanded core straightens within the vagina when drawn upon." The problem with other catamenial devices was that they "have been made to attach a tape or ribbon to a core of absorbent material but it was found that after the material expanded in the vagina it was exceedingly difficult to withdraw it owing to the restricted opening."[114] With the threads stitched right into the cotton longitudinally, so that the cord extended beyond the bleached cotton, it was then compressed so that could be inserted easily. It would then expand lengthwise inside the vagina as it absorbed fluid. In order to perfect the size of the cotton plug, he felt no compunction to measure the cervix or vagina, since he had "seen so damn many of them" that he felt he got the gist.

He believed Tampax would conform to any woman's vagina, regardless of shape, size, or angle of the vaginal canal.[115]

Luckily for Haas, his wife, a nurse, helped him to hone the final form of the tampon by wearing various modifications throughout the developmental process. She also helped him by distributing test samples to other nurses. Although the plug was unique in that it expanded lengthwise, its real advantage came from its patented dispenser: a telescopic applicator made of disposable cardboard cylinders (Figure 5). Haas considered a reusable metal applicator—along the schematics of a speculum—but the convenience, and profitability, of a disposable applicator held sway. With the disposable cardboard, women would continually repurchase the same item, boosting profits. The cardboard applicator allowed women to insert the tampon without their fingertips ever touching their bodies, and in theory flush the applicator down the toilet after they finished. Since cardboard was water soluble, "they may be discarded into a toilet bowl where they will dissolve or soften so that they may be flushed away."[116] Haas named his invention Tampax, for vaginal tampon packs, mimicking the hard final syllable of the brand Kotex.[117]

Tampons, however, exhausted Haas. As he put it, he "had a lot of trouble with this thing" and could not get anyone to buy the option for the company or the patent. In fact, by the time he found a buyer, he sold it outright with no possibility for royalties. By then he admitted, "I didn't want anything to do with it. I was so sick of it. After a while you get turned off on those things, boy."[118] Producing and selling the product became too troublesome, and Haas sold his patent and company for $32,000 to Gertrude S. Tenderich, a Denver businesswoman and a German immigrant. Organizing Tampax Sales Corporation in 1934, Ten-derich and her employees made small lots of tampons in a Denver warehouse. Personally delivering her sales pitch at drugstores, Tenderich tried to persuade pharmacists to purchase the tampons, but they often expressed little interest. Seeking to reach a wider market, Tenderich traveled to New York where she met prospective buyer Ellery Mann, who had been the president of Zonite Products Corporation, which manufactured douches.[119] Clearly Mann was no stranger to feminine or personal hygiene products—he was also responsible for the sale of toothpaste, soap, and mouth spray.[120] He helped propel sales and laid the foundation for the company, with the product roll out in 1936. Since tampons were once used for vaginal infections, and menstruation remained a medical debility, advertising again relied on medical expertise to legitimate the product. Tampax ads often mentioned that a doctor invented Tampax, and used his name and stature to elevate the product. Tampax ads also claimed that the American Medical Association endorsed the product because *Journal of the American Medical Association* accepted the ads in the publication.[121] This meant very little in terms of the product, but it created an impression that physicians not only accepted but also promoted Tampax tampons.[122] At medical conventions and trade shows, such as those sponsored by the AMA,

Tampax Inc. staffed an information booth that displayed its product and information. Mable Mathews, outfitted in a white uniform dress and cap, fielded questions and served as a medical authority. By her appearance and dress she resembled a registered nurse endorsing the product, but her training as an X-ray technician belied that representation. She later established the Tampax education department, but the company quietly continued to promote her legitimacy as a medically trained professional nurse.[123]

Besides seeking physicians to endorse its product, Tampax Inc. also targeted female consumers through women's magazines. One approach it used was to blitz women's magazines with cheap, concise, black-and-white column advertisements. These newspaper-like entries sharply contrasted with the artistic and colorful Modess and Kotex ads. Because of this cheap format, by 1940 Tampax Inc. placed ads in over 47 different magazines with a total circulation of over 45 million people.[124] In each *Good Housekeeping*, the ads were located on the left-hand side, page fourteen. Because the ads were cheap to produce, Tampax Inc. could advertise more often and more broadly, and attract a wider audience.[125]

Advertisements practically challenged women to find activities that they were prevented from engaging in while wearing sanitary napkins, thus drawing on the passing narrative to persuade potential customers of the merits. The ads repeatedly stated: "Gone forever are the cumbersome belt-pin-pad harness . . . the fear of telltale outlines . . . the risk of chafing. Tampax can't be seen or felt once it's in place."[126] Tampax allowed women to shroud their menstrual periods from public view. A woman could cast aside the "fear of telltale outlines" which gave her away, thus masking her menstrual condition. Another ad boasted, "You need never fear that *anyone* can detect anything if you wear Tampax."[127] Tampons were more comfortable because the rough cellucotton gauze of sanitary pads no longer chafed the inner thigh. Additionally, tampons released women from the cumbersome bathroom gymnastics required when managing a skirt, a sanitary belt, and a diaper-like pad between the legs while using the toilet.

Invisible Technology

The new menstrual hygiene products of sanitary pads and tampons more effectively concealed menstruation and helped to hide women's menstruating bodies. Literally bandaging the wound with scientifically developed dressings, the sanitary napkins concealed, controlled, and contained the blood better than menstrual rags, allowing women to pass as healthy. Women so readily accepted and purchased Kotex, and the call for "invisible protection" was so great, that Kimberly-Clark named its newly designed sanitary napkin "Phantom Kotex." Patented and marketed in 1932, the pads' special tapered ends were to lie more smoothly underneath clothing. The name implied that the pads were so thin that they were mere illusion. However, illusion created the exact circumstances of a successful pass. The ads drew out the scenario: "Maybe you weren't always aware of it. Maybe it was others who noticed that revealing outline, that telltale bulkiness. But no matter now! A new Kotex is here. A Kotex with ends flattened and tapered, so as to be completely invisible even under the closest-fitting gowns."[128] The brand name Phantom also referenced supernatural powers, as of those beyond physical reality and human endeavor. Phantom pads therefore seemed to hold technological power over women to control their unruly bodies.

Other advertisements for Fibs, "the Kotex Tampon," utilized a different tactic to sell a product: bandwagon. It was not bandwagon in an overt way, but bandwagon for an in-group to learn the technological techniques of passing. A 1941 ad in *McCall's* magazine depicted two young women in the pin-up Vargas style, clad in lingerie with decidedly noticeable nipples and buttocks cleavage discernable through the drape of the fabric (Figure 6). Through their conversation, they become in-members of the group who learn how to pass. One woman, called "The Blonde," says "*It's invisible* sanitary protection, thank heavens . . . 'cause Fibs are worn internally . . . keep my secret safe even in this bathing suit. Otherwise I'd be missing lots of fun this summer."[129] Her friend, "The Brunette," responds "*Whatta pal* . . . why didn't you tell me before? I had to miss the beach all last week!" Fibs kept her secret safe by accommodating the successful pass and inculcating a new technological passer.

The increased complexity of menstrual hygiene advertisements matched the variety of brand names, types, and shapes on the market, for example, Meds tampons manufactured by the Personal Products Corporation, Fax by Sanitary Products Company, and Curads sanitary napkins by Lewis Manufacturing Company. The sheer number attested to the profitability of a disposable technology and the possibility of women accepting such products in their array of daily toiletries. Menstrual hygiene technologies uniquely managed what ads referred to as a hygienic handicap, and sanitary napkins helped women to pass as normal, thus masking debility and presenting the appearance of a healthy female body. Sanitary napkin and tampon advertisements repackaged and appropriated feminism—while downplaying its more disruptive elements—and beckoned women to fulfill their modern roles by emancipating their bodies with disposable sanitary napkins. The emergence and acceptance of manufactured menstrual hygiene technologies, and the possibility of women using them for their own ends, fostered new discussions about the meaning of menstruation, and women's relationship to it.

Notes

1. Lillian Gilbreth, "Report of Gilbreth, Inc.," January 1, 1927, Papers of Frank and Lillian Gilbreth, Special Collections Purdue University, N-File, Box 95, 20–21; 70.

2. "Woman's Greatest Hygienic Handicap," *Liberty* 4, no. 52 (December 31, 1927): n.p.

3. Display Ad 152, *New York Times*, June 19, 1949, ProQuest Historical Newspapers, p. SM38.

4. Jennifer Scanlon, *Inarticulate Longings: The Ladies' Home Journal, Gender, and the Promises of Consumer Culture* (New York: Routledge, 1995); Carolyn Kitch, *The Girl on the Magazine Cover: The Origins of Visual Stereotypes in American Mass Media* (Chapel Hill: University of North Carolina Press, 2001); Janice Williams Rutherford, *Selling Mrs. Consumer: Christine Frederick and the Rise of Household Efficiency* (Athens: University of Georgia Press, 2003); Kathy Peiss, "American Women and the Making of Modern Consumer Culture," *The Journal for MultiMedia History* 1, no. 1 (Fall 1998), http://www.albany.edu/jmmh/vol1no1/peiss-text.html (accessed May 16, 2006).

5. Christine Frederick, *Selling Mrs. Consumer* (New York: The Business Bourse, 1929), 6.

6. Arnold Gingrich, "A Magazine for Men Only," *Esquire* 1 (Autumn 1933): 4; Kenon Breazeale, "In Spite of Women: *Esquire* Magazine and the Construction of the Male Consumer," *Signs* 20, no. 1 (1994): 1–22.

7. William Faulkner to Morton Goldman, June 1936, in *Selected Letters of William Faulkner,* ed. Joseph Blotner (New York: Random House, 1977), 94–95. Anne Goodwyn Jones, "'The Kotex Age': Women, Popular Culture, and *The Wild Palms*," in *Faulkner and Popular Culture: Faulkner and Yoknapatawpha,* eds. Doreen Fowler and Ann J. Abadie (University Press of Mississippi, 1990), 142–62.

8. Susan Faludi quotes Faulkner as lambasting *Gone With the Wind* as "a product of the triumph of 'the Kotex Age.'" "Afterward," in *The Women's Room*, Marilyn French (New York: Ballantine Books, 1993), 471.

9. Sut Jhally, "Image Based Culture, Advertising and Popular Culture," in *Gender, Race and Class in Media: A Text Reader*, eds. Gail Dines and Jean M. Humez (New York: Sage Publications), 249–57.

10. Ruth Schwartz Cowan, *A Social History of American Technology* (New York: Oxford University Press, 1997).

11. On technoscience see also Bruno Latour, *Science in Action: How to Follow Scientists and Engineers Through Society* (Cambridge: Harvard University Press, 1988).

12. Many studies have outlined the role of consumption at the beginning of the twentieth century and its ultimate influence upon modern society. See Roland Marchand, *Advertising the American Dream: Making Way for Modernity, 1920–1940* (Berkeley: University of California Press, 1985); Pamela Walker Laird, *Advertising Progress: American Business and the Rise of Consumer Marketing* (Baltimore: Johns Hopkins University Press, 1998); Jackson Lears, *Fables of Abundance: A Cultural History of Advertising in America* (New York: Basic Books, 1994); Lawrence Birken, *Consuming Desire: Sexual Science and the Emergence of a Culture of Abundance 1871–1914* (Ithaca: Cornell University Press, 1988); William Leach, *Land of Desire: Merchants, Power, and the Rise of a New American Culture* (New York: Pantheon Books, 1993).

13. Susan Strasser, *Satisfaction Guaranteed: The Making of the American Mass Market* (New York: Pantheon Books, 1989).

14. Laurel D. Graham, "Lillian Moller Gilbreth's Extensions of Scientific Management into Women's Work, 1924–1935" (Ph.D. diss. in Sociology, University of Illinois, 1992), 103.

15. Suellen Hoy, *Chasing Dirt: The American Pursuit of Cleanliness* (New York: Oxford University Press, 1995).

16. "Bathrooms and Civilization," *House and Garden* 30 (February 1917): 90, in *The Bathroom and the Kitchen and the Aesthetics of Waste*, Ellen Lupton and J. Abbott Miller (Cambridge: MIT List Visual Arts Center, 1992), 17.

17. Strasser, *Satisfaction Guaranteed*, 95.

18. Lears, *Fables*, Chapter 5; see also Gail Bederman on constructs of civilization, *Manliness and Civilization: A Cultural History of Gender and Race in the United States, 1880-1917* (Chicago: University of Chicago Press, 1995).

19. Lears, *Fables*, 137.

20. Lears, *Fables*, 165.

21. Using menstrual hygiene products symbolized a degree of civilization and also Americanization. See Joan Jacobs Brumberg, "'Something Happens to Girls': Menarche and the Emergence of the Modern American Hygienic Imperative," *Journal of the History of Sexuality* 4 (July 1993): 99–127. Jane Rothstein discusses the importance of retaining and reinforcing the mikvah—the purifying and ritual bath conducted after menses—to stave off forces of Americanization within the Jewish immigrant community. See Jane Rothstein, "The Religious Duties of the Daughters of Israel: American Jews, Sexuality, and the Jewish Family Purity Laws, 1900–1949," (paper delivered at the 112th Meeting of the American History Association, Seattle, Washington, 1998).

22. Vern Bullough, "Merchandising the Sanitary Napkin: Lillian Gilbreth's 1927 Survey," *Signs* 10 (Spring 1985): 614–27, cited on 625.

23. See Janice Delaney, Mary Jane Lupton, and Emily Toth, *The Curse: A Cultural History of Menstruation* (Urbana: University of Illinois Press, 1988), 138. For an extensive study of patented products see Laura Klosterman Kidd, "Menstrual Technology in the United States, 1854–1921" (Ph.D. diss. in Textiles and Clothing, Iowa State University, 1994). Navaho women used pieces of sheep pelt secured to their waists; Salish women used cattail down, and Kaska women wore pads of sphagnum moss layered within modified breechcloths. See Carolyn Niethammer, *Daughters of the Earth: The Lives and Legends of American Indian Women* (New York: Collier Books, 1977), 53. Japanese women often rolled paper tampons, while rolls of soft grass and roots served West African women. See Delaney, et. al., *The Curse*, 138.

24. William Robinson, M.D., *Sex Knowledge for Women and Girls: What Every Woman and Girl Should Know* (New York: The Critic and Guide Company, 1917), 51–52.

25. Robinson, *Sex Knowledge*, 52.

26. Robinson, *Sex Knowledge*, 52.

27. On the New Woman see Lois Scharf and Joan M. Jensen, eds., *Decades of Discontent: The Women's Movement, 1920–1940* (Westport: Greenwood Press, 1983); Kathy Peiss, *Cheap Amusements: Working Women and Leisure in Turn-of-the-Century New York* (Philadelphia: Temple University Press, Reprint edition, 1987); Carolyn L. Kitch, *The Girl on the Magazine Cover: The Origins of Visual Stereotypes in American Mass Media* (Chapel Hill : University of North Carolina Press, 2001); Jean V. Matthews, *The Rise of the New Woman: The Women's Movement in America, 1875–1930* (Chicago: Ivan R. Dee Publishers, 2003); Patricia Marks, *Bicycles, Bangs, and Bloomers: The New Woman in the Popular Press* (Lexington: University Press of Kentucky, 1990).

28. For an extended business history of Kimberly-Clark, including the early development and promotion of Kotex, see Thomas Heinrich and Bob Batchelor, *Kotex, Kleenex, Huggies: Kimberly-Clark and the Consumer Revolution in American Business* (Columbus: The Ohio State University Press, 2004).

29. Anne M. Spurgeon, "Marketing the Unmentionable: Wallace Meyer and the Introduction of Kotex," *The Maryland Historian* 18 (1988): 17–30; Joan Jacobs Brumberg, *The Body Project: An Intimate History of American Girls* (New York: Random House, 1997).

30. For a good discussion about the first advertisement campaigns in *Ladies' Home Journal*, see Spurgeon, "Marketing the Unmentionable." Wallace Meyer to Charles Reincke, April 8, 1944, Wallace Meyer Papers, Box 5, Folder 1, Wisconsin State Historical Archives. In 1923, Albert Lasker, of the Lord and Thomas advertising firm, acquired the account. He invested one million dollars in International Cellucotton, confident of its market potential. See *Time* (June 9, 1952): 94–95. See also Jennifer Scanlon, *Inarticulate Longings,* for a discussion of the relationship between women's magazines and the market.

31. "Meets the most exacting needs," *Ladies' Home Journal* 39, no. 1 (January 1922): 123.

32. "Traveling or at home—Kotex is almost indispensable," *Ladies' Home Journal* 39, no. 7 (July 1922): 118.

33. Susan Strasser argues that the modern product of Kotex ushered in the culture of trash and a truly disposable society. See *Waste and Want: A Social History of Trash* (New York: Metropolitan Books, 1999).

34. Kotex Advertisement, *Woman's Home Companion* 53 (March 1926): 85. Roland Marchand discusses the use of fabricated experts to serve as helpful "confidential advisers." See *Advertising the American Dream*, 355.

35. Kathleen Kane, "Feminine Hygiene Commercials: A Political and Symbolic Economy" (Ph.D. diss., Northwestern University, 1992), 137.

36. "Traveling or at home—Kotex is almost indispensable."

37. Class discussion, Angela Miller's "Women, Art, and Feminism" course, Washington University, fall 1993.

38. "It forms a new sanitary habit among women," *Ladies' Home Journal* 39, no. 11 (November 1922): 184.

39. Nancy Cott, *The Grounding of Modern Feminism* (New Haven: Yale University Press, 1987), chapter 5; Sharra Vostral, "Hidden Assurances: Tampons, Design, and the Question of Unruly Feminine Bodies," (paper presented at the annual meeting of the Society for Social Studies of Science, Pasadena, CA, October 22, 2005).

40. "Other women will tell you," *Ladies' Home Journal* 46, no. 4 (April 1929): 53.

41. "Wherever nice women gather," *Ladies' Home Journal* 39, no. 9 (September 1922): 128.

42. Elizabeth Kolmer, interview by author (October 15, 1993).

43. Mrs. V. V. Davidson to Johnson & Johnson, October 12, 1926, Gilbreth Collection, N-file, Box 95, Purdue University Special Collections.

44. Davidson to Johnson & Johnson, October 12, 1926.

45. Warren C. Middleton, "Is There a Relation between Kleptomania and Female Periodicity in Neurotic Individuals?" *Psychological Clinic* 22 (1933): 232–47.

46. Janet Lee and Jennifer Sasser-Coen, *Blood Stories: Menarche and the Politics of the Female Body in Contemporary U.S. Society* (New York: Routledge, 1996). See also Janet Lee, "Menarche and the (Hetero)sexualization of the Female Body," *Gender and Society* (September 1994): 348.

47. Gilbreth, "Report," 70.

48. "Silent Purchase, A Modess Advantage," *Ladies' Home Journal* 45, no. 6 (June 1928): 135.

49. Gilbreth, "Report," 62. Out of 1,037 women surveyed, their preferences broke down to: Kotex–788, Curads–86, Venus–36, Nupak–20, Lister's Towels–6.

50. Laurel Graham, *Managing on Her Own: Dr. Lillian Gilbreth and Women's Work in the Interwar Era* (Norcross, GA: Engineering & Management Press, 1998), 217.

51. Graham, *Managing on Her Own*, 85–105.

52. Union members of the American Federation of Labor accused the Gilbreths of promoting speed-ups on the manufacturing line, which in effect contributed to fatigue. The Gilbreths clung to the assurance that unnecessary motions reduced worker fatigue and improved working conditions, thus benefiting the laborer. See Brian Price, "One Best Way: Frank and Lillian Gilbreth's Transformation of Scientific Management, 1885–1940" (Ph.D. diss. in History, Purdue University, 1987).

53. Lillian M. Gilbreth, *As I Remember: An Autobiography* (Norcross: Engineering & Management Press, 1998).

54. Gilbreth, "Report," 9.

55. Gilbreth usually charged $300 per day, but because of the nature of the project, which extended several months including follow up, she agreed to this one-time fee (Gilbreth to R. W. Johnson, September 30, 1926, N-File, Box 95). Johnson & Johnson hired her for other studies as well, including a box and container study and a baby diaper study (Gilbreth to R. W. Johnson, June 3, 1927, N-File, Box 95).

56. Gilbreth, "Report," 11.

57. Gilbreth, "Report," 1.

58. Gilbreth, "Report," 1.

59. Gilbreth, "Report," 9.

60. Gilbreth, "Report," 12.

61. Gilbreth, "Report," 15.

62. Gilbreth, "Report," 2. She set about her work with two staff members from Gilbreth, Inc., to help her collect data: Investigator B, a college grad with ten years experience in the health and industrial fields, and Investigator C, a recent college grad with undergraduate contacts. Gilbreth identified herself as Investigator A, "president of the company with engineering, teaching and home experience."

63. Gilbreth, "Report," 9–10.

64. Gilbreth, "Report," 13.

65. Gilbreth, "Report," 37–44.

66. Gilbreth, "Report," 37–44.

67. Gilbreth, "Report," 41.

68. Gilbreth, "Report," 45.

69. Gilbreth, "Report," 46.

70. Gilbreth, "Report," 47.

71. Gilbreth, "Report," 12.

72. Gilbreth, "Report," 14.

73. Gilbreth, "Report," 5.

74. Gilbreth, "Report," 16.

75. Gilbreth, "Report," 16.

76. Gilbreth, "Report," 18.

77. Gilbreth, "Report," 18.

78. Gilbreth, "Report," 76.

79. Gilbreth, "Report," 22.

80. Gilbreth, "Report," 63.

81. Gilbreth, "Report," 64.

82. Susan Strasser, *Waste and Want*, 161-69.

83. Gilbreth, "Report," 66.

84. Gilbreth, "Report," 69.

85. Gilbreth, "Report," 75.

86. Gilbreth, "Report," 17.

87. Gilbreth, "Report," 22.

88. Gilbreth, "Report," 70.

89. "Don't Weaken Mother," *Ladies' Home Journal* 46, no. 4 (April 1929): 105.

90. "Never Mind, Mother—You'll Learn," *Pictorial Review* 30, no. 9 (June 1929): 87.

91. On the increase of housework see Ruth Schwartz Cowan, *More Work for Mother: The Ironies of Household Technology from the Open Hearth to the Microwave* (New York: Basic Books, 1983); Susan Strasser, *Never Done: A History of American Housework* (New York: Pantheon Books, 1982).

92. Gilbreth, "Report," 67.

93. Gilbreth, "Report," 130.

94. "Shaped to Fit," *Redbook Magazine* (1928), Ad*Access On-Line Project – Ad #BH0015, John W. Hartman Center for Sales, Advertising & Marketing History, Duke University Rare Book, Manuscript, and Special Collections Library, http://scriptorium.lib.duke.edu/adaccess/ (accessed May 5, 2005).

95. Ernst Mahler, United States Patent Office, 1,670,587, May 22, 1928.

96. "Shaped to Fit," *Redbook Magazine* (1928), Ad*Access – #BH0015.

97. "Amazing—so many women must learn this from others," *Holland's* (1929), Ad*Access – #BH0025.

98. "Hard to say, but I often have to warn the girls," *New York Daily News* (1929), Ad*Access – #BH0017.

99. Fax tampons, manufactured by Sanitary Products Company in the mid-1930s, referred to its product on packaging and advertisement copy as an "internal sanitary napkin." There is even less scholarship on tampons than sanitary napkins. See Delaney et al., *The Curse*; Joan Jacobs Brumberg, *The Body Project*; Karen Houppert, *The Curse: Confronting the Last Unmentionable Taboo: Menstruation* (New York: Farrar, Straus and Giroux, 1999); and Jane Farrell-Beck and Laura Klosterman Kidd, "The Roles of Health Professionals in the Development and Dissemination of Women's Sanitary Products, 1880–1940," *The Journal of the History of Medicine and Allied Sciences* 51 (July 1996): 325–52.

100. "3 Reasons Why Women Choose Fibs," *True Story* 40, no. 1 (March 1939): 35.

101. "To Tampon Users, Fibs is the Tampon," *Good Housekeeping* 115, no. 2 (July 1942): 162.

102. "Can you Trust Tampons?—and when?" *Ladies' Home Journal* (1942), Ad*Access – #BH0077.

103. Farrell-Beck and Klosterman Kidd, "The Roles of Health Professionals," 325–52.

104. Janet Brodie, *Contraception and Abortion in Nineteenth-Century America* (Ithaca: Cornell University Press, 1994), 224.

105. On electrical vibrators as medicinal therapy see Rachel P. Maines, *The Technology of Orgasm: "Hysteria," the Vibrator, and Women's Sexual Satisfaction* (Baltimore: Johns Hopkins University Press, 1999). On pessaries, see Harvey Green, *The Light of the Home: An Intimate View of the Lives of Women in Victorian American* (New York: Pantheon Books, 1983), 122–26.

106. Ives Marie Paul Jean Burrill, United States Patent Office, 1,726,339, August 27, 1929.

107. Marie Huebsch, United States Patent Office, 1,731,665, October 15, 1929.

108. Frederick S. Richardson, United States Patent Office, 1,932,383, October 24, 1933.

109. Display ad 84, ProQuest Historical Newspapers, *New York Times*, September 8, 1935, SM18.

110. "Save Embarrassment, Money . . . by Mail," *Sears Catalog* (Fall/Winter 1934), Museum of Menstruation, http://www.mum.org/wixsad.htm (accessed June 3, 2006).

111. Heinrich and Batchelor, *Kotex, Kleenex, Huggies*, 100.

112. Richard Bailey, "Small Wonder: How Tambrands Began, Prospered and Grew" (Produced for Tambrands Inc., 1987), 5.

113. *Michael L. Kehm v. Proctor and Gamble*, United States Courthouse, Cedar Rapids, Iowa, April 5, 1982, 1173.

114. Earle Cleveland Haas, United States Patent Office, 1,926,900, September 12, 1933.

115. *Kehm v. Proctor and Gamble*, 1179.

116. Earle Cleveland Haas, United States Patent Office, 1,926,900, September 12, 1933.

117. Tambrands Informational Flyer, Palmer, MA, and "Small Wonder," 5–6.

118. *Kehm v. Proctor and Gamble*, 1177–78.

119. As president of Zonite Mann took it upon himself to sell alcoholic beverages through the company's distribution network after prohibition. He tried to gain rights to import Russian vodka, and failed to the tune of $300,000. Due to pressure from the board of trustees, he resigned. The offer to produce tampons may have been his only option.

120. Bailey, "Small Wonder," 8–10.

121. Bailey, "Small Wonder," 14.

122. Bailey, "Small Wonder," 14. Bailey writes that the editor of *Journal of the American Medical Association* was a friend of Ellery Mann, who asked the favor to use the "endorsement." Bailey also notes that in 1943 the Federal Trade Commission asked Tampax Inc. to drop the phrase, and that they complied. However, I have found ads from the 1950s that continued carrying the pronouncement.

123. Bailey, "Small Wonder," 28.

124. Bailey, "Small Wonder," 24.

125. Bailey, "Small Wonder," 24.

126. "I just feel like hugging myself," *Good Housekeeping* 139, no. 2 (September 1954): 14.

127. "Sharp Eyes Cannot Tell with Tampax," *Ladies' Home Journal* 58 no. 1 (1941): n.p.

128. "Telltale Revealing Outlines Gone, the New Phantom Kotex," *Cosmopolitan* (1932), Ad*Access – #BH0037.

129. "Sh-h-h—Listen In!" *McCall's* (1941), Ad*Access – #BH0070.

Chapter 5

Private Technologies and Public Policies

Although the advertisements for menstrual hygiene technologies during the 1930s and 1940s painted a rosy picture of women cheerily masking their periods with new products such as Kotex, Modess, Meds, or Fibs, the reality was not so straightforward. Advertisements publicized menstruation, and certainly the products were not a secret. However, women's use of them was camouflaged, so one never really knew for sure if a woman was wearing a sanitary pad or tampon or not. This raised the uneasy question about the verity of women's actions, and menstruation as well as its technologies became political fodder by which to gauge women's bodies, their fitness as employees, and their reliability. In many ways, the products became symbols of women's liberation, fraught with different meanings depending upon one's political perspective. For example, Joe Breen, a Catholic morality crusader, member of the Legion of Decency, and architect of the 1930 Production Code in the film industry, took offense at Kotex. He was appalled at the report of a Hollywood party where the hostess used condoms and Kotex squirted with ketchup as place cards at the dinner table.[1] For Breen, this use of Kotex was just another piece of evidence displaying the wanton immorality of the Hollywood elite, and he used it as an example of their depravity. However, the hostess of the party must have thought the place cards a humorous snub at prudery, and clearly intended the sexualized innuendo. The technologies, surprisingly, held a great degree of interpretive flexibility.

Incidents like this contributed to public discourse about menstrual hygiene technologies, raising the question anew about the relationship of women's behaviors to their periods. If anything, the educational tone of some of the ads, the more nuanced marketing campaigns, and women's willingness to experiment with new products, indicated that practices and knowledge surrounding menstruation were changing. In addition, between the 1930s and the 1940s, academic studies of the biology of menstruation, the psychology of menstruation, and the efficacy of menstrual hygiene technologies emerged as legitimate areas of inquiry. Medical practitioners and psychologists interested in women's health resurrected Mosher's ideas about functional periodicity and called for an end to mandatory rest. Importantly, many employers adopted findings from these academic studies, so that the most current theories about menstruation and menstrual hygiene products were put into motion. Of course, there were economic stakes and security implications at play due to the need of the United States to supply female workforce replacements for male laborers during World War II. Employers used these new psychological understandings to manipulate women's attitudes about healthy menstruation, ensuring an able-bodied female workforce freed from menstrual problems.[2] The military provided different workplace challenges. For women pilots during World War II who were prevented from flying while menstruating, knowledge about menstrual hygiene technologies and the ability to hide their periods could help them defy orders to remain grounded. The time period of the 1930s and 1940s marked an important transition in menstrual hygiene technologies, from that of new products with limited use to those of overall general acceptance. Medical and psychological studies about menstruation, and women's menstrual experiences during World War II, culminated with manufactured menstrual hygiene products viewed as normal and a necessity to manage adult women's menstrual flow. And importantly, women themselves demonstrated a shrewd ability to manipulate menstrual hygiene technologies, as well as resist derogatory assumptions about menstruation, to assert personal agency and control of their bodies.

The New Science of Menstruation

By the 1930s, physicians and scientists began assessing menstruation somewhat differently than their earlier counterparts. Mary Putnam Jacobi and Clelia Mosher held conceptions of the body that were informed by vital force and the emerging belief that that body, mind, and nerves worked together dynamically.[3] Their concepts of the body were formed at the macro level. These concepts were challenged as psychology rose in stature to analyze human behavior, and more sophisticated research methods in biochemistry identified hormonal proteins. Now researchers had the ability to trace chemical agents that triggered bodily processes, such as ovulation, at the micro level. The discovery of hormones, especially sex hormones, caused physicians to ask questions about menstruation, and more importantly, the symptoms and behaviors surrounding menstruation.

Many wondered if painful periods were triggered by a chemical agent, or amounted to a psychosomatic response at an emotional level. The study of menstruation split, with physicians examining body chemistry and psychologists conducting case-study research on outward behaviors.

Although nineteenth-century physicians worked endlessly to derive the relationship between ovulation and menstruation, they had focused only upon physiology. Additionally, physicians understood very little about women's bodies, which partially explains why they blamed menstruation for so many problems and ailments. Clelia Mosher experienced resistance trying to prove that indigestion, for example, had no direct relationship to menstruation. By the early 1900s, however, scientists began studying sex endocrinology, the biology and chemistry of sexual functions. By 1920, scientists had isolated and located two sex hormones—estrogen and testosterone—one for women and one for men. Of course, this allowed for limited interpretations, and confounded scientists as to the appearance of testosterone in women. Yet, the discovery of hormones reinforced sexual duality and sexual differentiation, providing the foundation for biochemical constructions of sexual identity.[4] After 1925, sex hormones influenced research in psychology, for now both masculine and feminine traits could be studied in more than just terms of biological sex difference, but cultural behavior as well.[5]

Knowledge of sex hormones radically changed ideas about the body and made a vast difference in the way physicians viewed menstruation. The menstrual cycle could now be mapped in terms of hormonal changes within the body. Researchers abandoned the old theory of "spontaneous ovulation" because hormones better explained the relationship between ovulation and menstruation. Hormones seemed to be the answer to many female disorders as well, and were administered for all kinds of perceived abnormalities. In 1941, Dr. Emil Novak, a gynecologist at Johns Hopkins Medical School, reported that some physicians administered a serum of "progesterone, testosterone and chorionic hormones found in pregnancy urine" to adolescents suffering from excessive bleeding during their periods.[6] Physicians prescribed hormone treatment for adolescents with "breast abnormalities," defined as both "flat breasts" or breasts of "enormous size." Hormone treatments did not work as well as mechanical means for altering breast shape, they found. For young women with large breasts, "plastic operation" was the best solution. Novak reported that estrogen administration to flat-chested girls resulted in negligible improvement, that "frequent massage, designed to promote growth by increasing the blood supply" to the breast tissue worked better.[7] Physicians discovered that hormone treatment for dysmenorrhea proved to have promising applications, and was a radical departure from "cocainization"—application of a cocaine-derived sedative to the "'genital spot' in the nose."[8] The experimentation on adolescents with high doses of hormones raises ethical questions, and it demonstrates the extent to which categories of the

normal were policed and regulated through medical means. Hormones both explained physiology and opened up new questions for medical study.

While hormonal theories tended to fix sex differences—and therefore innate
behaviors—by affirming biomechanical and seemingly determined body systems, psychological theories about sex both agreed and disagreed with this assessment. On one level, many psychologists believed that human capacities were
"natural" and therefore relatively fixed, unable to sway much from a preset
course. On the other hand, some psychologists emphasized human capacity as
malleable, with humans able to shape and reshape their emerging individuality.[9]
The emphasis on self, personal motivation, and the ability to change provided a
more palatable, and ultimately commercially viable, form of psychology for
middle-class men and women to apply to their daily lives. The developing field
of psychoanalysis offered a means to describe "this new self and a technology
for treating it."[10]

Together, the modern sciences assessed humans from specific disciplines
and different vantage points. An important result of the hormonal and psychological understandings of the body was the dismantling of menstruation as a
catchall explanation for women's ailments. Physicians questioned which behaviors or symptoms could be linked with physiological, hormonal changes within
the body, and which were psychosomatic and part of a broader diagnosis of
mental disorder. Layered into this analysis was an assessment of normality,
gauging behaviors and symptoms from the common to the abnormal.[11] Of
course, the knowledge of hormones gave further legitimacy to the notion that
chemical components dictated women's bodies. But Mary Chadwick, writing in
1932, argued for the opposite. Her early work, *The Psychological Effects of
Menstruation,* pointed toward the influence that psychological components had
upon the chemicals of the body, thus explaining heavy, painful, or entirely
missed periods due to emotional factors.[12] Chadwick also interpreted symptoms
that often preceded the period—such as "the swelling and tenderness of the ovaries, back-ache, considerable abdominal distention and swelling of the
breasts"—as manifestations of pregnancy fantasies.[13] She believed that women
often experienced more psychological and emotional disturbances during their
periods, with young girls especially prone during menarche.[14]

Karen Horney, a psychologist who began to develop female-centered psychoanalysis models during the 1930s, also studied "feminine psychology" as
related to menstruation. She believed that the biology of menstruation and the
chemical changes that took place in the body must be studied in conjunction
with psychological models to garner a broader understanding of the individual
patient. By taking a more holistic approach that encompassed the body and the
emotions, she examined the subtle shifts in a woman's personality before her
period as linked to a woman's environment. She stated "the knowledge of these
biological events does not by itself give us any information about the particular
psychological content of premenstrual tensions, but it is nevertheless indispen-

sable to their understanding, because certain psychological processes parallel these physical events, or are caused by them."[15] By examining the biology of menstrual cycles alongside of psychological changes, Horney believed that she could better understand the whole woman.[16] Horney also accounted for social context, for she believed if women were devalued in society, these feelings of inadequacy might manifest in the feminine psychology of menstruation.[17] In such cases, knowledge of the rhythms of menstruation enabled psychologists "to therapeutically influence the manifold psychological and functional disorders of menstruation."[18] It is important to note that Horney believed women's psychological disorders could be treated because of the human potential for growth and change when placed in the proper environment.[19] For Horney, therapy proved to have long lasting and real effects.

With the changing fields of biochemistry and psychology, physiological problems could be addressed through medicine—namely hormone treatments—while psychological problems required varying degrees of behavior modification. It prompted psychologist Thea Goldschmidt, writing in 1934, to ask, "Are the ill effects of the menstrual period partly mental, as well as physical?"[20] Many more clinical psychologists began studying behaviors during menstruation to determine the scope and extent of menstrual disorders. They examined irritability levels in women by measuring the varying heights of their knee jerk reactions.[21] They tracked "the defensive function of menstrual bleeding," in which women spontaneously menstruated upon their first sexual encounter, thereby preserving their virginity via sex prohibition during menstruation.[22] They measured rates of kleptomania in relation to menstruation in neurotic women.[23] They also examined the learning process during the "destructive" phase and "nonmenstrual" stage of a woman's period.[24] Helen Deutsch studied abnormal psychological disorders, and she theorized that the loss of menstrual blood provoked feelings of loss and depression, because it equated to the loss of a child.[25] Menstruation leveled such a profound influence that she called for a special field studying the "psychology of menstruation" due to the unique "intermingling of biologic hormonal events and psychologic reactions."[26] For the most part, all the psychologists reported mixed results. Some women seemed to suffer more and exhibit highly irritable personalities while others continued on just the same as if they were not menstruating. Goldschmidt concluded no one diagnosis could be applied to all women; nervousness and depression, going to bed or not going to bed during a period, were manifestations "entirely individual, rather than common to women as a whole."[27] However, she believed that "effects of tradition upon the feminine mind" accounted for difficulties during menstruation. She surmised, "its effects are in part mental and traditional rather than biological, that women are still under the spell of the primitive taboo."[28]

These kinds of psychological assessments of menstruation found voice in popularly received books, too. How these menstrual traditions posed potential health risks formed the basis of Rachel Lynn Palmer and Sarah K. Greenberg's

1936 book, *Facts and Frauds in Feminine Hygiene: A Medical Guide Against Misleading Claims and Dangerous Products.*[29] Although Palmer and Greenberg were more concerned with dubious products intended for contraceptive use, such as Lysol disinfectant marketed as "feminine hygiene," they also interrogated the idea of menstruation as a disease. Like Jacobi and Mosher, Palmer and Greenberg concluded that the foundations of painful periods and the "sicktime" were often laid during childhood. They noted that "[m]any women who are today troubled by painful menstruation, when girls were rushed to bed by solicitous mothers whenever their periods appeared."[30] The girls learned to expect "special consideration from all the family at these times," during which they were excused from responsibilities. Palmer and Greenberg believed that since women expected pain, "it is almost inevitable that pain does develop." Furthermore, the women that exhibited this behavior "exercise a bit of subtle tyranny over their husbands, and sometimes children as well, by making the most of the traditional belief that at a particular time of the month women must be treated with special solicitude and tenderness and that any emotional or temperamental vagaries on their part should be met with special forbearance."[31] By using menstruation as a biological excuse to abstain from family responsibility, some women manipulated husbands and children. This same logic could be used against women in the end, they warned, for in the past many "argued that women should not go to college or participate in politics because they were emotionally unstable for a period every month."[32] Palmer and Greenberg urged women to exercise caution and judgment in deploying this excuse, and temper the dramatic performance of menstrual debility. In order to counter such behaviors, they suggested that women practice feeling healthy, which meant incorporating the technological use of sanitary napkins into their hygiene routines. Redirecting behavior toward consumption as well as newly conceived menstrual hygiene practices would presumably alter old patterns and promote healthy womanhood.

Tampon Efficacy

The incorporation of menstrual technologies into health regimes sounded like a good idea to many health practitioners, and even though there was a growing body of work on menstrual endocrinology and psychology, there was no systematic research on sanitary napkins and tampons. Yet, with the introduction and growing popularity of Tampax in 1936, physicians received queries from their patients and many lamented that there was negligible scientific research available to them concerning not only the performance of tampons but also the health risks. With so many women administering a technology once in the hands of physicians, what were the consequences of across the board use? By the late 1930s, medical journals began to publish research articles on this very issue, some submitted by independent researchers and others by corporate sponsored scientists. As such, the conclusions were highly dependent upon political loyalties.

Some physicians worried that women's "self tamponage," without the oversight of a physician, might lead to irritation of the vagina.[33] Harry Sackren, a physician practicing in Brooklyn, New York, compared Tampax to sanitary pads in his 1939 article "Vaginal Tampons for Menstrual Absorption," published in *Clinical Medicine and Surgery*, and concluded that tampons reduced the level of vaginal irritation. Furthermore, since sanitary pads worn externally could harbor more organisms from the rectum, tampons would decrease the likelihood of infection introduced into the vaginal tract in this manner. He reported that with a bit of practice and experience inserting and removing the tampons, "most women decided not to return to external pads" and "a few mentioned the comfort of urinating and defecating without the nuisance of removal of the protection."[34] Mary Barton, a medical practitioner with a Bachelor of Medicine practicing in England, tended to agree with the reasoning, as she had treated women with boils and lesions on the vulva from the abrasive covering on sanitary pads. In terms of using tampons, she felt too much was made about women forgetting to change their tampons with the result of possible infection. She noted in her 1942 article "Review of the Sanitary Appliance with a Discussion of Intra-Vaginal Packs" that "[t]he argument that internal pads may be left in indefinitely and forgotten applies also to birth-control appliances, and even, indeed, to false teeth, and we must hope that personal hygiene has reached a stage when such contingencies can only very rarely arise."[35] This argument has had a long shelf life. The rationalization of women's incompetence concerning reproductive health was repeated with the introduction of birth control pills in the 1960s as well as the contemporary debates about "the morning after pill," the consequence being highly regulated products whose distribution requires medical intervention.

Another study by A. W. Diddle and L. Boulware, physicians and researchers in the Departments of Obstetrics and Gynecology and Student Health, State University of Iowa, College of Medicine, entitled "Vaginal Tampons for Menstrual Hygiene" appeared in 1942 in the *Journal of Iowa State Medical Society*. They conducted research by sending out questionnaires to 569 single, white college women and nurses whose average age was 23. According to the researchers the group showed little experience with tampons: 412 used only sanitary pads and 27.6%, or 157, had used tampons for at least one month, with 73 using them for more than one year. The majority, 79.6%, found them acceptable and comfortable. Reasons for discontinuing their use included discomfort, inadequacy in controlling menstrual flow, difficulty of insertion, and that a physician advised against their use. Some used external sanitary pads or even vulval pads—small pads worn within the cleft of the labia—on the first heavier days of the period

Figure 1: An early proponent of women's health, Mary Putnam Jacobi, a trained physician, conducted scientifically-based medical research to disprove theories of menstrual-induced illness. Her 1877 book, The Question of Rest for Women During Menstruation, argued that forcible rest during the period was unnecessary for healthy women. This idea was counterintuitive to contemporary common knowledge, and was often dismissed by her male colleagues. Mary Corinna Putnam Jacobi, 1842-1906. Library of Congress, Prints and Photographs Division, LC-USZ62–61783.

Figure 2: Clelia Mosher used her medical degree to champion women's menstrual health. She wrote voluminously about menstruation, hygiene, and sexuality, and coined the term "functional periodicity" to develop a positive understanding of menstruation. Furthermore, not only did she make this point in medical journals, she put her ideas into practice by developing exercises and deep breathing techniques to relieve menstrual cramps that she taught to her students at Stanford. Clelia D. Mosher, 1863–1940. Palo Alto Historical Association Photograph Collection.

How Science Ends the Uncertainty
of Old-Time Hygienic Methods

*And gives women freedom, comfort, standards
of health never before possible*

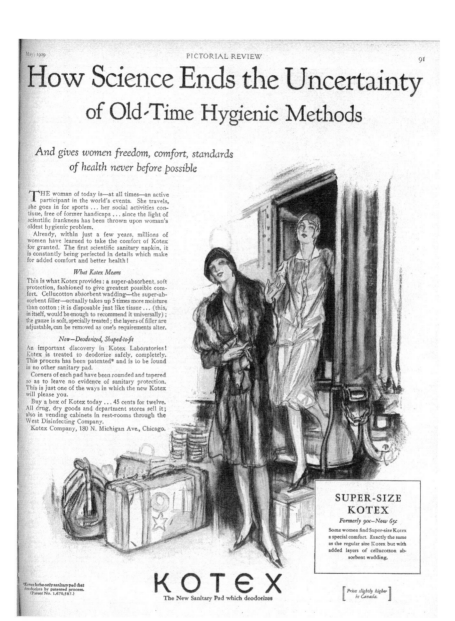

THE woman of today is—at all times—an active participant in the world's events. She travels, she goes in for sports ... her social activities continue, free of former handicaps ... since the light of scientific frankness has been thrown upon woman's oldest hygienic problem.

Already, within just a few years, millions of women have learned to take the comfort of Kotex for granted. The first scientific sanitary napkin, it is constantly being perfected in details which make for added comfort and better health!

What Kotex Means

This is what Kotex provides: a super-absorbent, soft protection, fashioned to give greatest possible comfort. Cellucotton absorbent wadding—the super-absorbent filler—actually takes up 5 times more moisture than cotton; it is disposable just like tissue ... (this, in itself, would be enough to recommend it universally); the layers are soft, specially treated; the layers of filler are adjustable, can be removed as one's requirements alter.

Now—Deodorized, Shaped-to-fit

An important discovery in Kotex Laboratories! Kotex is treated to deodorize safely, completely. This process has been patented* and is to be found in no other sanitary pad.

Corners of each pad have been rounded and tapered so as to leave no evidence of sanitary protection. This is just one of the ways in which the new Kotex will please you.

Buy a box of Kotex today ... 45 cents for twelve. All drug, dry goods and department stores sell it; also in vending cabinets in rest-rooms through the West Disinfecting Company.

Kotex Company, 180 N. Michigan Ave., Chicago.

**SUPER-SIZE
KOTEX**

Formerly 90c—Now 65c

Some women find Super-size Kotex a special comfort. Exactly the same as the regular size Kotex but with added layers of cellucotton absorbent wadding.

Kotex is the only sanitary pad that deodorizes by patented process. (Patent No. 1,670,587.)

KOTEX
The New Sanitary Pad which deodorizes

[*Price slightly higher in Canada.*]

Figure 3: Though Ladies' Home Journal *accepted the first Kotex advertisements into its publication in 1921, they soon became prevalent in many women's magazines. This advertisement relies on notions that link scientific progress with advancement, modernity, and even civilization to streamline the body and dispense with old-fashioned, out-of-date menstrual practices.* Pictorial Review *(May 1929): 91. Copyright Kimberly-Clark Worldwide, Inc., reprinted with permission.*

Figure 4: Lillian Gilbreth, well known for her book, Cheaper by the Dozen, made a career for herself as an efficiency expert. In her view, scientific management could be applied to any process, including menstruation. She analyzed the 1927 menstrual hygiene market in her report to Johnson & Johnson, in which she made numerous suggestions to improve the technologies offered for sale. Lillian M. Gilbreth. Rutgers University, Special Collections and University Archives, New Jersey Portraits Collections (Oversize), Box 2.

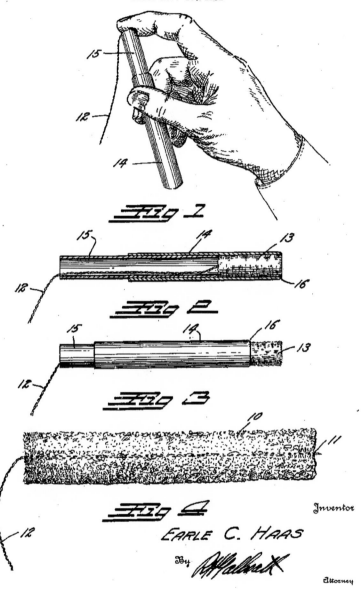

Figure 5: Cotton plugs tamped wounds for many years, but using a plug to absorb menstrual fluid became commercially viable when Earle Cleveland Haas developed not only a tampon that expanded lengthwise, but also a disposable telescopic applicator. Packaged together, the new product Tampax had appeal because it provided a new and innovative solution to manage menses. Earle Cleveland Haas, United States Patent Office, 1,926,900, September 12, 1933.

Listen in!

[The Girls are Talking about Tampons]

The Blonde: *It's invisible* sanitary protection, thank heavens . . . 'cause Fibs are worn internally . . . keep my secret safe even in this bathing suit. Otherwise I'd be missing lots of fun this summer.

The Brunette: *Whatta pal* . . . why didn't you tell me before? I had to miss the beach all last week! But why Fibs? . . . aren't all tampons alike?

The Blonde: *I'll say they're not!* For one thing . . . Fibs are easy to use . . . no gadgets needed, so naturally Fibs cost less. And what means even more to me—Fibs are the *Kotex* Tampon . . .

The Brunette: *That's the answer!* Fibs are a Kotex product . . . so it's Fibs for me! Now I remember . . . Fibs are the tampons that are "Quilted" for more comfort and safety. And you get a full dozen for just 20¢. 'Nough said!

FIBS' the Kotex Tampon

Not 8 - not 10 *but* 12 FOR 20¢

*Trade Marks Reg. U. S. Pat. Off.

Figure 6: Many menstrual hygiene products competed for consumers' attention. Kimberly-Clark's major product was Kotex, but it also introduced Fibs tampons for "the waning days of the period." Thus, women might use two different technologies. This ad also made clear that passing was both understood and desirable. Fibs Advertisement, McCall's (1941). Copyright Kimberly-Clark Worldwide, Inc., reprinted with permission. Ad*Access On-Line Project—Ad #BH0070, John W. Hartman Center for Sales, Advertising & Marketing History, Duke University Rare Book, Manuscript and Special Collections Library.

OBJECTIVE

REDUCTION OF FEMALE ABSENTEEISM

Statistics show that women absent themselves from work much more often than men; indeed, such absenteeism is said to be 50 per cent[1] higher among women.

Though available data do not clearly assign the responsibility for this marked differential, obviously menstrual inconveniences account for a considerable proportion of the days lost.

On this point Pommerenke[2] recently made the following observation before the American Association of Industrial Physicians and Surgeons: "With a better understanding of the purpose and nature of menstruation, and its recognition as physiological rather than as a pathological process, many a woman may be re-educated and come to regard the so-called difficult days as days in which she need not seriously curtail her usual activities."

Many physicians have discovered the contribution which *improved menstrual hygiene* (as with the intravaginal tampon Tampax) affords this reeducation process—since it provides such a welcome sense of security, freedom and poise by relieving the physical distress and emotional uncertainty caused by vulval irritation from perineal pads, or from olfactory offense, or conspicuous bulging under slacks or coveralls.

Tampax can be used easily and safely—it will not irritate delicate tissues nor block the flow. And its three different absorbencies permit individual regulation depending upon daily needs. Compressed into a one-time-use applicator, it may be inserted and removed simply and daintily.

Your patients should be grateful to you for recommending Tampax—and (in many cases) it may enable them to stay "on the job" where they are so vitally needed.

[1] Mod. Med., 11:120, 1943; (2) Ind. Med., 12:512, 1943

TAMPAX INCORPORATED · PALMER, MASS.

ACCEPTED FOR ADVERTISING BY THE JOURNAL OF THE AMERICAN MEDICAL ASSOCIATION

TAMPAX

TAMPAX INCORPORATED Palmer, Mass. Please send me a professional supply of the three sizes of Tampax.	Name	N 44
	Address	
	City	

59

Figure 7: Tampax promoted itself as a productive wartime technology during World War II. It claimed that women employees would take fewer "sick" days during their periods by wearing tampons, thus maintaining the efficiency of the assembly line and also bolstering patriotism. "Reduction of Female Absenteeism," Journal of Nursing (1944). Reprinted with permission from Proctor & Gamble. Ad*Access On-Line Project—Ad #BH0201, John Hartman Center for Sales, Advertising & Marketing History, Duke University Rare Book, Manuscript, and Special Collections Library.

You're the fun in his furlough

Will you ever forget how proud he looked as you glided down the long staircase? As though he'd been waiting for this moment all his life!

What he said wasn't nearly as important as the *way* he said it! And as you were dancing, his eyes told you that being with you is what makes a furlough worthwhile.

To think that at five o'clock you were ready to break your date! Because today's eight hours of defense work had seemed like eighty!

Then in stepped Destiny . . . her name was Diana. "Why let trying days of the month rule your life?"— she asked. "Why should *you* be a deserter when other girls carry on in comfort *every* day?"

You don't need a furlough!

"You don't need time-out," she explained . . . that is, if you choose Kotex sanitary napkins. And how right she was!

Because Kotex is made in soft folds, so it's naturally less bulky . . . more comfortable . . . made to stay soft while wearing. A lot different from pads that only "feel" soft at first touch.

Now that you know, you'll take Kotex for confidence, too . . . to put an end to edgy little worries that so often upset a girl. Because the flat, pressed ends of Kotex keep your secret safe. And a new moisture-resistant "safety shield" provides *added* protection!

Maybe it did take you until today to learn why Kotex is more popular than all other brands of pads put together.

But you're glad that you did! Because now you can breeze through work or play as millions do — with never a *thought* of deserting!

Keep Going in Comfort

—with KOTEX*!

(*T. M. Reg. U. S. Pat. Off.)

Tells All — Quickly!

Send today for the bright, new booklet—"As One Girl To Another". Lots of tips for keeping in the fun on "difficult days" . . . what to do and not to do. Mail name and address to P. O. Box 3434, Dept. WH-10, Chicago, for copy FREE!

*Figure 8: Kotex advertisements during World War II managed a delicate balance of promoting wartime employment of women, while encouraging them to remain feminine. Importantly, menstrual hygiene technology helped create this feminine identity. In addition, sanitary pads would help women pass as normal, thus enabling them to keep long scheduled dates with beaus returning home for a furlough. "You're the Fun in His Furlough," Woman's Home Companion (1942). Copyright Kimberly-Clark Worldwide, Inc., reprinted with permission. Ad*Access On-Line Project—Ad #BH0064, John Hartman Center for Sales, Advertising & Marketing, Duke University Rare Book, Manuscript, and Special Collection Library.*

"You're a young lady now"

Figure 9: After World War II, menstrual hygiene corporations gave renewed attention to teenagers and pre-pubescent girls. Menstrual hygiene pamphlets, films, filmstrips, and advertisements increasingly addressed young teenagers as consumers, who had the potential to become lifelong customers. Menstrual Education Pamphlet, Kimberly-Clark Corporation, 1952. Copyright Kimberly-Clark Worldwide, Inc., reprinted with permission. Personal possession of the author.

"Proportioned what?"

Proportioned Kotex napkins.

Now you can choose the length, width and depth that meets your special needs because Kotex comes in 4 proportioned sizes.

Each comes with the moisture-proof shield.

That's why nothing protects quite like Kotex.

Which proportioned Kotex napkin protects you best?

| REGULAR | JUNIOR | SLENDERLINE | SUPER |
| Medium width, depth and length | Regular length and depth—less width | Narrowest, deepest, shorter than Regular | Regular length, deeper, wider |

Now more than ever, Kotex is confidence.

Copy No. 62*1–L7906—Finished—page bleed—plate 10⅞ x 15½ in.—Ebony, November 1962
Printed in U.S.A.
Prepared by FOOTE, CONE & BELDING

Figure 10: This was the first color advertisement to feature a black woman, and appeared in Ebony magazine. The Civil Rights movement made clear, among other things, that black women were an untapped consumer market. Kotex advertisement, Ebony (November 1962). Copyright Kimberly-Clark Worldwide, Inc., reprinted with permission.

Figure 11: This advertisement mirrored the Ebony spread, and demonstrated parity in quality of layout, design, and production values, though the intended audiences for Kotex remained segregated. Kotex advertisement, general magazine placement (November 1962). Copyright Kimberly-Clark Worldwide, Inc., reprinted with permission.

because the tampons did not absorb enough fluid.[36] The researchers concluded that no serious damage would occur with sensible use of tampons.

Corporations sponsored other research. Significantly, the research underwritten by Tambrands only studied Tampax and no other readily available tampons. In their 1942 study "The Intravaginal Tampon in Menstrual Hygiene," Maurice O. Magid and Jacob Geiger ascertained, not surprisingly, that "evidence is conclusive that the tampon method of menstrual hygiene is safe, comfortable and not prejudicial to health."[37] Following Tambrands, the International Cellucotton Company, manufacturer of Fibs, granted research money to the Department of Obstetrics and Gynecology at the University of Wisconsin to study tampons, and the Personal Products Corporation, a division of Johnson & Johnson, who introduced Meds in 1940, underwrote research in the Department of Obstetrics and Gynecology at Columbia University.[38] The research conducted for the International Cellucotton Company had a study period of two years, during which researchers required women to undergo repeated pelvic exams, as many as twelve over the course of the study. Predictably, the researchers concluded that tampons were safe, and no women developed yeast infections or other problems due to tampon use. Tambrands quickly incorporated this positive research into its advertisements directed at medical personnel. It directly addressed these concerns in ads such as "Facts for the Patient Inquiring about the Safety of Internal Menstrual Protection," which claimed Tampax could be "soundly recommended" to patients.[39]

What set apart the study for the Personal Products Corporation was its reliance upon X-ray technology to evaluate tampon efficiency. In 1944, Irja Widenius, a physician in the Department of Obstetrics and Gynecology, Columbia University, published "A Study of Commercially Manufactured Catamenial Tampons" in the *American Journal of Obstetrics and Gynecology*. The X-ray images were supposed to assess the position of the tampon in the vagina, and how well they absorbed fluid versus merely plugging up the vagina. The technological difficulty of the study was developing a technique by which a radiopaque solution might mix well with menstrual blood, so that it would appear on the images. Not just the menstrual blood but also the tampons needed definition, so technicians brushed barium sulfate onto the tampons, which women then inserted into their vaginas. Widenius took X-ray images of women's pelvises before the insertion of the tampons, immediately afterward, and at an interval of half an hour later. She sampled different brands of tampons, and how well they absorbed blood in situ. Though only numbers identified the tampons, the images clearly revealed the brands, as with the outline of the cellophane sheath on Wix. The report included the results from examinations of twenty-five women, although more participated in the study. Of the twenty-five, five became pregnant of whom three delivered babies. The disturbing part of this was that these pregnant women and their fetuses were exposed to high doses of radiation as part of the study. Widenius interpreted these pregnancies as positive, because they showed that tampon use did not prevent conception.

J. Milton Singleton and Herbert F. Vanorden, physicians from the Department of Obstetrics and Gynecology, University of Kansas Medical School, and St. Luke's and St. Mary's Hospital, Kansas City, Missouri, respectively, flatly rejected the use of tampons for their patients. They detailed the findings of their study in the *Western Journal of Surgery, Obstetrics, and Gynecology* in 1943. Instead of conducting research on menstruating women, like previous healthcare practitioners, they sent out questionnaires to 3,400 doctors in the United States and Canada concerning the physicians' attitudes about tampons. Of the low yield of 251 replies, 157 opposed the use of tampons, and only 29 were completely favorable. The remainder suggested limited use for women in specific jobs, like dancing or athletics. They admitted that they had prejudice against tampons because "whenever there is free serum, blood, or discharge from a wound or body cavity, free drainage is desired and must be encouraged."[40] Tampons blocked the flow of fluid and contradicted common assumptions about the body. They recommended that their patients avoid tampons for this reason, and also because their application was aseptic, the chances of irritation great.

However, their opinions, as well as those of the majority of physicians that they surveyed, were based upon deeper assumptions about women and their bodies. These assumptions included the sanctity of the hymen as a symbol of virginity, the penis as the only acceptable object to enter the vagina, and the exclusive knowledge of physicians as experts about women's vaginas and their bodies. Although they did not state why, the doctors claimed that tampons "should never be used by virgins."[41] Although a common concern about tampons was they would break the hymen, these physicians did not employ such reasoning. They claimed that tampons brought about "pelvic consciousness," and "undue handling" of the genitals "may cause eroticism and masturbation." Furthermore, the physicians reported an "almost unanimous opinion against tamponage in virgins, with the expressed feeling that it created sex consciousness, may stimulate eroticism and the habit of masturbation."[42] As a hidden technology, tampons raised the question about women's, and especially virgins', sexual pleasure, and the ways and means by which women might satisfy themselves without heterosexual intercourse involving a penis. Because users of tampons were younger and often unmarried, Singleton and Vanorden blamed women's misjudgment on immaturity and the influence of attractive advertising. In their view, women not only transgressed appropriate outlets for their sexuality—heterosexual marriage—but sanctions against touching their genitalia. They reasoned "[i]f traditionally, even the physician is not supposed to invade the vagina during menstruation, let alone the husband or consort, why should the woman be authorized to do it herself by an absolutely unskilled technic?" Here, the physicians relied upon a belief that women should abstain from sex during their periods, which has its roots in biblical tradition. If husbands, who typically had marriage ownership over their wives' bodies, could not have access to the vagina, and physicians who were mostly men should not have that male privilege either, then women who were granted even less status had no right to enter their own vaginas. That Singleton and Vanorden referred to the tampon user as "an absolutely unskilled technic" highlights the point that tampons were technologies, and as technologies—including knowledge, practice, and artifacts—they were generally believed to belong to the domain of men. The responses of the physicians are noteworthy because they represent some of the fears about the unintended consequences of tampon use, and how women might deploy the technology. Put into the hands of women, tampon use raised questions about women's right to their bodies, and the fears of their liberated sexualities.

The effect of these studies about tampon efficacy was that practicing physicians and nurses had mixed results to contend with. Simply put, physicians could choose the results that aligned with their own sensibilities about menstrual hygiene products. The conflicting results also represented the different shades and contours of menstrual politics, and how menstruation was to be understood in terms of women's general trustworthiness, as well as their expected behaviors. The more women challenged these norms, the more some physicians redoubled their efforts to gain back control of the tampon. It symbolized a powerful, even threatening, shift in women's personal autonomy and agency.

Menstruation and the Workplace

Despite earlier ideas dictating rest during menstruation, there were clearly benefits to liberating female bodies, with the proper guidance and grooming. Encouraging women to manage their periods responsibly became the hallmark of advice doled out by corporations, physicians, and some employers of women in the 1930s and 1940s. Since tampons, and even sanitary napkins to some degree, raised the question about women's secretive behavior, if a model for women's menstrual practices could be promoted, the behavioral outcomes might be more predictable, and even beneficial to employees. Much attention was given to women in the workplace concerning their compliance with menstrual practices deemed appropriate to the work environment.

The Metropolitan Life Insurance Company, located in New York City, became a research site for women's use of menstrual hygiene practices as well as attitudes concerning menstruation. In part, the insurance company had a stake in assessing ranges of normality in its issuance of insurance policies, and attention to menstrual disorders was just another medical condition to further understand. However, the sheer number of women employed meant that issues of menstruation were the business of the company on a day-to-day level if they affected productivity. By the 1920s, the workplace environment at the Metropolitan Life Insurance Company incorporated the notion of functional periodicity. Mrs.

Brockaway, head of the Welfare Department, was responsible for employee health at the company and noticed marked absenteeism in women. Although she had no evidence, her suspicion pointed toward menstrual debility as the culprit. She reasoned "having been brought up to believe that they were 'sick' at such a time, they simply stayed away from work and would not offer explanation to the men doctors."[43] In order to decrease absenteeism, Brockaway experimented by hiring two female physicians for her female employees. When the employees visited the female physicians, they were given advice about exercise, and "told that they are not sick" during their menses. To Brockaway's delight, absenteeism decreased. However, the employees may have felt pressured to return to work by management, or threatened that they would lose their jobs because of their menstrual absences. Regardless, Brockaway perceived a notable change due to the female physicians. She believed that "the trouble with menstruation today is the result of the fact that few industries provide women physicians for their workers."[44] Therefore, the problems associated with menstruation might be solved with scientifically based medicine, delivered by female physicians.

Miss Harris, the head nurse of the dispensary of the Metropolitan Life Insurance Company in the late 1920s, reported to Lillian Gilbreth for her 1927 Johnson & Johnson survey that 7,000 women employed in one building consumed approximately 4,500 napkins in one month. The primary concern for the workers was comfort, so that napkins with fiber-like filler that frayed were "very unsatisfactory for file clerks, mail girls, and others who must be moving about constantly." Since women could not easily change their pads, and only had the opportunity "before 9 a.m., during their thirty-five-minute noon-hour, and after 4:30 p.m.," they needed soft napkins or would suffer irritation from the rough napkins. Another related problem was the quality of the sanitary napkin dispenser in the restroom. According to Harris, only the Hygienic brand held up to the bangs and jostling of the women dropping slugs, instead of coins, into the machine. Kotex slot machines failed to withstand the wear and tear, and fared much worse.[45]

In 1931, Dr. Ruth E. Ewing conducted a study of dysmenorrhea at the Metropolitan Life Insurance Company.[46] The medical staff at the company observed that dysmenorrhea caused "a great deal of discomfort to the patient and a real loss of time and impairment of efficiency" to the company.[47] Between June and December of 1927, there were 1,151 absence days and 2,670 trips to the rest room due to dysmenorrhea among 7,390 female clerks. The company physicians isolated those women exhibiting menstrual disorders and subjected them to a course in functional periodicity. They taught women about diet, regular bowel habits (induced with mineral oil) and fluid intake, how Mosher exercises worked to improve strength and posture, and how deep breathing reduced painful periods. According to their survey, 90% of the women in the program believed they benefited from the treatment. More importantly for Metropolitan, trips to the rest room decreased, the company lost fewer days to absenteeism, and the amount of time clerks spent away from their desks decreased 53%. Ewing concluded, "the saving in time was real" and "directly attributable to the treatment."[48]

Due to women's growing economic relevancy, ideas about menstruation which de-emphasized menstrual debility were particularly important. This was due in part to employers' needs for a reliable, healthy workforce, freed from ideas about mandatory rest during menstruation. To promote health and curtail absenteeism, employers began sponsoring health campaigns intended to change women's attitudes about menstruation. By addressing both physiological ailments as well as psychological behaviors, employers sought to create a more productive workforce (albeit based upon the model of a universal male). Besides improving women's attitudes about menstruation, the campaigns influenced the commercial market of menstrual hygiene products. The model of an able body held economic, commercial, and patriotic meanings in 1940s America.

With the outbreak of World War II and the strain upon wartime industry, manufacturers turned to women to fill jobs traditionally held by men. In the name of patriotism and duty, many women joined the ranks of paid labor, nudged onward by propaganda campaigns. As women began working full time and overtime, some struggled with the difficulties of finding adequate day care for their children and time to grocery shop. Others gladly worked at industrial jobs that offered them newfound confidence and exceptional pay compared to secretarial work. Regardless of their reasons, the number of women employed changed the face of labor during the war.[49]

Many wondered if women were capable of doing "man's work." Yet, with few men to turn to, women suddenly accomplished work tasks once thought unimaginable. The sheer number of women employed, however, created unforeseen troubles for managers. Everything from footwear, face shields, and work uniforms needed to be redesigned to fit women's generally smaller frames.[50] Not only was appropriate work clothing an issue, but also women's bodies did not conform to a regimented schedule like men's bodies. Women often became pregnant, which was grounds for dismissal.[51] Women's menstrual cycles also interfered with the clockwork precision of shift work, and many who had cramps avoided work, thus leaving an empty space on the assembly line. Because this ultimately slowed down production, women's issues—once quickly dismissed as esoteric—now took on greater meaning to production quotas. Childcare, pregnancy, and menstrual cycles were suddenly not just women's concerns; they were industrial concerns which managers needed to address.

Sometimes a woman's family needs took precedence over her responsibilities at the factory. *Harper's Magazine* reported that housework, not menstruation, proved to be the most common reason for fatigue, lost days, and safety issues at the manufacturing plant. Because women were responsible for daily income and maintaining home life, they had little time to accomplish their many tasks. Male workers usually did not have this problem, and often benefited from the luxury of a wife to cook, clean, and take care of the children after a long day at work. Ideally, he rejuvenated himself each night, ready for work the next day. Women workers were not so lucky, and often needed to take days off—absences attributed to menstruation—in order to take care of household matters.[52]

One of the chief ways that companies sought to deal with the "problems" of female employees was counseling. Recognizing their own shortcomings, managers began to hire female counselors to help trouble shoot and reduce absenteeism. Counselors dealt with finding transportation for women who lived in cities with poor public transit and could not afford cars. They found temporary housing and connected employees with landlords and real estate agents to find apartments. They also served as representatives to community agencies, and often supported federal assistance for day care programs.[53] Although the counselors often acted like therapists, and probably even offered sound advice, most were neither trained in psychology nor formally educated at all. One reporter noted that "she is likely to have been chosen simply for her sympathetic attitude," and she was most often a mother as well.[54] Susan Laughlin, a counselor within the Personnel Division at Lockheed, fit this description. She recalled that the personnel manager chose her over a "psychologist who had written a book" because "he liked my answers better than hers." The psychologist also had no children, and the manager believed that because Laughlin was a mother, the other employees could better relate to her.[55]

Laughlin recalled helping women with very personal issues, such as providing employees information about physicians who performed abortions.[56] This was very important economically, since managers usually fired a woman once they found out about her pregnancy. Counselors held powerful sway over many workers, but some viewed them more suspiciously because of their ties to management. If the union could provide these same services and tap into the funding and assistance provided by the Office of Labor Production (through the War Production Board), they could attract support by displaying the benefits of union membership.[57] Women's issues became the focus of the union counselors, and their programs proved to create loyal members. Female workers challenged counselors to help find solutions to childcare, sexual harassment, and even the availability of sanitary napkins in the restrooms.[58]

Trained psychologists also took note of women's wartime labor experiences. Georgene Seward, who held a doctorate in psychology, provided a unique set of skills to assess the relationship of women's labor, psychology, and menstruation. Seward's major professor while working on her doctorate at Columbia was Leta Hollingworth. Hollingworth, a contemporary of Clelia Mosher, wrote *Functional Periodicity: An Experimental Study of the Mental and Motor Abilities of Women During Menstruation* in 1914 as her dissertation, in which she argued that menstruation did not impair women's mental or motor efficiency during their periods. Hollingworth was particularly concerned with broad-based discrimination based upon woman as a sex, and it is clear that her ideas re-emerged in the work of Seward. Seward wrote a publication for the Columbia

University Council for Research in the Social Sciences entitled "Effect of Menstrual Cycle on Sensitivity to Pain" prior to her work on laborers.[59] She later wrote *Sex and the Social Order* (1946) to scientifically discern the relationship between sex, reproduction, and social life. Her political message rang out in the final chapter, "Sex in Postwar Society." She argued "by confusing women's biological function with their social role and maintaining male monopoly in the world of achievement, it has been possible to keep half of the population from competing for the insufficient jobs available."[60] One reviewer noted that other than the "slightly feministic bias" the book did not suffer from moral overtones as did so many others on this topic.[61]

Seward's 1944 article "Psychological Effects of the Menstrual Cycle on Women Workers" encompassed much of her feminist ideas. She recognized that the role of menstruation in relation to attitudes about women workers and women's efficiency at their jobs held political meaning for women's rights before the war, and more importantly, took on national meaning during the war. Attitudes about menstruation being an illness had potential repercussions on Allied troops, and Seward pointed out "[w]ith female employment in essential war industries at an unprecedented peak, the question of possible menstrual effects becomes acute."[62] Seward sought to determine how much of women's absenteeism was "due to factors intrinsically associated with sex, and how much is socially conditioned."[63] Although she witnessed dysmenorrhea on the decline due to women's participation in the work force, she believed that "menstrual handicaps" persisted among women because of "a paternalistic attitude toward them, emphasizing their 'need' for special protection." As a result, she concluded, "[t]hese protective devices actually have 'protected' only economic inequalities between the sexes, justified on the assumption of biological inequalities."[64] She viewed her work as challenging such notions, with an eye toward economic equality and parity of pay free from sex bias.

Seward surveyed a variety of employers, including Sears and Roebuck, AC Spark Plug Division of General Motors, and Vultee Consolidated Aircraft Corporation. All reported that "any systematic therapeutic program which concentrates attention on the employee" improved morale, and consequently, decreased absenteeism. Some businesses like Metropolitan Life Insurance and the American Telephone and Telegraph Company implemented "progressive" health programs aimed at creating "healthy psychological attitudes toward menstruation."[65] On the contrary, other companies spied upon their employees, accusing women of loitering in the bathrooms.[66] An unnamed life insurance company reported reduced absenteeism after it withheld pay from women, punishing them for taking time off for menstrual cramps.[67] These manipulative tactics used menstruation as a foil to regiment and discipline the female workforce.

Seward believed that some women experienced severe medical problems, but that "the incapacitation of menstrual cripples should not be charged against the great majority of working women."[68] In fact, the menstrual cycle had little effect on the average worker. Yet, "the persistence of a code of menstrual invalidism, however, has contributed to industrial absenteeism." What women needed was "a broad program of sex education begun in childhood and directed toward healthy psychosexual development as a whole" to engender more positive attitudes about menstruation. She believed, though, that as women continued to gain experience and be valued as workers, it "should free them from the cultural burden of invalidism" and make them confident "to assume their places beside men in the work of the world."[69] Seward's desire to eliminate women's inferiority based upon sex difference was not easily attained.

Hygeia, the medical publication sponsored by the American Medical Association and directed toward the lay public, also addressed the female laborer in its article, "Health for the Working Girl," and repeated assumptions about difference based on sex.[70] The article noted "[w]hile women have proved themselves as capable as men in the industrial world, women have unique physical problems because of their sex." This included decreased efficiency due to pregnancy and menstruation, which amounted to "a worry to the woman herself and to the company for which she works."[71] Statistics showed that women were often absent twice as often—14 days compared to 8 days for men—and that they were absent on average for only one day at a time. This the United States Public Health Service attributed to menstruation.[72] Reiterating much of the contemporary medical and psychological research, the article recommended that factories and businesses provide a restroom and a cot for women to lie down. Bathroom architecture even supported menstrual debility, with building space accommodating this ideology. Fainting couches and chairs decorated the lounge section of the restroom, offering women a private place to recline.[73] Attended by a nurse who could administer hot drinks and a "pain-easing drug" such as aspirin, the women could return to work more quickly. The factory would only lose a few hours instead of an entire "sick" day. The article reported on the trend in business to implement educational programs, in the form of "posters, pamphlets, and movies" to promote healthy diet, exercise, good posture, and lessons in "feminine physiology."[74] These educational programs set out to break women of the belief that they were sick, and increase their work attendance. Interviewed for the "Health for the Working Girl" article, Dr. W. T. Pommerenke of the Department of Obstetrics and Gynecology, University of Rochester School of Medicine, believed education promoted healthy menstruation. Respected as a researcher, he wrote about subjects ranging from sterility and fertility to the characteristics of cervical mucus, as well as the effects of nuclear radiation transmission in breast milk.[75] Sounding much like Clelia Mosher, he encouraged women "to think of menstruation as a natural process like digestion" so that "much of the nervous tension and distress will be overcome."[76]

Many factory managers became aware of menstrual liability and through health counselors worked to alter attitudes about it. The North American Aircraft Company reported an 80% reduction in absenteeism after its medical department sponsored a physical education class that taught women exercises to relieve cramps.[77] Consolidated Vultee Aircraft Company instituted an exercise and stretching program to reduce cramps in its female workers. Women enrolled in a ten month "Work to Win" program, and the supervising doctor found that not one woman reported absent during that time. *Newsweek* magazine called the exercise program a "cure for cramps," with detailed descriptions of the stretching routines.[78]

The programs to reduce menstrual debility were tacitly reinforced through campaigns to eliminate absenteeism. Directed at troops in the field and workers in the factories, pointed posters warned that one day's absence might cause a soldier's demise. Posters such as "We'll lick absenteeism or we'll lose the war" and "Knifed! Willful absenteeism strikes at our liberty!" reminded workers that their job was not only about a wage, but also about victory in war.[79]

The Military Workplace and Women's Periods

The question of the female worker extended beyond wartime industrial production to women enlisted in military service. Just as industrial managers wondered if women were strong enough or physically capable, Army officers had doubts about women's reliability. Of course, women were already performing well at secretarial or detail-oriented tasks, but what about jobs that required physical rigor? Major L. W. McIntosh reminded his colleague Major Everett S. Hughes that women possessed a "psychological handicap which renders her abnormal, unstable, etc., at certain times."[80] Due to this belief, Army planners cautiously protected sensitive positions in which "reliability" proved to be a critical component. Because of this distrust of menstruation and its effects on women, officers took extra precautions to either avoid situations in which a woman's period might interfere with her performance, or to quell menstrual debility altogether.

In particular, the military scrutinized the health of women serving in the Women's Army Corps (WAC), the Women's Auxiliary Ferrying Squadron (WAFS), and the Women Airforce Service Pilots (WASP). Congress approved the Women's Army Auxiliary Corps (WAAC) in 1941 after much acrimonious debate. It later became the WAC, integrated with the regular Army in 1943. Enlisted women served in support roles to male troops, often providing clerical help as stenographers, typists, clerks, and communication specialists staffing switchboards or transmitting short-wave radio messages. WAFs, initiated in 1942, had already earned their commercial pilot's licenses, and transported goods and supplies as well as Army Air Force trainees to their stations. By 1943, all women flying for the Air Force were brought into the WASP program. Besides just ferrying supplies, they served as flight instructors, participated in test flying, towed gliders, and flew airplanes during gunnery practice.[81] They fulfilled a support role as pilots, and deliberately so.

Army quarters and assignments provided a different set of challenges to women and unit managers. Unlike female factory workers who could go home at the end of the workday or use sick days if absolutely necessary, enlisted women in the Women's Army Corps had no such luxury. Since they were always on duty they could not go to bed with menstrual cramps. In fact, a report concerning women's medical treatment noted that standard operating procedures prohibited "sick in quarters"; women could not simply retreat to bed for a couple of hours. Instead, they were required to report to the infirmary, but Dr. Margaret Craighill of the Army Medical Corps reported that "many subterfuges are practiced to get around this, however, some of which have more disadvantages than actually permitting the practice."[82] Because of Army rules, if a woman was sick and could not return to work, she needed to be admitted to the hospital. Many women concealed their cramps because release from the hospital often took two or three days, by which time their periods were nearly over. Women's medical records followed them to each assignment, and repeat admittance to the hospital pointed toward a history of menstrual disorder—a diagnosis providing sufficient grounds for discharge.[83] Near the end of the war, the rules were relaxed a bit so that women could obtain a "twenty-three hour pass" at some locations to remain off duty if experiencing headache, cramps, or even a cold. A short rest proved more productive, and prevented a great loss of time.

Physicians attributed almost one-fourth of the hospitalizations to "female complaints," which prompted an Air Force surgeon to recommend, "women with menstrual disorders should be eliminated prior to their dispatch to a Theater of Operations."[84] Whether through coercion or necessity, many WACs reported improved menstrual cycles once they began service. By 1943 mandatory training sessions included sections on health, with discussions of anatomy, physiology, and the process of menstruation, which may have contributed to this shift. The reception of this information encouraged instructors to include a general hygiene film that addressed menstruation, with the idea of addressing superstitions and teaching women how to manage their bodies.[85] What also improved dramatically was women's willingness to disguise their periods, and carry on without claiming the rights of menstrual debility.

Rules of the Women's Auxiliary Ferrying Squadron specifically forbade "women to fly from one day before the beginning of the menstrual period until two days after it," resulting in a week of lost work.[86] The official reason for this ruling was that women sometimes fainted while piloting during their periods, ending in "fatal results."[87] This proved to be more myth than fact; nonetheless the no-fly rule remained. The only way to enforce it was to police women's periods, or rely on the pilots to self-enforce the policy. A report from the Ferrying Division noted, "without the rather intimate cooperation of the women pilots concerned, it is difficult to understand just how the Group Commander could tell when a WAF was in a period." The report concluded, "there was little anyone could do if a WAF denied being in that condition."[88] Although regulations officially removed them from service, research on the female pilots, such as a study conducted by Raymond S. Holtz entitled "Should Women Fly During the Menstrual Period?" (1941), proved that women were quite capable of piloting during their menses.[89] Like many other physicians he believed that women with abnormally painful periods or other endocrine problems should not fly, but for most the menstrual period was a "normal physiologic process." Having interviewed endurance and racing pilots, he concluded that menstruation did not threaten women's ability to fly. He also concluded that "to regulate or attempt to regulate a woman's flying activities in this connection would be an utter impossibility inasmuch as some women are reluctant to admit their weakness, especially when the admission might result in an interruption of their flying."[90] It was in women's own best interest to represent their bodies in a healthy, perpetually non-menstrual state.

After the WAF merged into the WASP, officials were just as anxious about women's wartime performance and the effects of the menstrual cycle upon their duties. An entire report, entitled *Medical Consideration of WASPS,* examined such concerns for the female pilots. One of the goals was to evaluate the "experiences peculiar to feminine pilots" and how their bodies might adapt to flying.[91] This included everything from the ultimate height and weight for a female pilot to the pragmatics of urinating while in the cockpit. It also addressed the commonly held notion that "[p]hysiologically, [women] were said to be handicapped, that due to menses they would be off flying for so many days that their services would be undependable as ferry pilots and other military assignments in aviation."[92] The medical officer made observations about menstrual effects on concentration, coordination, and reaction time by evaluating how well they read flight instruments and were able to navigate. To his surprise, the findings, as subjective as they were, showed that women reacted better during the ten days surrounding their periods. The study found "the percentage of girls grounded for menstruation to be less than heretofore popularly supposed."[93] Furthermore, "of the 11 fatal accidents, 112 major, non-fatal accidents, there were no demonstrable contributing menstrual factors."[94] The flyers reported that menstrual tension decreased after they flew, and that they generally felt better after flying.[95] In addition, in terms of absenteeism, six woman instructors reported fewer missed days than their male counterparts. Unlike recommendations from the other divisions, the medical report concluded, "menstruation, in properly selected women, is not a handicap to flying or dependable performance of duty" and "there is no relation demonstrated between accidents and menstruation."[96]

Like other women during World War II, the WASP trainees endured courses in "sex morality, personal hygiene and health" which may have helped to account for the low incidence rate of dysmenorrhea, though the pilots were chosen in part due to their overall health. However, as subjects of military orders, they were required not just to receive educational training but routine physicals, including vaginal exams. The exams served a means of regulating their bodies, especially in terms of sexuality. Of the sixty-four gynecological exams conducted on graduating members in 1944, none had venereal disease, unlike comparable samples of male pilots. Advocates interpreted it as a measure of women's health in relation to men's, and a mark of females' dependability since they were not losing work time due to diseases of sexual intercourse.[97] However, medical paternalism characterized the advice given to the pilots, and Lucile Doll Wise, a WASP who flew during World War II, recalled that a physician told one of her friends "if she went into the WASP she might not be able to have children."[98] Jean McCreery, another pilot, reinforced this notion. "I was nineteen years old and unmarried and had *no idea* of what was going on . . . the Doctor told me (this I have never forgotten) that 'Well, you young people are playing at war, but just remember after the war is over, that a Doctor at Patterson Field told you that you would have difficulty having babies!'"[99] McCreery went on to have ten children, disproving the doctor, but the physician's comments left her very concerned about her fertility upon being discharged from the military.

Lucile Doll Wise also recalled studies about WASP menstrual periods. According to her, Dr. Nels Monesrud, the flight surgeon, "issued the order that we were to report the date of our periods to the infirmary." She thought that they wanted to study how periods affected their flying ability. However, "most of us ignored that order, and I have heard that the doctor concluded jokingly that we were a very unusual group of women because we did not menstruate."[100] The unnamed medical officer (most likely Monesrud) who compiled the report *Medical Consideration of WASPS* expressed similar sentiments. The physician devised a survey about menstruation for the trainees to complete. However, the practitioner soon discovered that "they were filling these out and giving replies that they thought would be proper, that would enhance the percentage in favor of women pilots, etc.," thus finding it necessary to gleen information by other means.[101] In some ways, the menstrual re-education campaigns worked too well for the doctor's taste. The pilots exercised careful manipulation of information to enhance their representation and decrease impediments against them, since they were particularly attuned to prejudice. WASP pilot Starley M. Grona summarized it clearly by explaining the reactions that their sex elicited which then overshadowed their identity as pilots. She said, "We feel at all times under a certain nervous strain because of being civilians and women. The well-known belief so common to so many men, that women are inferior to men in fields ordinarily presumed to be exclusively male, works strongly against us, so that we find it necessary to be especially circumspect in all our sections, particularly in flying in order to prove our worth."[102] The pilots had every reason to hide their periods from the gaze of unsympathetic officers.

The pilots also had powerful tools to do so: technologies of menstrual hygiene. Lucile Doll Wise thought that they must have been supplied to her at the base, since she did not go "to a drugstore in Sweetwater [Texas] for this purpose. That would have been inconvenient, since we were restricted to base except on weekends."[103] Personal supplies including hand lotion and toothpaste were often difficult to procure, and Major Margaret Craighill, part of the medical corps and a consultant for women's health and welfare, reported the "entire supply of Kleenex is saved for women."[104] However, pilots and WACs did not just use Kotex, but tampons, which in some cases were actually foisted upon them. The Navy procured Tampax for wartime nurses, as they required less storage space in tightly designed transport ships. Russ Sprague, a mechanical engineer at Tambrands, described the recollections of a friend who served as petty officer on board a naval ship. During the war, Navy ships transported enlisted women and nurses to India and other ports abroad. On one particular trip, so many women flushed sanitary pads through the plumbing that "crewman had to go in with fire axes to break up the jam." Since the sanitary pads put the ship at risk, the captain ordered that only tampons be used for the duration of the trip, forcing women to alter their menstrual hygiene patterns. This was a real boon for the company, and Sprague acknowledged, "once the girls had used tampons they weren't going back to pads."[105]

Tambrands reported skyrocketing orders and had difficulty filling them. Wartime prosperity accounted for women's expendable income, but women workers and women in the military who changed their menstrual practices explained the product's popularity.[106] Sales increased nearly five fold from 1937 to 1943, and by 1945 tampons claimed 10% of the catamenial market with sanitary napkins accounting for the other 90%.[107] Between 1942 and 1943, sales increased nearly 50%.[108] Of those purchasing tampons, about half were married and half single, and women between the ages of 20–24 demonstrated a greater proportion of "exclusive use" than any other age group. These figures indicated that young women invested in concealment, and that they purchased the products to support and maintain their jobs and lifestyles.

Tampax ads quickly incorporated themes of patriotism, production, and duty during the war, and directed the ads to women workers. Ads also reinforced the necessity of reduced absenteeism, and how Tampax would help women stay at work during their periods. One ad suggested that Tampax "Helps them to forget 'Time of the Month,'" which "naturally increases efficiency—on the 'off days.'"[109] In essence, the technologies discouraged even a random thought about menstruation so that women might reclaim their non-menstrual selves and waste no time worrying about their periods. The ads promoted the notion that by using a tampon a woman could still remain productive despite her period. A more pointed ad ran in the *American Journal of Nursing* in 1944 and encouraged nurses to recommend Tampax to patients (Figure 7).[110]

The ad incorporated the new approach of menstrual education and counseling as a platform to promote tampons. The ad cited an article from *Industrial Medicine* to support this contention, and quoted it extensively: "With a better understanding of the purpose and nature of menstruation, and its recognition as physiological rather than as a pathological process, many a woman may be re-educated and come to regard the so-called difficult days as days in which she need not seriously curtail her usual activities."[111] Because the event of menstruation was physiological, it could be treated with better material products to reduce physical discomforts. The ad argued for the use of tampons to reduce absenteeism in the workplace. Since "menstrual inconvenience" proved to be the reason for the majority of worker absenteeism, the ads suggested that a successful "reeducation process" depended on the introduction of improved menstrual hygiene. Tampons relieved "physical distress and emotional uncertainty" related to irritation, odor, and "conspicuous bulging under the slacks or coveralls."[112] Repeated advertisements placed in a variety of sources—*Women's Home Companion* and the *American Journal of Nursing* for example—pushed forward the use and sale of Tampons during the war. Kotex advertisements also capitalized upon women's wartime productivity, and reminded them to remain patriotic and work hard, and not disappoint their soldier boyfriends. Through a passing narrative one Kotex ad remarked, "To think that at five o'clock you were ready to break your date! Because today's eight hours of defense work seemed like eighty!" The ad questioned, "Why should you be a deserter when other girls carry on in comfort every day? You don't need a furlough!"[113] By using menstrual hygiene technologies, women could mask their symptoms "with never a thought of deserting" (Figure 8). The menstrual hygiene products provided a technological solution to the troublesome bleeding body, formerly required to retreat from work and social activities.

The narratives of such wartime advertising reflected the prevailing shift toward menstrual ability, and the success of public health programs and training courses initiated by employers to change women's attitudes about menstruation. The programs increasingly affected women as they became more valued as paid laborers. Undoubtedly, many still clung to the benefits of menstrual debility, and felt compelled to stay at home the first few days of their periods. On the other hand, a regimented workday was unforgiving to the vagaries of their menstrual cycles, and hardly sympathetic to three or four pad changes a day. However, the necessity of female employees, particularly during World War II, compelled manufacturers to encounter and accommodate women's menstruating bodies.

Armed with new psychological theories, employers sought out ways to improve absenteeism and productivity. In order to prevent sick days lost to menstruation, health counselors worked to convince women that they were not sick, and informed them about the best course to attain healthy menstruation. A further result of this menstrual reform was an acceptance of tampons by many working women. Advertisements capitalized upon women's mobility, freedom, and status, and a surge in the usage of tampons correlated with women's entry into employment during World War II. Labor shortages and economic pressures forced women and men to evaluate their misgivings about menstruation, and promote instead menstrual health as one means to bolster patriotism. By shedding menstrual debility, women were encouraged to contribute to national security, freedom, and democracy. Importantly, women used menstrual technologies as tools of empowerment, for both personal gain and political independence.

Notes

1. Frank Walsh, *Sin and Censorship: The Catholic Church and the Motion Picture Industry* (New Haven: Yale University Press, 1996), 84.

2. For a discussion of the rise of psychological experts and "human engineering" see Ellen Herman, *The Romance of American Psychology: Political Culture in the Age of Experts* (Berkeley: University of California Press, 1995); as related to women see Elizabeth Lunbeck, *The Psychiatric Persuasion: Knowledge, Gender, and Power in Modern America* (Princeton: Princeton University Press, 1994); and Joel Pfister and Nancy Schnog, eds., *Inventing the Psychological: Toward a Cultural History of Emotional Life in America* (New Haven: Yale University Press, 1997).

3. For a late nineteenth-century framework about sexuality and health see Helen Lefkowitz Horowitz, "Victoria Woodhull, Anthony Comstock, and Conflict over Sex in the United States in the 1870s," *Journal of American History* (September 2000): 403–34.

4. Nelly Oudshoorn, *Beyond the Natural Body: An Archeology of Sex Hormones* (New York: Routledge, 1994), 15–39. See also Anne Fausto-Sterling, *Sexing the Body: Gender Politics and the Construction of Sexuality* (New York: Basic Books, 2000), on the scientific creation of gender difference.

5. Oudshoorn, *Beyond the Natural Body*, 15–39.

6. Emil Novak, M.D., "Gynecologic Problems of Adolescence," *Journal of the American Medical Association* 117 (December 1941): 1950–53.

7. Novak, "Gynecologic Problems of Adolescence," 1953.

8. Ruth E. Ewing, M.D., "A Study of Dysmenorrhea at the Home Office of the Metropolitan Life Insurance Company," *Journal of Industrial Hygiene* 13 (1931): 244–51.

9. Jill G. Morawski, "Educating the Emotions: Academic Psychology, Textbooks, and the Psychology Industry, 1890–1940," in *Inventing the Psychological*.

10. Morawski, "Educating the Emotions," 219.

11. Lunbeck, *The Psychiatric Persuasion*.

12. Mary Chadwick, *The Psychological Effects of Menstruation* (New York: Nervous and Mental Disease Publishing Company, 1932), 27–28.

13. Today these symptoms would be diagnosed as Pre-Menstrual Syndrome. Chadwick, *The Psychological Effects*, 45–46.

14. Janice Delaney, et al., *The Curse: A Cultural History of Menstruation* (Urbana: University of Illinois Press, 1988, rev. ed.), 74–77.

15. Karen Horney, *Feminine Psychology* (New York: W.W. Norton, 1973, c. 1967), 101.

16. For a discussion of the "open-system" and holistic approach taken by Karen Horney and how it contrasted with Sigmund Freud, see the introduction by Harold Kelman in *Feminine Psychology*. Horney also departed from Freud by challenging the male model of psychoanalysis and its conspicuous absence of the female subject. For a brief biography see Janet Sayers, *Mother of Psychoanalysis: Helene Deutsch, Karen Horney, Anna Freud, Melanie Klein* (New York: W.W. Norton Company, 1991).

17. Delaney, et al., *The Curse*, 78.

18. Horney, *Feminine Psychology*, 99.

19. Horney, *Feminine Psychology*, 13.

20. Thea Goldschmidt, "The Menstrual Taboo and Woman's Psychology," *Journal of Abnormal and Social Psychology* 29 (1934): 218–21.

21. W. W. Tuttle, "Changes in Irritability in Women during the Menstrual Cycle," *Journal of Laboratory and Clinical Medicine* 11 (1925): 60–62.

22. Michael Bálint, "A Contribution to the Psychology of Menstruation," *Psychoanalytic Quarterly* 6 (1937): 346–52.

23. Warren C. Middleton, "Is There a Relation between Kleptomania and Female Periodicity in Neurotic Individuals?" *Psychological Clinic* 22 (1933): 232–47.

24. Orpha Maust Lough, "The Effect of Functional Periodicity on the Learning Process," *Journal of Genetic Psychology* 50 (1937): 307–22.

25. Delaney, et al., *The Curse*, 74–75.

26. Helen Deutsch, *The Psychology of Women: A Psychoanalytic Interpretation, Vol. I* (New York: Grune and Stratton, 1944), 149.

27. Goldschmidt, "The Menstrual Taboo," 220.

28. Goldschmidt, "The Menstrual Taboo," 221. Her use of the word "primitive" reflected her sense that these menstrual mores were out of date, and unnecessary in a modern society.

29. Rachel Lynn Palmer and Sarah K. Greenberg, M.D., *Facts and Frauds in Woman's Hygiene: A Medical Guide Against Misleading Claims and Dangerous Products* (New York: The Vanguard Press, 1936).

30. Palmer and Greenberg, *Facts and Frauds*, 53–54.

31. Palmer and Greenberg, *Facts and Frauds*, 53–54.

32. Palmer and Greenberg, *Facts and Frauds*, 54.

33. Lloyd Arnold and Marie Hagele, "Vaginal Tamponage for Catamenial Sanitary Protection," *Journal of the American Medical Association* 110 (March 1938): 790–92.

34. Harry S. Sackren, "Vaginal Tampons for Menstrual Absorption," *Clinical Medicine and Surgery* 46, no. 8 (August 1939): 329.

35. Mary Barton, "Review of the Sanitary Appliance with a Discussion on Intra-Vaginal Packs," *British Medical Journal* 1 (April 1942): 524–25.

36. A. W. Diddle and L. Boulware, "Vaginal Tampons for Menstrual Hygiene," *Journal of Iowa State Medical Society* 32, no. 6 (June 1942): 256–57.

37. Maurice O. Magid and Jacob Geiger, "The Intravaginal Tampon in Menstrual Hygiene," *Medical Record* 155, no. 9 (May 1942): 320.

38. Madeline J. Thorton, "The Use of Vaginal Tampons for the Absorption of Menstrual Discharges," *American Journal of Obstetrics and Gynecology* 46 (August 1943): 259–65; Irja Elizabeth Widenius, "A Study of Commercially Manufactured Catamenial Tampons," *American Journal of Obstetrics and Gynecology* 48 (October 1944): 510–22. On the introduction of Meds see "Advertising News and Notes," *New York Times*, June 29, 1940, ProQuest Historical Newspapers, 25.

39. "Facts for the Patient Inquiring about the Safety of Internal Menstrual Protection," *Medical Women's Journal* (1944), Ad*Access On-Line Project – #BH0203, John W. Hartman Center for Sales, Advertising & Marketing History, Duke University Rare Book, Manuscript, and Special Collections Library http://scriptorium.lib.duke.edu (accessed April 18, 2006).

40. J. Milton Singleton and Herbert F. Vanorden, "Vaginal Tampons in Menstrual Hygiene," *Western Journal of Surgery, Obstetrics, and Gynecology* (April 1943): 146–49.

41. Singleton and Vanorden, "Vaginal Tampons," 146.

42. Singleton and Vanorden, "Vaginal Tampons," 149.

43. Gilbreth, "Report," 105.

44. Gilbreth, "Report," 105.

45. Gilbreth, "Report," 20.

46. Ewing, "A Study of Dysmenorrhea," 244.

47. Ewing, "A Study of Dysmenorrhea," 245.

48. Ewing, "A Study of Dysmenorrhea," 245–49.

49. For a discussion of women at work during World War II see Nancy Gabin, *Feminism in the Labor Movement: Women and the United Auto Workers, 1935–1975* (Ithaca: Cornell University Press, 1990); Karen Anderson, *Wartime Women: Sex Roles, Family Relations, and the Status of Women during World War II* (Wesport: Greenwood Press, 1981); Alice Kessler-Harris, *Out to Work: A History of Wage-Earning Women in the United States* (New York: Oxford University Press, 1982); Susan M. Hartmann, *The Home Front and Beyond: American Women in the 1940s* (Boston: Twayne Publishers, 1982).

50. A. G. Mezerik, "The Factory Manager Learns the Facts of Life," *Harper's Magazine* 817 (September 1943): 291.

51. Mezerik, "The Factory Manager," 293–97

52. Mezerik, "The Factory Manager," 289–97.

53. Meserik, "The Factory Manager," 294.

54. Meserik, "The Factory Manager," 293.

55. For the oral history of Susan Laughlin, see Sherma Berger Gluck, *Rosie the Riveter Revisited: Women, the War, and Social Change* (Boston: Twayne Publishers, 1987), 241–55.

56. Gluck, *Rosie the Riveter Revisited,* 251. In the *Harper's* article Mezerik details the difficulties of raising the issue of abortion, and how management discriminated against pregnant women by relocating, dismissing, or unfairly treating them.

57. Gabin, *Feminism in the Labor Movement,* 92.

58. Gabin, *Feminism in the Labor Movement,* 83.

59. John and Georgene Seward, "Effect of Menstrual Cycle on Sensitivity to Pain" (1932–1935), Records of the Columbia University Council for Research in the Social Sciences (1925–1968), Series 5, Box 7, No. 69, Columbia University Archives and Columbiana Library.

60. Georgene H. Seward, *Sex and the Social Order* (New York: McGraw-Hill Book Company, Inc., 1946), 249–50. Although the book received strong reviews in the *American Sociological Review* and *Marriage and Family Living,* Margaret Mead was not so kind in her review published in *American Anthropologist* 49, no. 2 (April–June 1947), 309–11.

61. Robert Winch, Book Review, *Sex and the Social Order, American Sociological Review* 11, no. 6 (December 1946): 780–81.

62. Georgene H. Seward, "Psychological Effects of the Menstrual Cycle on Women Workers," *Psychological Bulletin* 41 (1944): 91–102.

63. Seward, "Psychological Effects," 92.

64. Seward, "Psychological Effects," 93. Seward cited Jacobi as evidence to support this contention.

65. Seward, "Psychological Effects," 96.

66. Emily Martin, *The Woman in the Body: A Cultural Analysis of Reproduction* (Boston: Beacon Press, 1992), 97, and chapter 6, "Menstruation, Work and Class."

67. Seward, "Psychological Effects," 95, and also Martin, *The Woman in the Body*, 120.

68. Seward, "Psychological Effects," 95.

69. Seward, "Psychological Effects," 99.

70. J. V. Sheppard, "Health for the Working Girl," *Hygeia* 26 (April 1948): 250–99.

71. Sheppard, "Health for the Working Girl," 250.

72. Sheppard, "Health for the Working Girl," 251.

73. Emily Martin describes the restroom as the private and "complex backstage area in contrast to the school, factory, or firm's public front stage area." This privacy also allowed a degree of freedom and autonomy away from those "stages" where supervisors controlled women's physical movements. See Martin, *The Woman in the Body*, 94.

74. Both *Hygeia* and *Newsweek* reported the importance of good posture upon alleviating dysmenorrhea; see "Cure for Cramps," *Newsweek*, October 4, 1943, 89–90.

75. W. T. Pommerenke, "Cyclic Changes in the Physical and Chemical Properties of Cervical Mucus," *American Journal of Obstetrics and Gynecology* 52 (1946): 1023–31; W. T. Pommerenke P. F. Hahn, W. F. Bale, W. M. Balfour, "Transmission of Radio-Active Iron to the Human Fetus," *American Journal of Physiology* 137, no. 1 (1942): 164–70; W. T. Pommerenke, "Artificial Insemination: Genetic and Legal Implications," *Obstetrics and Gynecology* 9, no. 2 (1957): 189–97; W. T. Pommerenke and P. F. Hahn, "Absorption of Radioactive Sodium Instilled into the Vagina," *American Journal of Obstetrics and Gynecology* 46 (1943): 853–55.

76. "Health for the Working Girl," 299.

77. Gluck, *Rosie the Riveter Revisited*, 241.

78. "Cure for Cramps," *Newsweek*, October 4, 1943, 89–90.

79. "Powers of Persuasion: Posters from World War II," National Archives and Records Administration, Control numbers NWDNS-44-PA-1224 and NWDNS-179-WP-843, http://www.nara.gov (accessed October 20, 2000).

80. Major L. W. McIntosh to Major Everett S. Hughes in Mattie Treadwell, *The Women's Army Corps* (Washington, D.C.: Office of the Chief of Military History, Department of the Army, 1954), 5.

81. Judith A. Bellafaire, "The Women's Army Corps: A Commemoration of World War II Service," Center of Military History 72–15, http://www.history.army.mil /brochures/wac/wac.htm (accessed June 12, 2005); National Museum of the United States Air Force, http://www.wpafb.af.mil/museum/ (accessed June 14, 2005).

82. Margaret Craighill to Surgeon General, U.S. Army, "Health Conditions of Nurses and WACs in MTOUSA," 20 December 1944, HD 333 – Health Conditions of Nurses and WACs, WWII Administrative Records, MTO (Geographic File 1917–1949); Record Group 112, Stack 390/17/8/3, Box 13, 11.

83. Treadwell, *The Women's Army Corps*, 603–604, 613.

84. Treadwell, *The Women's Army Corps*, 398.

85. Treadwell, *The Women's Army Corps*, 612.

86. Treadwell, *The Women's Army Corps*, 614.

87. *Medical Considerations of WASPS* (1945), Woman's Collection, Texas Woman's University Library, 13.

88. Treadwell, *The Women's Army Corps*, 614

89. Raymond S. Holtz, M.D., "Should Women Fly During the Menstrual Period?" *Journal of Aviation Medicine* 12 (1941): 300–303.

90. Holtz, "Should Women Fly?" 303.

91. *Medical Consideration of WASPS*, 1.

92. *Medical Consideration of WASPS*, 9.

93. *Medical Consideration of WASPS*, 11.

94. *Medical Consideration of WASPS*, 12.

95. *Medical Consideration of WASPS*, 6.

96. *Medical Consideration of WASPS*, 13–14.

97. *Medical Consideration of WASPS*, 51.

98. Lucile Doll Wise, correspondence with author, May 26, 2005.

99. Jean T. McCreery, correspondence with author, June 2, 2005.

100. Lucile Doll Wise, correspondence with author, May 26, 2005.

101. *Medical Consideration of WASPS*, 9.

102. Army Air Forces Central Flying Training Command, *History of the WASP Program*, 20 January 1945, 145.

103. Lucile Doll Wise, correspondence with author, May 26, 2005.

104. Margaret Craighill to Surgeon General, U.S. Army, "Health Conditions of Nurses and WACs in MTOUSA," 20 December 1944, HD 333 – Health Conditions of Nurses and WACs, WWII Administrative Records, MTO (Geographic File 1917–1949), Record Group 112, Stack 390/17/8/3, Box 13, 8.

105. Ronald H. Bailey, *Small Wonder*, 36.

106. Dickinson, "Tampons as Menstrual Guards," *Journal of the American Medical Association*, June 16, 1945, 493.

107. Dickinson, "Tampons as Menstrual Guards," 492.

108. Ronald H. Bailey, *Small Wonder*, 37.

109. "War Duties Lead Many Women to Use Tampax," *Parade* (1943), Ad*Access – #BH0187.

110. "Reduction of Female Absenteeism," *American Journal of Nursing* (1944), Ad*Access – #BH0201.

111. Pommerenke, *Industrial Medicine* 12 (1943): 512, from advertisement "Reduction of Female Absenteeism," Ad*Access – #BH0201.

112. "Reduction of Female Absenteeism," *American Journal of Nursing* (1944), Ad*Access – #BH0201.

113. "You're the Fun in his Furlough," *Woman's Home Companion* (1942), Ad*Access – #BH0064.

Chapter 6

Virgin Bodies, Menstrual Hygiene Technologies, and Sex Education

If working women coped with managing their menstrual flow at the office or the factory, teenage girls and young women enrolled in the institutional setting of school struggled in different ways. For adult women after World War II, menstrual hygiene technologies became widely accepted as part of their daily purchases and bodily maintenance routines. In many ways, the products helped to so normalize passing that notions of rest and menstrual debility began to wane and Pre-Menstrual Syndrome took its place as a disability of women after it was named and agreed upon in 1953.[1] However, an unintended consequence of menstrual hygiene technologies was that they landed in the hands of the young because they menstruate, too. Tampons, in particular, were intended for adult women. Yet once a technology is deployed, it takes a great deal of policing to maintain its intended use. In addition, menstrual hygiene products as technologies are not necessarily self-evident in their use nor do users possess intuitive knowledge of them. As such, adolescent females and unmarried young women received much attention and instruction about proper menstrual hygiene habits from the 1930s onward. Part of the concern stemmed from meanings of menstruation, which as a marker of fertility often served the purpose of delineating girls from mature women. Yet there remained the fact that the maturation process that produces a fertile body brings with it a developing sexual persona. What to do with this nascent sexual being with erotic potential is a matter of cultural

115

interpretation, and oftentimes cultural policing. In the United States during most of the twentieth century, Americans have been uncomfortable with the assignment of womanhood to an eight-year-old, for example, even if she is already menstruating. Therefore, menstrual hygiene technologies, especially in terms of passing, forced a confrontation between the cultural denial of sexual maturation and the public pronouncement of menstruation as a consumer event. In essence, access to menstrual hygiene technologies offered teens the possibility of hiding their periods from adults and mothers if they so desired. As one mother lamented, "she got into wearing these tampons without even me knowing. And I see the box underneath the sink and I'm like, 'you went and bought tampons. What, are you wearing tampons up you [your vagina]? You're supposed to wear the pads.'"[2] This loss of parental control, as well as the hiding of the tampons, had the potential to raise further questions about a daughter's sexual development, and ultimately her sexual activity.

A girl's first period symbolizes important physiological changes within her body from child to adult. However, the way that society interprets this biological event reveals much about the definition of childhood and adulthood, and the steps in between. The use of menstrual hygiene technologies by pre-pubescent girls, teenagers, and young women touched a societal nerve at different levels. First, on a very pragmatic level, there were practical issues about how a teen should manage her period while in the institutional setting of school and even college. From gym class and swimming, to getting a bathroom pass, to going to the nurse's office, a private bodily event acquired scrutiny and regimentation within the public domain of schools. Second, the push by companies to promote menstrual hygiene products through health class or in sex education class raised questions about the appropriate knowledge of human development and reproduction for presumably innocent children. Third, the products themselves forced a discussion about adolescent sexuality, as tampons in particular were deemed a threat to a girl's virginity and further vilified as a potential sexual stimulant. At the center of this concern about teenagers' use of technology was also how much personal agency and decision making young women should possess. If technologies provided the pragmatics for a pass, proved efficacious, and empowered teens, then teens were far savvier that many adults wanted to acknowledge. By using technologies, adolescents challenged assumptions about girlhood while asserting new meanings of autonomy.

The encroachment of menstrual hygiene advertisements onto younger audiences challenged constructions of childhood and the myth of their innocence, while helping to create adolescence as a recognized stage of development.[3] Print advertisements, informational brochures, advice columns to mothers, menstrual hygiene filmstrips, and short films were the new venues to reach girls and teenagers.[4] By addressing girls while at school and using mothers as conduits for information, companies hoped to create lifetime loyalty amongst those girls just reaching menarche. The narrative ads and pamphlets continued to address these girls as they progressed through high school and reinforced their purchasing patterns. However, the more liberalizing aspects of menstrual health prompted during the war gave way to an emphasis on menstruation in terms of fertility for future motherhood.[5] Couched in lessons on femininity, the booklets taught girls not only how to pass but how they should act as young ladies. The narratives provided tools for self-diagnosis of bad behavior and how to self-correct a sour attitude concerning menstruation. They also taught girls about the performance of gender; menstrual hygiene campaigns taught young women about societal expectations, constructions of femininity, and the importance of regulating the body through menstrual hygiene. By dislodging menstruation as a symbol of physical maturity, the education campaigns served to strip menstruation as a signifier of adulthood, while reinscribing it in terms of adolescence.

The Theater of School

Schooling of one sort or another proves to be a near universal experience for most modern American children, especially after World War II. Because girls and teens spend so much of their time in the physical and public space of school buildings, there is a high probability their monthly periods will begin there too. For most girls this is less than ideal. Managing a period at home is one thing, with supplies for menstrual hygiene and even a change of underwear nearby if necessary. At school, access to a public restroom or the nurse's office necessitates some finagling. One big problem is how to tote around a pad. Many teens start carrying a purse when they begin menstruating, because there is no other way to hide a sanitary napkin. Cindy, born in 1960, recalled it was at that time she started carrying a purse, "so that you would be able to hide the fact; you wouldn't have it hanging out of your pocket."[6] This method was not failsafe. Toni Anne, who attended high school in the 1980s, remembered that in tenth grade "I had mini-pads in my purse and this kid knocked my pocket book over and the mini-pads came out and he's like 'What do you have foot pads in your pocket book for?'"[7] Though Toni Anne had the foresight to carry around mini-pads in her pocket book, Faye, a generation older, felt she was always caught off-guard. She simply forgot, and complained of numerous accidents because "every time it surprised me."[8] Cindy, Toni-Anne, Faye, and Wendy, born in different eras during the twentieth century, all spoke about adolescence, and how their periods affected their daily patterns of behavior. Though these women came from different generations they still shared the anxiety of publicly managing a menstruous body by covering both their menses and the technology.

Adding to the strain imposed by the cultural milieu of school, adolescent bodies are characteristically unpredictable, which adds to girls' anxieties. Some periods last three days, others eight or ten. Some periods are five weeks apart, and others only three. The chances of getting caught off-guard were pretty good, and most likely happened to girls and young women all the time. Other girls found it entirely objectionable to go to the nurse's office, because it was too embarrassing to ask for a sanitary pad. Additionally, they were apt to receive a hospital pad or something so bulky and untoward that it was not worth the hassle. Wendy, aged forty-seven, humorously described the pads she remembered from the 1970s. "Back then, the pads were like an inch and a half thick. We're talking this was enough if someone was hemorrhaging through their artery." She re-emphasized the point of their bulk and discomfort, and how much blood the pads were meant to hold, "you could lose your arm and put it on and it would hold the blood." Adding to the discomfort were the tabs that she described as having "these really long things on the end, and that's what you would attach to your underwear somehow or to a belt."[9] Wendy chose to avoid the belt, and instead used safety pins, attaching the pads to her underwear that way. Between the pad, the belt, the bulk, and the trip to the school nurse, the environment of school provided different hurdles for young women than those faced by adult women in the workforce.

Besides the physical challenges presented to teens and younger women in school, there were also the politics of educating them about their periods. To understand the incorporation of menstrual hygiene education into school curriculums it is fruitful to revisit the origins of sex education. As early as the 1920s there were two main groups with vested interest in sex education. The first was progressive reformers. Composed mainly of educators, nurses, and physicians, they sought to educate young people in order to prevent encounters with sexually transmitted diseases, namely gonorrhea and syphilis. They believed that by enforcing codes of middle-class morality, discouraging premarital sex, and conducting purity campaigns, youths would receive a dose of fear and postpone sex, instead looking forward to the joy of marital sexual relations.[10] In contrast, religious traditionalists, mainly spearheaded by the Catholic Church, opposed such notions, and worked not only to curtail but also to expunge such discussions from public schools. Topics of sexuality were deemed inappropriate for public conversations, let alone pliant young minds. They believed that discussions about syphilis necessarily led to acknowledgement of prostitution (consistent with the commonly held assumption that prostitutes spread venereal diseases), and this discussion was entirely inappropriate for young minds. It only increased curiosity and encouraged experimentation instead of preventing it.[11]

Early sex education books often took the form of marital advice manuals, morality tales, and physiology literature.[12] The social hygiene movement influenced much of the writing. Social hygienists sought to curtail individuals' sex lives and redirect that sexual energy into marriage. They sought to enlighten the ignorant and reduce the transmission of venereal disease. By World War I, educators and social workers comprised the membership of the American Social Hygiene Association. Besides leading an educational campaign against venereal disease, it also advocated state-mandated blood testing before marriage (with cases of syphilis infection being reported to the state), and the inclusion of civic and social institutions to pressure and presumably shape an individual's opinions about sex through sex education. The campaigns stressed prevention, rather than promotion, of sexual behavior.[13]

However, many parents, educators, and Catholic traditionalists were troubled by sex education. The Catholic response ranged from abhorrence to acceptance. Some felt that sex education was a scheme "to substitute a pagan philosophy . . . for a positive Christian morality." On the contrary, by 1944 Sister Mary Jessine argued that children needed sex education.[14] However, other Catholics disagreed, perceiving sex education to indiscriminately "ladle out" information that had nothing to do with true education.[15] The question, then, was who should teach the children? Although educators from the social hygienist tradition believed that parents should take responsibility for this task, parents often failed. Because schools often pressed forward with some form of sex education, many argued that the clergy should collaborate, to incorporate ideals of moral virtue and chastity into the curriculum. According to Father Kilian J. Hennrich, collaboration was difficult and virtually impossible to accomplish unless the public schools decided to allow religious instruction within their domain.[16] Overall, religious traditionalists believed that in the best world, sex education might be accomplished both at home and at school, with "strong moral habits and thought control" emphasized.[17]

Regardless of the disputes, teachers forged ahead with some sort of education. By 1943, Ruth E. Beach, Supervisor of High School Girls' Physical Education within the Pittsburgh Public Schools, indicated that "sex education should not only be taught in high schools: sex education is being taught in the twenty-eight Pittsburgh junior and senior high schools very successfully."[18] She believed parents had a duty to teach their children about sex, but for the most part they were either unwilling or unqualified to assume that responsibility. Due to what Beach termed parental "neglect," she believed offering sex education in the schools posed the only option for the present crisis in sex hygiene.

Topics Beach discussed with the students included "Physiology of the Sex Organ; How Life Begins; How Life Develops; Marriage Laws."[19] In order to promote discussion and begin with the "least embarrassing" subject, the instructors started with the topic of menstruation. By beginning with menstruation, "the subject would pave the way for a friendly, frank, unemotional discussion of the other topics."[20] Beach reported that this method elicited trust, and even improved mother/daughter relationships. She recalled one student, who "stood up and in a rather defiant tone of voice said, 'Why don't our mothers tell us these things? My mother didn't tell me, and I will never forgive her.'" Beach responded that the student's mother probably did not know how to tell her, but that the student would now know how to talk to her own daughter in the future, thus breaking the cycle of silence. Since her mother gave written permission for her daughter to attend the class, Beach encouraged her to talk to her mother about everything she had learned.[21] Beach reported that the student spoke to her mother with positive results, which Beach interpreted as a sign of success and evidence to continue the progressive reform.

Concurrent with the development of sex education curricula were menstrual hygiene education campaigns, which had an underlying agenda of sales, yet the appearance of a means to resolve some of the tension about sex education and parental omissions of knowledge. Menstrual education campaigns sponsored by corporations followed the creation and promotion of mass-produced sanitary napkins.[22] In 1928, Kimberly-Clark Corporation published one of the first pamphlets directed at pre-pubescent girls entitled "Marjorie May's 12th Birthday."[23] The content and tone of the pamphlet shared similarities with other prescriptive advice books; the difference was that instead of persuading girls to embark on a path of social hygiene, it worked in tandem with advertising to sell the product of sanitary napkins. Additionally, Kimberly-Clark Corporation relayed advice in the form of a short story, rather than a physician's heavy-headed warnings.

Although the story presented a sugarcoated, consumer approach to menstruation, it encouraged mothers to talk to daughters. One of the assumptions was that there was a code of silence about menstruation and for many girls this was true. "Marjorie May's 12th Birthday" made clear that menstrual hygiene could be discussed without mentioning sexuality or sexual development. The story ended with Marjorie's mother remarking that "soon I must tell you the purpose which menstruation has in Nature's creative plan—but not today."[24] She provided an enticement to curiosity, and alluded to the role of motherhood lurking on the horizon. The pamphlet walked the tightrope between teaching about menstruation and triggering thoughts about sex. Sexuality, fertility, and pregnancy remained protected by a seeming conspiracy of silence. The story demonstrated a model that mothers could comfortably and easily mimic, thereby discussing menstruation with their daughters without bringing up the uncomfortable subject of sexuality.

A pamphlet published in 1940 by Kimberly-Clark Corporation entitled "As One Girl to Another" promoted the model of mothers cooperating in the process of introducing menstrual hygiene to their daughters. This brochure also depicted a companionate mother/daughter friendship, in which their relationship shared so much fun that they could talk to each other "as one girl to another."[25] By referring to the mother as a girl it infantilized the mother, reducing her status to that of a young child. Yet it also made the discussion seem like innocent chatter between two school age friends. This assuaged any fears a mother might have in bringing up menstruation as a subject of discussion for now it simply was a "fun" conversation stripped of any reference to sexuality. Even though the booklet was dedicated to mothers and daughters, it used mothers as the vehicle to reach teenagers. Mothers usually requested the brochures from the companies and delivered them to their pubescent daughters.

Susan Brandt's mother employed this recommended approach in 1958. One afternoon, ten-year-old Susan sat in the back seat of her mother's car as they returned home from a shopping trip. She noticed a beautifully wrapped package sitting next to her mother on the front seat, and asked her if it were a present for somebody. Her mother curtly replied that it was not a present at all, but sanitary napkins. Susan then asked what sanitary napkins were for. Her mother responded even more sharply, "for blood." Perplexed, Susan asked another question: "Where does the blood come from?" Angered and having lost all patience, her mother blurted out in frustration, "your bottom!" quickly ending the conversation. Confused, Susan longed to ask more questions, but judging by her mother's response, decided to the contrary. The next day, a small booklet called "Now You Are Ten" appeared on Susan's bed.[26] It explained menarche and periods, and announced to Susan that she was "now a woman." Susan poured over the pages, wondering if she really had become a woman. The booklet raised new anxieties for her. When would she become a woman, and when, exactly, would her period begin? Susan worried from that day forward—for six years until her period began at age sixteen—that something was wrong with her body.[27] The booklet, meant to assuage her fears, promoted others in the end.

Susan's mother most likely responded to her daughter's questions the best way she knew how to, and the way experts encouraged: through menstrual education booklets. Even though Susan's mother obviously used Kotex during her period, this acceptance did not necessarily correlate into comfort discussing menstruation, especially in regard to her pre-pubescent daughter's developing sexuality. Regardless of her mother's discomfort, Susan's body would soon experience menarche, a sign of fertility and an indicator of a developing sexual persona. Susan's mother used a menstrual education guide as a framework to acknowledge—without discussing—her daughter's fertility, while circumventing a conversation about sexuality. Thus, menstrual hygiene education helped mothers to negotiate uncomfortable conversations with their daughters about menstruation and the questions about sex that were sure to follow.[28]

Kimberly-Clark Corporation, the makers of Kotex, provided a self-interested service by developing education materials to be used within health and hygiene or sex education courses. Kimberly-Clark Corporation produced menstrual hygiene education pamphlets, filmstrips, and films to be freely distributed to schools and shown to pre-pubescent girls. The contents described a girl's reproductive physiology, what to expect during menstruation, and how to attend to it with manufactured sanitary napkins. Kimberly-Clark Corporation claimed success with its methods, especially with the 1946 Walt Disney-produced film entitled "The Story of Menstruation." According to the company, it was used for over thirty-five years and viewed by more than 105 million girls.[29] Sex education films usually utilized actors and actresses, but Kimberly-Clark Corporation radically departed from this standard by commissioning Walt Disney Productions to animate "The Story of Menstruation."[30] This ten-minute film, provided free by the company, was widely distributed throughout schools, Parent Teacher Associations, YWCAs, and nurses' hospitals.[31] In fact, it received the famous "Good Housekeeping Seal of Approval," further bolstering its reputation. In addition, Encyclopedia Britannica Films adapted a filmstrip version of the ten-minute movie, accompanied by a teacher script to narrate with the frames.

According to a film reviewer writing for the *Journal of the American Medical Association*, the success of the film came from a need to present "material related to the reproductive processes without creating an atmosphere of tension, not to say fear and disgust."[32] The film offered a means for school board members to acquiesce to the teaching of human reproduction without falling into the trap of prurience. One school board member lamented, "I wish it were possible to present sex to girls in such a way that they would not thereafter associate the whole subject with old bewhiskered doctors threatening venereal disease."[33] The reviewer writing for *JAMA* claimed, "this film is the answer to the problem." The animation, information, and narration combined to present menstruation with "an air of good cheer."[34] Of course, it was not merely menstruation and reproductive physiology being taught, but how to teach adolescents to be feminine teenagers, manage menstruation, and learn the tools and techniques of passing with menstrual hygiene products.

The film depicted the process of menstruation, and began by introducing "growth hormones," which sent messages to the pituitary gland, and "maturing hormones," which signaled the ovaries to "turn on." Drawings displayed the egg traveling through the fallopian tubes, ready to lodge within the uterus. The film flirted with fertility with a reference to pregnancy: "if the egg becomes fertilized, which happens when a woman is going to have a child, the egg will stay within the uterus."[35] The film avoided mention of how a woman became pregnant, but alluded to a girl's pre-determined role as mother. For many girls this was enough information, yet it left others perplexed. The narration continued that since there was "no use for the potential nourishment in the built-up lining of the uterus" it "passes from the body" and was called menstruation.[36] It provided no indication of what body part this "potential nourishment" might pass through, nor what color it would be or what to expect (the film depicts menstrual blood as gray). For girls with absolutely no idea about puberty, the film was a significant introduction to human development, but also remained so vague as to raise very basic questions about reproduction and sexuality. The narration asserted that menstruation was a "normal and natural part of nature's eternal plan for passing on the gift of life," affirmed by the representation of a woman in a wedding dress, followed consecutively by an image of her cooing over a baby in a bassinet.[37]

Besides reinforcing heteronormative social structures, the filmstrip advised girls how to manage menstruation. The protagonist, a girl with a large head and puny body much like the Tinkerbell character from Walt Disney's "Peter Pan," participated in rituals of menstrual health. The filmstrip showed her keeping clean by taking warm showers, breathing better through good posture, and avoiding extreme physical exertion (like picking up a large chair with one hand to vacuum underneath it) during her menses. By following these simple steps the film assured a girl "once you stop feeling sorry for yourself and accept menstruation as routine, you'll find it easier to keep smiling and even-tempered."[38] Kotex for adolescents helped to create the model of a happy, well-adjusted teenager, and not an adult woman. Bleeding meant an introduction to adulthood, not participation in it.

By using animation, Kimberly-Clark Corporation succeeded in infantilizing menstruation as well as presenting it as mere entertainment, thus minimizing stereotypes of debility. The education campaigns abandoned laws of bed rest, and viewed menstruation as effortless if girls assumed a quiet demeanor while reigning in outbursts of emotion. The film served to dislodge menstruation from sexuality by redefining menstrual meanings in terms of hygiene and the regulation of the post-pubescent body. The film alluded to a growing girl's biologically determined role as a child bearer, but also severed links between meanings of menstruation, sexual maturity, and sexual desire, focusing instead on hygiene. Thus, the campaigns helped to teach girls about the importance of containing their sexually mature, menstruating bodies by understanding their bodies in terms of asexual adolescence.

Menarche and Sexuality

During World War II and afterward, there was a growing concern about out-of-control teenagers, teen sexuality run amuck, and heretofore-unknown freedoms both granted to and usurped by teens.[39] Because parents—usually mothers—were occupied with wartime industrial jobs and spent less time looking after the children, a small percentage of young teens took advantage of the freedoms afforded to them, and challenged social expectations. The Victory Girls, better know as V-Girls, earned the reputation of being sexually fast and free, and were blamed for the transmission of venereal diseases to enlisted men in rates higher than those of prostitutes.[40] The freewheeling sexuality of girls as young as thirteen prompted concern about young women's proper behavior and the importance of restraining them. Teenaged girls signified burgeoning sexuality and eroticism, and in an American society afraid of illegitimate pregnancy and teenage motherhood, advice literature worked to curtail curiosity about sexuality and uphold the importance of virginity.[41] Many believed that appropriate training could provide the antidote to counteract this behavior in future generations, and women's consumptive power was one means to do so. Advertisements published in popular magazines such as *Ladies' Home Journal, Redbook, Good Housekeeping,* and *Woman's Home Companion* targeted both mothers and daughters as readers. According to the narrative, a teenager, having read her mother's magazine subscriptions, desired the social ease and confidence portrayed in the advertisements. *Good Housekeeping* printed monthly advice columns that reinforced gender roles, such as "It's Your Date," "Brides and Brides to Be," and "Man Talk," further reifying women as wives and helpmates. [42] Advertisements selling blenders, Pond's Cold Cream, Veto deodorant, and S.O.S. scouring pads also buttressed the idea of the feminine, beautiful, white, suburban housewife, producing idealized images of well-adjusted young women in their day-to-day activities, functioning normally with the help of consumer products, including sanitary napkins.

But menstrual hygiene advertising for adolescents shouldered important meanings about psychological development. Since menarche marked the beginning of sexual development, nurses, educators, and parents worked hard to forge together menstruation with menstrual hygiene as the dominant means to understand this bodily process. Menstrual education, coupled with widespread print advertisement campaigns, reinforced this meaning even further. If a mother slipped from her parental duties, now was the time to reestablish authority over her daughter. By influencing her daughter's first experience of menstruation, she could fulfill her successful role as mother within American society. Scientific motherhood reared its heavy hand in attempting to convince mothers that the experts knew more than they did in this regard. In essence, it continued the trajectory of scientific menstruation, now in the form of advice to mothers about how to give advice to daughters. Ads encouraged a mother's participation not only in her daughter's first period, but also in the promotion of menstrual hygiene products. Advice literature calmed mothers by reassuring that "[n]o mother need be shocked to discover that her daughter has not waited for her explanation of the process of menstruation, but has already a fund of information." [43] The article advised mothers not to "condemn" this, but to understand their daughters' curiosity "as natural and normal as the phenomenon of menstruation itself." [44] It was a mother's role now to gently correct "false ideas" and provide accurate information to her daughter through material provided by Kimberly-Clark Corporation. [45] If mothers were unwilling or unable to do this, Kimberly-Clark Corporation encouraged them to renounce responsibility for educating their daughters about menstruation.

This scenario was not so far-fetched. Lillian, born in 1931 and from the Bronx, New York, remembered learning about Kotex from her older sister. Her mother told her sister and her nothing, so her sister took it upon herself to find out. She read the Kotex ads, and followed the directions to receive a booklet by sending Kimberly-Clark ten cents. It arrived in the mail soon thereafter, and when Lillian's mother found out, she tore it up in front of the girls. Lillian reiterated, "I still can't believe she was upset enough to tear it up." Lillian referred to her mother's attitude as "a closed door" and believed that she must have thought that the reading materials "just gives them ideas," about sex presumably. She did however use Kotex and Modess for her periods, and remembers feeling horrible at least one day a month due to severe cramps. Around the age of twenty, she remembered self-administering "blackberry brandy and a heating pad" to help start the flow. She also did not like purchasing pads because "it was embarrassing to go to the drugstore," and in retrospect, she pondered how "stupid" it was. She wondered aloud if her cramps were related to the psychological stigma of purchasing products understood to be shameful.[46]

With anecdotes such as these, it is no wonder that physicians and psychologists informed mothers "it is every mother's profound duty to give her daughter the full facts about menstruation and menstrual hygiene."[47] Dr. Marjory Nelson, a faculty member and college physician at Barnard College from 1948 to 1971, believed that a mother needed to assess her own knowledge and evaluate her own attitudes because "it is her duty first to check her own beliefs and practices, so as to make sure her information is up to date." Ultimately, "since the girl's menstrual health may depend on it," a mother held the responsibility "to present the physical facts in a healthy, positive way."[48] Nelson suggested that if a mother had not spoken to her daughter beforehand, then at the first signs of maturation she could initiate a conversation. The talk might begin by telling her that "the cycle that will make it possible for her to have babies is soon to begin."[49] The article suggested that discussing the possibility of motherhood would help women describe the meaning of menstruation. Of course, this vague reference to pregnancy sometimes had the opposite effect, with girls believing that they could become pregnant by merely kissing a boy.

Nelson warned that mothers who were ignorant about their own physiology ran the risk of perpetuating menstrual stereotypes to their daughters. She excoriated these mothers, saying "[t]ime and again it becomes apparent that the most important fact in establishing a normal menstrual cycle is the attitude of the girl's mother."[50] She cautioned that "[i]n this modern day mother is seriously to blame if she allows her deficiencies to warp her daughter's life."[51] Menstrual attitudes extended to the entire sexual persona that the girl was to become. That a mother's inadequacies could "warp" her daughter's life implied not only negative attitudes toward cramps and bloating, but also the very approach a young woman may take concerning socialization and heterosexual relationships.

Elizabeth Woodward harbored equally accusatory opinions about mothers. The author of a nationally syndicated parenting advice column, she reprimanded mothers' inadequacies and announced: "Maybe you're the one who has filled her with fear and superstition! You passed on to her what information you had. You dug into your own experience . . . and shared with her some of the bogey ideas you picked up when you were a teen-ager."[52] Woodward did not identify these "bogey" ideas, such as the menstrual "sicktime," menstrual "congestion," bearing the "curse" of humanity, being unable to wash one's hair, and avoiding exercise or social events when necessary. Woodward lamented, "[n]o wonder your daughter may be afraid to talk things over with you." She did not want to learn about the negative aspects of the "curse" or her "monthlies."[53]

In her article, Woodward begged mothers "if *you* can't tell her what she wants to know adequately, sanely, unemotionally, scientifically . . . why not choose the source of her information?"[54] She bought into and promoted the corporate version of menstrual hygiene. Disney and Kimberly-Clark Corporation at this early date had skillfully merged product placement into the classroom and other media venues such as women's magazines. Woodward sang the praises of "The Story of Menstruation" as the cornerstone of a menstrual hygiene education program, calling it a "common-sense and entertaining solution to a girl's problem of living with (and in spite of) menstruation."[55] That elements of menstruation could be entertaining marked a clear departure from its solely medicalized understanding, yet still left much to be desired in terms of imbuing a biocultural event with substantive meaning. Coupled with the reviews from *JAMA*, the advice columns directed at mothers encouraged them to consider purchase of menstrual hygiene products as a means to deal with issues of fertility and adolescence.

Menstrual hygiene advertisements aimed at teenagers helped to reinforce standards of feminine behavior, and teach girls that they could possess confidence by using Kotex to conceal menstrual blood, thereby masking their periods from others.[56] One particular series of advertisements directed at teenaged girls was called "Are you in the know?"[57] It presented potentially awkward social situations and then asked, in the form of multiple-choice questions, which answer would be the most appropriate for the situation. The ad continued by providing the rationale for the correct answer. For instance, one ad presented a teenage girl's dilemma in ordering an entree while on a date at a French restaurant. The ad warned, "better not stab at just *any*thing listed. It might turn out to be snails' brains—when you were drooling for duck!" The ad discouraged her from ordering, even if she understood the menu and wanted to impress her date by speaking French and ordering on her own. Instead, the ad insisted, "let him pollyvoo for you." This reinforced her subordinate role to her date. Besides letting him speak for her, the ad assumed that the readers would not be able to interpret the French spelling of *parlez vous*, replacing it with the phonetic "pollyvoo." The relation to sanitary napkins hinged upon a universal understanding of Kotex as offering confidence: "In any language, *confidence* (on certain days) means Kotex."[58] The ad reinforced the notion that confidence stemmed from the authoritative decision making of a man, because men know best. The ad prompted a reader to associate the confidence of a male protectorate with that of using Kotex sanitary napkin technology, which also offered protection from embarrassment and ensured appropriate behavior. Thus the ads previewed up-coming adult roles and prescribed a scenario in which a young woman's pass was secure.

The ads also encouraged the feminine traits of cooperation and friendliness. One ad posed the question: "When a gal's not 'one of the gang' – why? [A] She's shy [B] She's a glow worm [C] She's a vacuum cleaner." The ad went on to explain "[s]hyness is only one reason why a cutie's out of the fun. She may be a glow worm (self-centered). Or a vacuum cleaner (picks up all the dirt). Any answer above can be right. The cure. More interests! Learn to get along with others. Good way's to join a dramatic club. Be a good trouper, *whatever* the day—for Kotex is made to stay soft while you wear it."[59] Directing attention inward, being selfish and generally diffident were all traits contrary to cooperation—but they were also the traits of a developing teenager. The solution for such an outcast was for her to join a group or club that fostered cooperation, and be a good sport. This encouraged deference and team play. Of course using Kotex would help her be a resilient "trouper" in the face of discomfort, cramps, and chaffing. The ad made clear that she had no reason to be cranky since Kotex was soft. Furthermore she could not use menstruation as an excuse to avoid group participation for it was no longer a legitimate excuse. She only had herself to blame, because Kotex supposedly helped her to keep her social calendar events because it hid the signs of menstruation. The ad lauded her ability to squelch her feelings and place the greater good before her own needs, thus proving her worth as a productive member of the group, as a young woman, and subsequently as a member of American society.

Through the ad campaigns and the materials distributed by Kimberly-Clark Corporation, teens looked toward the experts for personal advice. One troubled teen, worried that her period might have adverse effects on her social life, wrote to the nurses at Kimberly-Clark Corporation's education department. She asked, "What explanation shall I give a boy if he wants me to swim or dance and I don't feel like doing so? He may not understand if he has seen me doing other things that day."[60] Clearly, she expressed confusion about the mixed messages being sent about menstruation. On one hand, she was active and functional at school, seemingly able and normal. Yet, her period rendered her "sick" and required her to refrain from strenuous activities. How was she supposed to act? Her question revealed the fear of her pass being exposed and unveiled. It was difficult to exhibit a healthy attitude about menstruation and practice restricted activity at the same time. Her confusion exemplified her desire to pass but also her desire to adhere to gendered behavior codes.

The advertisements also reflected the creation of specifically girl teen culture, and how products might be part of that identity. Though companies sold the products, they also sold the affluent teen ideal, obtainable by wearing menstrual hygiene technologies. Popular, pretty, white, and fun loving, the ideal girl and the real girl reconstituted one another through behavior, preferences, and purchases.

Teenagers and Tampons

Teenagers had a more tenuous association with tampons than sanitary pads. The insertion of a long, slender object into the vagina of a young girl raised anxiety about prematurely breaking the hymen, thereby violating her virginity. Through word of mouth, cultural fears spread to limit teenagers' purchases of tampons. Advertisements, articles in *Consumer Reports*, and studies in *JAMA* worked to dispel this trend, but myths continued to circulate. Many women and girls shared this vernacular knowledge about tampons, their safety, and their propriety.[61]

However, expectations about young women and their bodies were changing, so that tampons were a contested technology. Wartime women's work, activities, and able-bodied attitudes trickled down to adolescent girls. They helped to challenge long held beliefs about limited gym class exercise, especially the ban on swimming during menses. Even though the gym instructors were supposedly some of the most updated individuals concerning the latest medical perceptions of menstruation, many still clung to conservative views during the 1940s.[62] The vestiges of Dr. William Clarke remained, and physicians continued to warn against strenuous exercise because they projected that the vital energy required to menstruate would be redirected to muscle tissue. They prescribed a trip to the nurse's office, or curtailed gym exercises. Swimming proved controversial because cold chills of any kind were to be avoided, and women were warned that "care about keeping the feet dry and wearing adequate clothing in bad weather" would help to prevent "congestion" which hindered the flow. Advice columns cautioned against swimming in particular because "a sudden chill is apt to stop the flow and that may cause pain and discomfort."[63] The vernacular knowledge concerning menses and cold chills prohibited many women and girls from swimming during their periods. On a pragmatic level, a sanitary napkin miserably failed in a swimming pool, for it immediately absorbed water and became a soggy mess. Additionally, the fear of blood contamination in the shared environment of the pool stemmed from concerns over hygiene.

Grace Thwing, a boarding school physical education instructor at George School, Pennsylvania, wrote a 1943 article concerning "Swimming During the Menstrual Period" and took a different approach.[64] Once she started stocking tampons in the supply closet, she noticed students' increased usage of them. Additionally, "girls who used them at home" brought "the question of internal tampons" to her attention. In fact, her students forced her to question her own misgivings. They asked, "Why can't girls who use tampons swim in the pool at school?" She had no good answer. The pressure from students and the swim team persisted since they were forbidden to compete at swim meets during their menses. She rationalized her approval of the tampons because the students "were used to exercise, the water and room were warm, and the use of tampons would prevent any possible contamination of the water." Each girl needed parental permission to use tampons while swimming, which indicated a concern on her part that some parents might disapprove of their use. Thwing noted that within her twenty-seven years of teaching (1915–1943), she sensed "a definite change in attitude toward this function and activities of girls during their periods." She continued, "[t]he modern attitude seems to be trying to get rid of the old taboos and unnecessary restrictions, and to encourage girls to live normally during their periods as at other times."[65] Importantly, menstrual hygiene technologies were an integral part of a teen's "normal" identity.

However, one gym instructor's approval did not amount to whole-hearted acceptance. The distrust of adolescents and adult sexuality via the tampon emerged to control and limit behavior. It points toward a general trend, defined by historian Elaine Tyler May as the "troublesome potential of female eroticism."[66] The problem was as much about what this potential sexuality would do to a man, as how women would wield it. In an interview, Faye recalled that in the late 1950s her home economics sewing teacher told the girls if they ever had to sit on a man's lap, to make sure to put down a newspaper first.[67] The newspaper was a protective barrier between the young women's chastity and the threat of a "dirty old man." The troublesome potential of a young woman's eroticism was what it might do to men; the woman's comportment was responsible, which also accounted for the push to channel women into marriage, to safely contain their sexuality.

The tampon threatened to secretly release this sexuality. Critics of the tampon warned of the slippery slope to masturbation—that if one gave approval for the use of tampons for menstrual hygiene, one might condone the very sin of masturbation. This was a serious issue because penetration—in this case in the form of a tampon—was understood as a way for women to experience sexual pleasure without a man, which amounted to masturbation. According to a Catholic theologian during the 1930s, masturbation was a "moral aberration" and "a person who sets [sex] in motion separately, robs it of its entire meaning, acts against nature, and reverses the order established by God." At root it is "a sin against the absolute, primary law of nature, and is a radical interference with the natural order."[68] Tampons pointed to the Church's desire to interpret heterosexual intercourse as solely procreative, not as an independent, leisure time activity. For the theologian, the tampon controversy was a religious one, for he could never really be certain if a woman was indulging in licentious behavior or not with "invisible protection." Therefore, tampons threatened to cut short a girl's childhood, quickly moving her into the realm of adulthood. Undoubtedly, for young women who had not masturbated or spent much time exploring their labia, learning how to insert a tampon amongst the skin's flaps and folds could be traumatic and difficult, and an introduction to a whole new awareness—and even sexual awareness—about the body. Faye received a similar message, though not so explicitly stated. Her college roommate at Cornell University in 1966 had a physician mother who warned her against tampons because they were not safe, with the implication being they were a cause of sexual arousal. For Faye, it was the first time it occurred to her not to use tampons.

Concern also stemmed from the phallic-like tampon threatening a young girl's virginity. Many believed that a tampon could damage an intact hymen—the physical evidence of sexual purity—forever tarnishing the reputation of an unsuspecting girl. Her claims of chastity might not hold up without evidence, and her trustworthiness would never really be certain. Therefore, tampons should be avoided and condemned to hedge the future reprimands of a duped husband. Mary Barton, a medical practitioner with a Bachelor of Medicine practicing in England, confirmed the problem of a falsely lost virginity in "Review of the Sanitary Appliance with a Discussion on Intra Vaginal Packs." She explained "it is difficult for virgins to use any internal pad without causing partial or total rupture of the hymen with regular use." She indicated that the "rupture has only forensic significance" but that "it is worth considering from the individual standpoint."[69] Protecting one's virginity was a serious matter, for as Alfred Kinsey documented in his famous reports on Americans' sexual behaviors, almost half of the men surveyed wanted to marry a virgin.[70] With this sort of pressure, it is no wonder that the tampon gained the reputation of threatening a woman's chastity.

Some physicians seemed perplexed by this turn of events. As late as the 1940s, Dr. Robert Dickinson noted, "antagonism to tampons presents a curious reversal on the part of gynecologists." Dickinson, an obstetrician and gynecologist at Brooklyn Hospital, edited obstetrics text books, authored and illustrated genre atlas handbooks on sex and birthing, served as secretary of the National Committee on Maternal Health, 1923–1937, and later held a position as honorary chairman of that same group. He used his notoriety to speak about many topics related to sex and sexuality, and therefore the tampon became the focus of a few articles. He claimed, "the tampon used to pay the office rent. A tampon saturated with glycerin or ichthammol supplemented the old iodine swab to the raw cervix twice a week, month after month" for vaginal infections and discharge.[71] Dickinson challenged the unwarranted "antagonism" and instead touted the merits of the tampon, its effectiveness, and its service to improved hygiene. He confronted the issue of masturbation and defended tampons, authoritatively stating "the sensory nerve fibers in the portion of the vagina in which [the tampon] lies are largely non-existent. The erotic stimulus of the stationary internal tampon should be, therefore, negligible." Not surprisingly, he made no mention about asking women their opinions on the matter.

Though he discounted the notion that tampons encouraged sinful behavior, he perpetuated a different accusation. Because a pad must be forced between the legs into "a cleft so narrow there is not room for it," it necessarily "produces some degree of triple-surface rubbing" while a woman walks and "every jounce when sitting produces upward pressing."[72] With so much external stimulation, Dickinson claimed that sanitary pads, not tampons, were the culprits for clitoral stimulation. He stated: "Any external menstrual guard, in addition to applying some degree of heat within a confined space, is responsible for the rhythmic play of pressure against surfaces uniquely alert to erotic feeling."[73] Besides the alleged erotic feeling, the sanitary pads also increased the chance for urinary tract infections, vaginal infections, and general odor. Tampons could not be held responsible for any of these liabilities.

Consumer Reports addressed the vernacular knowledge of tampons that linked them to sexual stimulation and sullied virginity, and emphatically answered a series of questions in its 1949 report on "Sanitary Pads and Tampons." To each of the following questions, 1) "Are they likely to result in injury to the unbroken hymen?" 2) "Are they likely to suggest or encourage masturbation?" 3) "Won't tampons stop or dam up the natural menstrual flow?" 4) "Won't the tampon get lost?," the answer continued be "no."[74] That *Consumer Reports* explicitly listed the questions indicates that vernacular knowledge strongly influenced young women's decisions about trying and using tampons.

In response to the vernacular knowledge circulating about tampons, Dr. Robert Dickinson came to their support once again. He reassured a suspicious audience that the hymen could not be injured or nicked by a tampon. He spent much effort in his 1945 *JAMA* article explaining the flexible properties of the hymen. With "douching, gentle stretching or good lubrication of the tampon tip" the hymen would become pliable and tolerant "without any nick or damage" as a result.[75] In fact, he proposed that a "good educator" for adolescent girls was "the douche," which would not only stretch the vaginal walls for a tampon, but also presumably condition the vagina for more enjoyable sexual penetration in the future.

Accompanying his text were schematic drawings that indicated the circumference of a tampon compared to a douche nozzle, demonstrating each was much smaller than the vaginal opening. He also compared the "caliber of distended hymen in virginal, married and parous women, in relation to tampon and douche tube diameters."[76] However, the prominent standard by which to compare each was the average size phallus, indicated in bold outline. Although he lamented that there was little published on "diameters and dilatability of the hymen," after digitally examining hymens of virgins and childless married women, he concluded, "the tampon has a caliber that does not impair standard anatomic [sic] virginity."[77]

Other evidence concerning the medical value of tampons was found in physicians' advice columns published in magazines such as *Parents* and *Hygeia*. Here, doctors responded to many queries about the legitimacy of the tampon.

One reader asked, "[w]hat is the present medical view of the use of internal sanitary napkins? Those of us in our college who use them find them convenient and comfortable, but some of the other girls tell rumors of harm from their use. Is there some danger attached to their use?"[78] The physician responded that there was no danger associated with tampons. If the reader liked them, then she should use them. Individual experience could be "considered a safe criterion" for tampon use. That the girls asked about their "harm" indicates an assumption about their danger. An article entitled "What a Mother Should Tell Her Daughter," appearing in *Parents Magazine* in 1950, also raised the issue of the tampon. The article cautioned middle-class mothers against perpetuating myths and fears concerning menstruation and tampon use. This ignorance included the belief that tampons caused cancer, that all exercise should cease during menstruation, and that tampons may get lost within the vagina or uterus, never to be recovered again.

Companies also worked to alleviate this suspicion, and Tampax advertisements alluded to this misperception. An ad entitled "Miss . . . or Mrs.?" piqued the attention of both married women and, presumably, unmarried virgins.[79] The ad implied that the product was meant for both sets of women, reassuring them that their upstanding reputations would remain intact. An ad for Meds tampons, manufactured by Personal Products Company, part of Johnson & Johnson, solicited interest by asking, "Can Single Girls Wear Tampons?" Their answer was an emphatic "yes."[80]

Tampax advertisements took a soft-peddled approach to tackle politely this potentially indecorous subject. One ad began by asking, "Has anyone ever told you that you cannot feel the Tampax while wearing it?"[81] Seeking to quell concerns about the impropriety of tampons, the ad's authoritative tone made clear that the lack of sensation was absolute. Reassuring an audience that the fingers would not provide accidental stimulation, the ad continued, "[y]our hands need not touch the Tampax while inserting it." It concluded that because "so dainty are the patented applicators that contain the absorbent cotton," a young woman would be protected from any unspeakable transgression she might commit by inserting a tampon. The language implied that a tampon was comparable to a cotton swab—innocuous, scientific, and medicinal—not at all worthy of such hype and exaggerated fear.[82] The ads worked to set aside any misgivings about tampons, and assuaged a nervous audience about preserving chastity while using them.

Tampax further assured teenagers, "Of course you can go swimming with Tampax. Why envy others at that certain time of the month? You can wear Tampax in the water on sanitary-protection days and no one will be the wiser!"[83] Teenagers took on the trickster role in this advertisement. Through deception, Tampax hid menstruation and made others believe that a woman was not disabled by her period. Her body had freedom of movement, the ability to swim, and was released from the menstrual stereotypes of sickness and debility and could pass as normal. On a pragmatic level, the technology offered an immediate physical freedom during menstruation previously unavailable by using sanitary napkins. However, the problem of swimming with tampons during menses is long lived. Many swimmers still have concerns about water pressure pushing a tampon into the vaginal canal. Here, a different problem arises; that of the tampon getting wedged or lodged into place and therefore becoming difficult to remove.

This was not an entirely unreasonable fear. When young women experimented with the technology, the results were not always successful. Rose, aged 70, started nursing school in the 1950s and was on a rotation at the mental hospital when she first tried them. "I had a friend standing outside the toilet telling me what to do in order to insert the tampon. Unfortunately, I must have done something wrong—the tampon came out but the cardboard stayed in." She continued, "[n]ow we had a problem, and we had to hurry up because we had class. I couldn't get it out and I didn't want to run to the emergency room so I laid down on the bed and my friend had tweezers and got it out."[84] Rose's trouble with using the tampon echoed some experts' warnings about women's inability to manage such a technology. However, this did not stop Rose from trying again.

This story only justified another interviewee's distrust of tampons. Rebecca Moore, my student researcher who conducted some interviews with family friends in New York, shared Rose's story with Beverly, born in 1958, and Cindy, born in 1960. They discussed the incident after they heard it.

Beverly: Oh my god! OWWWW! How can you put that [in] and the cardboard stay up?

Moore: I don't know.

Beverly: No good.

Moore: She must have done something wrong.

Cindy: Pulled it right out and left the cardboard up there.

Beverly: Oh my god! But it's not cardboard anymore. The ones I see are plastic . . .

Beverly: [My daughter] always wants me to buy her the ones that are plastic.

Cindy: There's one you use [with] your finger.

Beverly: Oh boy! No way![85]

The women's conversation reveals empathy about the frustrations of inserting a tampon with little knowledge about how to do so. It also displays the discomfort of inserting a foreign object into the vagina, the reticence about even uttering the word *vagina*, as well as the general feeling there is just something not right about tampons.

An influential and celebrated work that captures the anxiety about first periods and the use of menstrual hygiene is the book *Are You There God? It's Me, Margaret* (1970) by Judy Blume, intended for an audience of adolescent readers. Written within the context of the women's rights movement and the near passage of the Equal Rights Amendment, the book openly and honestly portrays the hopes of young Margaret to experience her first period. She is slow to get it, and prays for its fast delivery to help her fit in with the other girls. The book still has currency, as my local library had to special order it from another because only three of the sixteen books accessioned still remained. I dutifully read it for a book report in seventh grade, and for my assignment created a collage representing the plot, characters, and themes from the book. Importantly, I selectively omitted images of Kotex and Tampax, which seemed to unveil both her and me. However, negotiating these technologies of identity represented some of the most salient parts of the whole book. How Margaret encounters her Jewish faith as well as her burgeoning female body remained an issue then and now, and the book's popularity speaks to the deep need that young women and girls have to be validated in their new bodies.

Whether or not a young woman was inserting a tampon for the first time, or experiencing menarche, there was and continues to be great concern about her period and how she manages it. The concern is manifest in the relationship between menstrual hygiene technologies and adolescents. It is apparent in the narrative, prescriptive literature, and in education booklets reminding girls to "stay neat and sweet," clearly a hope for an idealized daughter who would develop into a feminine wife and mother (Figure 9).[86] Teaching girls about their period, and in essence their burgeoning womanhood, emerged in a variety of forms at different times. In some families, a young Jewish girl was slapped across the face to ward off evil or mark the transition to the liminal phase between childhood and adulthood.[87] During the 1920s, my grandmother Martha Vostral was commanded "off floor" in gym class, in order to protect her developing body from the expenditure of energy required during exercises. While some girls dutifully followed such cultural practices, others interpreted the dictates quite differently. During the late 1950s when the nuns told Pat she was "paying for the sins of Eve" when her period began (presumably understood by most people as a bad thing), she instead thought she had been chosen by God, and said her prayers with renewed vigor.[88] And, in a final example of re-imagining dictates of menstrual incapacity for young women, one of my colleagues, Sally, who attended Tufts University in the early 1960s, explained that she was allowed three excused absences from gym class each month for her period. Instead of using them during menstruation, she shifted her excused absence days to correlate with up-coming exams or term papers to garner more study time, and instead attended gym class during her period.[89] And, she wore hidden artifacts of menstrual hygiene to facilitate her pass and her practice of time management.

In some cases, young women manipulated the rules about menstruation to serve their own ends. In other cases, adults' attitudes profoundly influenced the formation of ideas about menstruation. In addition, the rhetoric provided by ads and corporate-sponsored education material shaped menstrual experiences. At stake was appropriating adolescent bodies to cultivate lifelong consumers. The unspoken anxiety that society expressed concerning girls' sexual development manifested itself in attention to menstrual hygiene—in the advertisements, mother/daughter advice columns, and menstrual education materials. This anxiety also emerged in folklore about tampons, which also reflected societal concerns about teenagers' expanded and ever-growing physical freedoms after World War II. The use of menstrual technologies served as a passage only to adolescence and not to mature adulthood, and the technologies served as a compromise, for it was easier to discuss the artifacts of menstrual hygiene rather than sex in many sex education classes. Ironically, the technologies helped teenagers pass as happy-go-lucky girls, and hedge their representation as sexualized adolescents. Ads even declared that by using Tampax, a menstruating woman could be "as free as though [she] were ten years old."[90] A non-menstruating ten-year-old female was idealized as the preferred physical state, because she had not acquired the burdens of womanhood, including menstruation. And, menstrual hygiene technologies could help all women pass as such.

Notes

1. Characterized by symptoms recurring at monthly intervals, PMS incorporated conditions such as fatigue, weight gain, edema, acne, depression, migraine, and breast swelling, to name just a few. Researchers studied incidents of epileptic seizures, "transient nymphomania," crimes of violence, and emotional instability, tracing them all back to the time preceding the menses. Menstruation itself provided the relief, with the more pernicious aspects of the cycle occurring *before* the appearance of blood. It was not coincidental that PMS appeared simultaneously with celebration of women's "traditional" roles in the 1950s. PMS helped to redefine menstruation as a problem, and again to control women's bodies and identities by invoking menstrual debility. Raymond Greene and Katharina Dalton, "The Premenstrual Syndrome," *British Medical Journal*, May 9, 1953, 1007–14; Carole Tavris, *The Mismeasure of Woman* (New York: Simon and Schuster, 1992), 129–69; John T. Richardson, "The Premenstrual Syndrome: A Brief History," *Social Science of Medicine* 41, no. 6 (September 1995), 761–67.

2. Beverly, interview with Rebecca Moore (August 13, 2005).

3. On the changing notions of girlhood see Jane H. Hunter, *How Young Ladies Became Girls: The Victorian Origins of American Girlhood* (New Haven: Yale University

Press, 2002); on medicalized constructions of adolescents see Heather Munroe Prescott, *A Doctor of Their Own: The History of Adolescent Medicine* (Cambridge: Harvard University Press, 1998).

4. On teenagers as consumers see Grace Palladino, *Teenagers: An American History* (New York: Basic Book, 1996), especially chapter 7; on children as consumers see Lynn Spigel, "Seducing the Innocent: Childhood and Television in Postwar America," in *The Children's Culture Reader,* ed. Henry Jenkins (New York: New York University Press, 1998), 110–35; Ellen Seiter, "Children's Desire/Mothers' Dilemmas: The Social Contexts of Consumption," in *The Children's Culture Reader,* 297–317.

5. On the relationship of the Cold War to domesticity see Elaine Tyler May, *Homeward Bound: American Families in the Cold War Era* (New York: Basic Books, 1988); Susan M. Hartmann, "Women's Employment and the Domestic Ideal in the Early Cold War Years," in *Not June Cleaver: Women and Gender in Postwar America, 1945–1960,* ed. Joanne Meyerowitz (Philadelphia: Temple University Press, 1994), 84–100; Eugenia Kaledin, *Mothers and More: American Women in the 1950s* (Boston: Twayne Publishers, 1984); on the mixed messages which celebrated both domestic and non-domestic women's roles, see Joanne Meyerowitz, "Beyond the Feminine Mystique: A Reassessment of Postwar Mass Culture, 1946–1958," in *Not June Cleaver,* 229–62.

6. Cindy, interview with Rebecca Moore (August 13, 2005).

7. Toni Anne, interview with Rebecca Moore (August 12, 2005).

8. Faye, interview with the author (April 13, 2005).

9. Wendy, interview with Rebecca Moore (August 13, 2005).

10. Jeffery Moran, *Teaching Sex: The Shaping of Adolescence in the Twentieth Century* (Cambridge: Harvard University Press, 2000), 25. Although Moran provides a much-needed analysis of the history of sex education, he fails to incorporate any references to menstrual education.

11. Moran, *Teaching Sex,* 23–40.

12. See Patricia Campbell, *Sex Education for Young Adults 1892–1979* (New York: R. R. Bowker Company, 1979) for an analysis of advice literature for teenagers. Other titles conveying similar information include William D. Robinson, *Sex Knowledge for Women and Girls: What Every Woman and Girl Should Know* (New York: Critic and Guide Company, 1917); Frances B. Strain, *New Patterns in Sex Teaching* (New York: D. Appleton-Century Company, 1934); Edith Hale Swift, M.D., *Step by Step in Education* (New York: MacMillan Company, 1938); and George W. Corner, *Attaining Womanhood: A Doctor Talks to Girls About Sex* (New York: Harper & Brothers, 1939).

13. John D'Emilio and Estelle Freedman, *Intimate Matters: A History of Sexuality in America* (Chicago: University of Chicago Press, 1997, 2nd ed.), 205.

14. Simon A. Baldus, "A Frank Discussion of Sex Education," *Catholic Action* 19 (November 1937): 6; Sister Mary Jessine, "Our Children Need Sex Education," *America* 85 (July 1951): 376–78.

15. Editorial Notes and Comments, "Sex Education," *Journal of Religious Instruction* 14 (January 1944): 428–29.

16. Kilian J. Hennrich, "Pastoral Musings, VII. Sex Education in the Public Schools," *Homiletic and Pastoral Review* 42 (April 1942): 645–52.

17. Sister Mary Anthony Wagner, "Sex Education and the Catholic Girl," *Catholic Educator* 1 (1950): 250–53.

18. Ruth E. Beach, "Should Sex Education Be Taught in High School?" *Journal of Health and Physical Education* (March 1943): 152–53.

19. Beach, "Should Sex Education Be Taught?" 152.

20. Beach, "Should Sex Education Be Taught?" 152.

21. Beach, "Should Sex Education Be Taught?" 153.

22. Although Personal Products Company (Modess) sponsored menstrual education pamphlets, teacher guides, and a film called "Molly Grows Up" (1953), Kimberly-Clark Corporation maintained dominance. Kennard lists no non-corporate sponsored films until 1972. See Margot Kennard, "The Corporation in the Classroom: The Struggles for Meanings of Menstrual Education in Sponsored Films" (Ph.D. diss. in Curriculum and Instruction, University of Wisconsin, 1989), 231–32.

23. Mary Pauline Callender, "Marjorie May's 12th Birthday" (Chicago: International Cellucotton Products Co., 1938). Harry Finley, curator of the Museum of Menstruation, has a nearly complete 1928 edition, and the series ran from at least 1928–38. Roland Marchand notes that ad agencies created "fictitious personal advisers" who offered helpful advice, and Callender was among them. See Roland Marchand, *Advertising the American Dream: Making Way for Modernity, 1920–1940* (Berkeley: University of California Press, 1985), 305. Her last name, Callender, must also reinforce the need to count "calendar days" between menstrual cycles.

24. Callender, "Marjorie May," 12.

25. "As One Girl to Another" (Chicago: International Cellucotton Products Company, 1940).

26. "Now You Are Ten" (Kimberly-Clark Corporation, 1958).

27. Interview with Susan Brandt, "Body and Spirit," National Public Radio Weekend Edition, February 12, 2000.

28. Joan Jacobs Brumberg, *The Body Project: An Intimate History of American Girls* (New York: Random House, 1997).

29. Kennard, "The Corporation in the Classroom," 35.

30. Robert Eberwein, *Sex Ed: Film, Video, and the Framework of Desire* (New Brunswick: Rutgers University Press, 1999), chapter three, "Youths and Their Bodies." Eberwein does not include menstrual hygiene education films within this genre, or even as a sub-genre of sex education. However, for many women, the menstrual education program sponsored by corporations was their first introduction to sex education, and marked a significant difference from sex education directed at boys.

31. "The Short Story of Menstruation," filmstrip (Burbank, CA: Walt Disney Educational Media, 1977); "The Story of Menstruation," Kimberly-Clark Corporation and Walt Disney Productions (1946), in *It's Wonderful Being a Girl!* A/V Geeks Video Series, n.d. The film was produced in tandem with a 63-frame filmstrip and a companion booklet entitled "Very Personally Yours" (1946).

32. "Medical Motion Pictures, The Story of Menstruation," *Journal of the American Medical Association*, April 5, 1947, 1033.

33. "Medical Motion Pictures, The Story of Menstruation," 1033.

34. "Medical Motion Pictures, The Story of Menstruation," 1033.

35. "Very Personally Yours," filmstrip, frame 19.

36. "Very Personally Yours," filmstrip, frame 20, 21. See also Emily Martin, *The Woman in the Body: A Cultural Analysis of Reproduction* (Beacon Press: Boston, 1992)

on constructions of menstruation as failed conception, offering a pessimistic view of menstruation as only serving models of pregnancy.

37. "Very Personally Yours," filmstrip, frame 44.

38. "Very Personally Yours," filmstrip, frame 34.

39. Wini Breines, *Young, White and Miserable: Growing Up Female in the Fifties* (Chicago: University of Chicago Press, 2001); Susan Douglas, *Where the Girls Are: Growing Up Female with Mass Media* (New York: Times Books, 1995).

40. Palladino, *Teenagers*, 73–77; D'Emilio and Freedman, *Intimate Matters*, 260–65; Richard R. Lingeman, "The Home Front During World War II," in *The Social Fabric: American Life from the Civil War to the Present, Vol. II*, eds. John Cary, Julius Weinberg, Thomas L. Hartstone, and Robert A. Wheeler (New York: Longman, 1999).

41. Rickie Solinger, *Wake Up Little Susie: Single Pregnancy and Race Before Roe v. Wade* (New York: Routledge, 1992).

42. Roland Marchand, *Advertising the American Dream*.

43. Dorothy V. Whipple, M.D., "How to Tell Your Daughter," *Parents* 22 (December 1947): 35.

44. Whipple, "How to Tell Your Daughter," 137.

45. Whipple, "How to Tell Your Daughter," 137.

46. Lillian, interview with Rebecca Moore (August 12, 2005).

47. Marjory Nelson, M.D., as told to Clementine Wheeler, "What a Mother Should Tell Her Daughter," *Parents* 25 (March 1950): 66.

48. Nelson, "What a Mother Should Tell Her Daughter," 66.

49. Nelson, "What a Mother Should Tell Her Daughter," 66.

50. Nelson, "What a Mother Should Tell Her Daughter," 68.

51. Nelson, "What a Mother Should Tell Her Daughter," 68.

52. Elizabeth Woodward, "Do You Scare Her to Death?" *Parents* 24 (1949): 52.

53. "Growing Up and Liking It" (Milltown, NJ: Personal Products Corporation, 1944), 5, at Museum of Menstruation, Menarche Education Booklets, http://www158.pair.com/hfinley/guli44a.htm (accessed November 6, 2000).

54. Woodward, "Do You Scare Her to Death?" 52. See also Kennard, "The Corporation in the Classroom."

55. Woodward, "Do You Scare Her to Death?" 53. "The Story of Menstruation" was part of a larger genre of twentieth-century industrial, safety, and educational films, known as ephemeral film, taught viewers how to become better citizens and better consumers. These short films promoted products such as automobiles, gave advice about how to avoid kissing on the first date, and displayed the consequences of drunk driving. See Rick Prelinger, multi-volume CD-ROM series, *Our Secret Century: Archival Films from the Darker Side of the American Dream* (Voyager Company, 1995). See also Ken Smith, *Mental Hygiene: Classroom Films 1945–1970* (New York: Blast Books, 1999).

56. For a general discussion of advertising for teens see Debra Merskin, "Adolescence, Advertising, and the Ideology of Menstruation," *Sex Roles* 40, no. 11/12 (June 1999): 941–57.

57. The ad copy from "Are you in the know?" ran from 1944–64. Besides being published in women's magazines, Kimberly-Clark also published at least one booklet, "Are you in the know? About Dating, Grooming, Fashions, This and That" (Kimberly Clark Corporation, 1956), at the Museum of Menstruation, Ads for teens, http://www158.pair.com/hfinley/inthekb1.htm (accessed November 6, 2000).

58. "Are you in the know?" *Good Housekeeping* (July 1954): 119.

59. "Are you in the know?" *Redbook Magazine* (November 1948): 67.

60. "Teaching Guide – Menstrual Education," Education Department, International Cellucotton Products Company (Chicago, IL: n.d.).

61. Helen Lefkowitz Horowitz describes this as the *vernacular*, which she defines as the popular and "unofficial culture, seldom noted and never regarded as legitimate." Her framework is quite useful in assessing tampon use, especially as it relates to prescriptive literature for teenagers. Because it is difficult to capture the vernacular myths spread by word-of-mouth, letters to advice columns provide an indirect means to access some of these conversations. Articles in *Consumer Reports* also provide second-hand evidence about the misinformation that circulated concerning tampons. Helen Lefkowitz Horowitz, "Victoria Woodhull, Anthony Comstock, and Conflict over Sex in the United States in the 1870s," *Journal of American History* 87, no. 2 (September 2000): 403–34.

62. Martha Verbrugge, "Gym Periods and Monthly Periods: Concepts of Menstruation in American Physical Education 1900–1940," in Mary M. Lay, et al, *Body Talk: Rhetoric, Technology, Reproduction* (Madison: University of Wisconsin Press, 2000): 67–97; Martha Verbrugge, "Recreating the Body: Women's Physical Education and the Science of Sex Difference in America, 1900–1940," *Bulletin of the History of Medicine* 71 (Summer 1997): 273–304.

63. "How to Tell Your Daughter," *Parents Magazine* 22 (December 1947): 138.

64. Grace Thwing, "Swimming During the Menstrual Period," *Journal of Health and Physical Education* (March 1943): 154.

65. Thwing, "Swimming During the Menstrual Period," 154.

66. May, *Homeward Bound*, 63.

67. Faye, interview with author (April 14, 2005).

68. Ernest Graf, O.S.B., "A Survey of Reviews: A Moral Question," *Homiletic and Pastoral Review* 39 (January 1939): 402.

69. Mary Barton, "Review of the Sanitary Appliance with a Discussion on Intra-Vaginal Packs," *British Medical Journal* 1 (April 1942): 524–25.

70. Alfred C. Kinsey, Wardell Pomeroy, and C. E. Martin, *Sexual Behavior in the Human Male* (Philadelphia: W. B. Saunders Co., 1948), 364.

71. Robert Latou Dickinson, M.D., "Tampons as Menstrual Guards," *Journal of the American Medical Association*, June 16, 1945, 494. For use of tampons in vaginal packs, see George Austin, *Perils of American Women: Or, A Doctor's Talk with Maiden, Wife and Mother* (Boston: Lee and Shephard, 1883), 179.

72. Dickinson, "Tampons as Menstrual Guards," 490.

73. Robert L. Dickinson, M.D., "Tampons as Menstrual Guards," *Consumer Reports* (September 1945): 246–47.

74. "Sanitary Pads and Tampons," *Consumer Reports* (August 1949): 352–55. See also Delaney, et al., *The Curse: A Cultural History of Menstruation* (Urbana: University of Illinois Press, 1988), 109–10; Brumberg, *The Body Project*, 163.

75. Dickinson, "Tampons as Menstrual Guards," 492.

76. Dickinson, "Tampons as Menstrual Guards," 491.

77. Dickinson, "Tampons as Menstrual Guards," 492. The term "anatomic virginity" implied that women could be virgins with a broken hymen, for many adolescents broke that membrane through sports or other activities. The term also implied that virginity must be "lost" through heterosexual, penile penetration.

78. "Tampons for Menstruation," *Hygeia* 27 (September 1949): 593.

79. "Miss . . . or Mrs.? (This Tampax message applied to both)" (1949), n.p. (Advertisement enclosure included with letter to the author from Kathleen B. Makrakis, Tambrands, Inc., January 24, 1995.)

80. "Can Single Girls Wear Tampons," *Motion Picture Magazine* (1952), Ad*Access On-Line Project – Ad #BH0094, John W. Hartman Center for Sales, Advertising & Marketing History, Duke University Rare Book, Manuscript, and Special Collections Library, http://scriptorium.lib.duke.edu (accessed November 4, 2000).

81. "Miss . . . or Mrs.?" 1949, n.p.

82. "Miss . . . or Mrs.?" 1949, n.p.

83. "Of course you can go swimming with tampax" (1951), n.p. (Advertisement enclosure included with letter to the author from Kathleen B. Makrakis, Tambrands, Inc., January 24, 1995).

84. Rose, interview with Rebecca Moore (August 13, 2005).

85. Beverly and Cindy, interview with Rebecca Moore (August 13, 2005).

86. "You're a Young Lady Now," pamphlet, Kimberly-Clark Corporation (1952).

87. Mark Zborowski and Elizabeth Herzog, *Life Is with People: The Culture of the Shtetl* (New York: Schocken Books, 1952), 347–48.

88. Pat, interview with author (March 27, 2007).

89. Sally, interview with author (November 5, 1999). Sally attended Tufts University from 1963–67.

90. "As free as though you were ten years old," *Cosmopolitan* (1937), Ad*Access – #BH0155.

Chapter 7

Civil Rights, Women's Rights, and Technological Options

In 1959, Karl Karnaky, a gynecologist and researcher at the Obstetrical and Gynecological Research Institute, Houston, Texas, began a journal article with the following sentence: "For many years, man has been seeking ways to absorb the menstrual flow during a woman's menstruation, so that during this period she could live her normal life."[1] This sentence is provocative because of the assumptions inhabited in it. From the former chapters, is clear that menstruation has been construed as a problem, for which inventors devised new technologies to absorb menstrual flow. This was also a predominantly male occupation, although there were some women granted patents. Furthermore, the technologies were deployed so that a woman "could live her normal life" unfettered by the burdens of, and those associated with, menstruation. Technology, and technologies of passing, proved to be the solution to this bodily and cultural problem.

However, by the 1960s and 1970s, many people began to question the technologies of menstruation. These questions took different forms, and had different social and political consequences. First, cultural changes wrought by the Civil Rights movement and women's movement pushed the envelope on a few different accounts. Besides access to political rights, disfranchised groups had new visibility with the effect that they were identified as potentially underserved consumers. When companies began to ask if they were reaching all their potential markets, many concluded that they were not, and it was in their financial interests to address black women and include them in print advertisements. Beginning in 1962, *Ebony* magazine published advertisements from Kimberly-Clark in which images of black women were used to pitch Kotex to black readers. Second, this changing audience for products was also reflected in new advertising venues. The representation of menstrual hygiene in sanitary napkin television commercials, which began in 1970 with Confidets manufactured by Scott Paper Company, generated new questions about how to talk about menstruation. Third, inspired by the women's movement, the Boston Women's Health Collective took the opportunity to demystify the process of menstruation in *Our Bodies, Ourselves* and reinterpret it as productive, positive, and a unique celebration of womanhood. Fourth, scientists and engineers began to ask how the technologies might be improved. For example, the explosion of new compounds, the promise of herbicides and pesticides, and the chemical engineering of polyester clothing all seemed to demonstrate the successful application of science to modern living. In terms of menstrual hygiene product design, engineering advances in materials made possible the production of removable adhesives, so that adhesive-backed sanitary napkins could be stuck to the underpants instead of being strapped to the body with a belt. The new products, named "New Freedom" and "Stayfree" in reference to notions of women's expanded political and reproductive rights, exploited themes from the women's movement. The limits of the new technologies were put to the test with the failed Rely tampons, linked to growing numbers of Toxic Shock Syndrome cases in menstruating women and manufactured by Proctor & Gamble in the late 1970s. The issues of design, culture, media, and feminism intertwined to reveal how menstrual passing took a decidedly life-threatening twist, with the deadly consequence of problematizing women's bodies, not the menstrual technologies themselves.

African-American Women and Advertising

By the 1960s, companies no longer questioned whether or not women would purchase sanitary napkins and tampons. Adult women, girls, and teenagers were accustomed to using menstrual hygiene technologies to manage their menstrual flow. The larger question for companies was how to garner new loyal customers. Factors such as price, quality, and improved features tended to be reasons that women switched to a different brand name. Preferences shifted, but new consumers were not necessarily created. However, black women in particular proved to be an untapped market which afforded companies opportunities for expanded economic growth. It is not surprising that companies began to recognize black people as potential consumers in the 1960s and 1970s. The Civil Rights movement put a real face on the two-tier system of segregation, in which black people felt the brunt of second-class citizenship. The more adamant demands of Black Nationalists made clear that black people should use their economic power to support black run businesses. It was no longer economically feasible to entirely disregard black people. Of course, representations of black people in mainstream advertising were slow in coming and also somewhat contrived, as well as deliberate. Companies avoided any connection with the Black Power movement and the image of clenched fists raised in the air, as with Tommie Smith and John Carlos from their gold and bronze medal performances in track and field during the 1968 Mexico City Olympics. This sort of boycott and image proved too dangerous for most mainstream companies catering to the dollars of white consumers. More often than not, lighter skinned black women who could emulate the white "All-American Girl" offered both white and black readers a seemingly benign and respectable image of black people, more aligned with notions of white aesthetics and beauty.

Daniel J. Edelman and Associates, Inc., a public relations firm, presented its findings to Kimberly-Clark in 1964 concerning advertising campaigns directed at black women consumers. The arguments and approach first had to convince executives at Kimberly-Clark that a market even existed. Prejudice about black people being poor and not spending money were addressed with statements like "[t]here are more that 20 million Negroes in the United States with a purchasing power exceeding 22 billion dollars annually." Following on this notion the report stated, "[n]egroes earn money, spend money, and are free to make their own choice of most consumer products." Common assumptions by many white people were that black people were told what to purchase by their white employers or that they were not smart enough to make informed decisions. In addition, the firm noted, "[s]mall merchants have made handsome profits by cultivating the good will of Negroes, and enlightened national companies now are adopting, to their economic advantage, the same techniques through a more sophisticated approach."[2] Once it was clear that black people earned and spent money, the greater difficulty arose concerning what approach to take. First and foremost, Kimberly-Clark needed to maintain its current clientele, and anything to harm that was considered foolish. Daniel J. Edelman and Associates, Inc. recommended, "'softening' the Negro market," which was "best done by not disturbing the general market." This meant targeting advertisements in pre-existing black newspapers and magazines, not necessarily mainstreaming images of black people in magazines targeted at white audiences.

Black newspapers enjoyed a long tradition of independent readership, and were also characterized as supportive of black-owned local businesses. The papers were known to be more openly critical of government policies and local rule, and exercised a high degree of freedom of expression, in part because the black press was generally ignored and dismissed by white people. For white executives, the black newspapers might as well have been foreign. Therefore, Daniel J. Edelman and Associates, Inc. suggested many techniques to engender support from the black readership of black newspapers. The firm recommended that the goodwill created for Kimberly-Clark at the local level might "withstand any wild or organized selective buying programs that may occur in the future." This perceived threat was not withstanding. Black people organized many successful boycotts in the past, one of the most effective and celebrated being the Montgomery bus boycott during 1955 and 1956, in which Martin Luther King, Jr. rose to acclaim and white-owned businesses were hurt by black shoppers taking their business elsewhere. By 1964, executives would have been concerned about rumblings from the South, and the effects of the mass movement of black people for events like the March on Washington Movement held in August of 1963. The researchers at Daniel J. Edelman and Associates, Inc. were aware of the volatility of black and white relationships, and therefore recommended tempered entrance into advertising targeting black women.[3]

The firm had many concrete suggestions. First, Kimberly-Clark should place "small product ads in selected Negro newspapers in key cities through one representative." A manager for all accounts dealing with black newspapers would engender a sense of trust and continuity. Besides the more personal contacts, the content of the ads would need to be specially directed toward young black women. The firm suggested changing the "Miss Deb" column (as in "Miss Debutante," who was presumably white) to "Personally Yours," a question and answer column directed to adolescents. Advertisers changed the images from white people to black people, and focused more upon personal hygiene. The firm suggested using "in the mast a Negro physical education teacher counselling [sic] two girls" on topics such as "Junior Miss etiquette, grooming, and interests."[4] Kimberly-Clark followed through on this suggestion. The columns printed similar questions to those run in white magazines, concerning weight, nail biting, and even study habits. They also included questions such as: "All my heels are sort of ground down at the outside edges. Does that mean there's something wrong with the way I walk?" The response was to shift the weight to the inside of the foot, and to take the heels "to the shoemaker for a beauty treatment."[5] Implicit within the questions was an assumption linking blackness with poverty—thus not being able to afford new shoes—and the need for black people to have some guidelines about how to become respectable through proper dress and hygiene.

Since education about hygiene was an element emphasized by the ads, the team at Daniel J. Edelman and Associates, Inc. suggested that at the end of "Personally Yours" the girls reading the letters and questions contact their physical education teachers for more information and literature about Kotex. In addition, newsletters should be sent to all home economics teachers. Besides addressing adolescents and young women, the firm addressed the importance of blanketing the staff of black newspapers with information, including mailing "Personally Yours" as well as the product information sheets. In addition to using newsprint to reach black consumers, the convention circuit offered another avenue. The firm believed that "servicing such annual Negro conventions as National Medical Association, National Dental Association, National Beauty Culturist League, Women's Editors of all Negro Newspapers, Negro Sororities (3), and United Beauty School Owners and Teachers Association" would also benefit Kimberly-Clark.[6] By addressing black professionals who were often segregated from their white counterparts, the company hoped to gain access to educated audiences with money to spend, and who seemed to have some sort of influence over other black consumers. Finally, the public relations firm recommended that Kimberly-Clark plan "seriously for any integrated television or general market magazine ads" with images of both black and white people, which pointed to the changing face of advertising for menstrual hygiene.

Kimberly-Clark followed many recommendations, such as running the "Personally Yours" column in black newspapers. By 1967, Daniel J. Edelman and Associates, Inc., created a more detailed plan for reaching markets outlined in "An Advertising Plan for Kimberly-Clark in the Negro Press." Interestingly, it called for modest advertising with a public relations bent in order to create a positive identity for Kimberly-Clark and their brands, including Kleenex. In addition, public relations with black presses and other venues would "reinforce and strengthen Kimberly-Clark's position as an equal opportunity employer, in effect providing insurance for the company's future employment and customer relationships with the Negro market."[7] This approach included emphasis on urban, metropolitan areas where a density of black people worked and lived, in cities such as New York, Chicago, St. Louis, and Detroit. It was in these metropolitan cities where they felt there was a larger black middle class who could afford to purchase products manufactured by Kimberly-Clark. In addition, the analysts incorporated elements from the 1965 "Moynihan Report," a congressional study of the social and economic conditions experienced by black people spearheaded by Senator Daniel Moynihan (D-NY) which, amongst its various and now controversial conclusions, demonstrated that women, not men, were the typical head-of-household.[8] The importance of the statistics and data, whether or not they were accurate, was how the information was used in terms of government programs as well as business models. For Kimberly-Clark, it meant that black men were virtually invisible as purchasers. It was black women who controlled a family's finances and needed to be addressed as the decision makers about money.

By addressing middle-class black families who read newspapers published by the black press, Kimberly-Clark hoped to acquire better name brand recognition and goodwill amongst black consumers. Since Kimberly-Clark was concerned about its company brand name recognition, there was some discussion about putting products such as Kleenex and Kotex in the same ad. The public relations firm could not recommend this approach, and emphasized "[n]either group of women—the older or the younger working women—are, in our opinion, sophisticated enough to react favorably to the combination of both household and feminine hygiene products in the same ad."[9] This they assumed would create "a negative reaction" because one product was meant for the family, while the other for her personally. Of course, also implicit was an assumption of black people as naïve and simple, unable to discern elements of visual representation and textual rhetoric in the advertisements. Daniel J. Edelman and Associates, Inc. did however recommend that black families, and not white families, be used in the advertisement images, because it would have more impact. "An ad with a family unit gives the reader a sense of identification with the use of the product in his or her own situation." The advice continued, "the home or family unit concept is currently in high regard in the Negro market, and every effort is being made to further it."[10] Therefore, the black newspapers, which tended to focus on church, civic, and business affairs, proved to be the outlet for Kimberly-Clark. That its competitor, Johnson & Johnson, ran ads for Modess sanitary napkins in the *Baltimore Afro-American* certainly motivated Kimberly-Clark to jump on the same bandwagon.[11]

The report continued by examining the newspapers of sixteen cities, the price charged for running an ad, the circulation, and the characteristics and tone of the papers. The researchers noted the *Michigan Chronicle*, published in Detroit, "was the only paper on the scene and continued to balance the news that was published" during the Detroit riots of 1967, which lasted five days leaving 43 dead and 1189 wounded.[12] The *Dallas Express* "was chosen because of the affluence of the Negroes in the city," who presumably could afford to purchase disposable products from Kimberly-Clark.[13] The report outlined two plans: one for year-long advertising in all the targeted newspapers, which amounted to $10,577.25, and a more modest plan with limited runs of the ads totaling $6,039, which could also be broken down into smaller segments. Through this "relatively modest expenditure" the firm felt that Kimberly-Clark could "strengthen its position with a minority group market."[14] The amount allotted was very meager. In comparison, the 1967 budget for Kotex Regular Sanitary Napkin magazine print advertising alone was $1,746,763.[15]

The firm also warned not to forget Balm Leavell, who founded the *Crusader* newspaper in Chicago and later the *Gary Crusader*, of Gary, Indiana. Leavell also represented the Negro Newspaper Publishing Association, and was disgruntled by the lack of advertising by large corporations in black newspapers. Since many accounts were handled through advertising agencies, and not the company itself, he directed his efforts there. Because Kimberly-Clark did not want to buckle to agitators, the firm suggested that "[t]o quell current pressures and to create a stronger position for Kimberly-Clark in refusaling [sic] future pressures, we do recommend a minimum number of insertions in some of the newspapers represented by Mr. Leavell and Mr. Mouchett," another black publisher.[16] Apparently these gestures were insufficient. According to an internal memo by Dean J. Hewitt of Kimberly-Clark's public relations department, Leavell was "the same guy who shook up Foote, Cone and Belding" advertising agency "with boycott threats."[17] Leavell felt that "the agency was not sympathetic to the Negro Press viewpoint" and Hewitt reported that Leavell wanted an invitation to present this perspective to the corporate executives. Whether or not the meeting occurred is unclear; Leavell died that same year in 1968 and his wife Dorothy R. Leavell took over their publishing legacy.

The other important avenue of advertising was *Ebony* magazine, founded in 1945. Though the newspaper ads were cheap to produce and quick to get in print, the advertisements in glossy magazines were more dramatic in color and clearly more expensive to produce. The first ad for Kotex placed in *Ebony* ran in its November 1962 issue (Figure 10). Prepared by the advertising firm Foote, Cone, and Belding, it introduced to black readers a campaign for various-sized sanitary pads, which varied three-dimensionally in length, width, and depth. Four sizes were designated—regular, junior, slenderline, and super—followed by descriptions of the four styles. The ad's header asked, "Proportioned *what*?" with the rejoinder, "Proportioned Kotex Napkins."[18] The black model possessed a medium-light complexion, with straightened coifed hair. She tied an orange ribbon around her hair, as if to hold it in place with a headband. Her orange dreamsicle-colored sweater matched her bow and her glossy lips, parted to insinuate she was caught off-guard by the announcement of newly sized Kotex. She was cut from the same cloth as the trim and neat Diana Ross from her early days in the Supremes. The ad itself was not particularly noteworthy in terms of style or content. However, a mirror image of the ad using a white model ran in its counterpart magazines. Foote, Cone, and Belding designed the same campaign and design layout, introducing proportioned Kotex to a white audience, this time with a white model (Figure 11). In her hair she too tied a bow, yellow instead, which complemented her apple green sweater. Her lips were also parted, and she had a similar doe-eyed expression for the camera, projecting youth and naivety as well as an appealing all-American look.[19] The parallel ads demonstrate the acceptance of black women as consumers, and the recognition that ads for black magazines needed the same attention to quality as their white counterparts.

Television and Menstrual Hygiene Commercials

Concepts in advertising were quickly shifting. Not only were black women represented in print advertisements, changes in the code of standards for television commercials in 1972 allowed products related to internal bodily processes to be aired, which raised the stakes for selling menstrual hygiene products. The change was driven by the National Association of Broadcasters (NAB), the trade organization for radio and television, comprised of due-paying member stations. Its board regulated content and programming by establishing guidelines, also known as the Code, in terms of "decency" and "taste" to be maintained on radio and television airwaves. Within these highly subjective parameters, personal-product advertising, which included feminine hygiene sprays, sanitary belts and napkins, tampons, vaginal diaphragms, jellies and foams, as well as hemorrhoid treatments, were banned in both television shows and in advertising.[20] As participating members, stations were required to follow the Code to remain in good standing. However, swayed by advertising money, stations in Minneapolis, Minnesota; Milwaukee, Wisconsin; Sacramento, California; and Columbus, Ohio participated in test marketing of FDS feminine deodorant spray during the summer of 1967. Many abhorred the abrogation of the Code, and Donald H. McGannon, president of Westinghouse Broadcasting, decided to resign from the NAB instead of condoning the new ads. He charged "we have now crossed the line where there is no practical obstacle to products being aired on television irrespective of their personal, intimate, or sensitive nature."[21] He also characterized these ads as "the last straw," presumably opening the floodgates for even more offensive products. However, the television commercials were aired, and proponents characterized them as "less offensive than many spots for acceptable products," further supported by the lack of complaints from viewers.[22] This break with allegiance to the NAB proved to be the path for product commercials dealing with bodily functions, including menstruation.

In June of 1970, the trade publication *Broadcasting* reported in a headline: "30-Second Time Bomb."[23] This time bomb referred to the first commercial for sanitary napkins ever to be aired by non-member stations, produced by the advertising firm BBDO for the Scott Paper Company and its product Confidets. Likening the sanitary napkin to a bomb demonstrated the shock of the televisual representation of menstrual hygiene products, which abrogated the cultural mores of silence around such public discussion. Stunned viewers, in fact, would not know what had hit them. Scott Paper Company, however, had a strong financial motivation for breaking into a new advertising arena. Its sales ranked third behind Kotex and Modess, whose companies were not so anxious to elevate the stakes. In February of 1970, BBDO forged ahead with advertising at non-code stations, after running two marketing samples at stations in Minneapolis, Minnesota (KMSP-TV) and Erie, Pennsylvania (WICU-TV, WJET-TV, WSEE-TV). Scott Paper Company kept a record of complaints about the commercials, and logged 24 phone calls and eight letters over a 16-week period. The firm of Marketing Studies Inc. conducted consumer attitude studies prior to the commercials and then six weeks after they aired. The firm interviewed 908 women who then ranked whether or not the sanitary napkin ads were in good taste or poor taste, as compared to similar commercials for bath tissue, bras and girdles, and feminine hygiene spray. Between 76.4% and 79.8% of women judged commercials for bath tissue, bras and girdles, and feminine hygiene spray all to be presented with good taste. Sanitary napkins enjoyed 35.4% of women discerning the ads in good taste, and only 10.5% in poor taste, with 54.1% not able to judge either way. After they actually viewed the ads, and were asked again six weeks later, the women were more decisive, with 42.9% finding them in good taste, 12.3% in poor taste, and 44.8% still unsure. Interestingly, Marketing Studies Inc. reported that of the women who found sanitary napkin advertising offensive, "69% also found one or more of the other product categories in questionable taste."[24] They dismissed this group as "chronic complainers" and continued to push ahead with comprehensive advertising on television. This overall hesitancy in accepting the commercials can be interpreted in a variety of ways. Certainly, many women were uncomfortable seeing these ads on television, and the media itself established a more direct intimacy with the viewer than a print advertisement. For those women who wanted to avoid thinking about menstruation, the commercials seemingly imprisoned them. In addition, even with the shrouded language, the commercials seemed to unveil menstruation and menstrual technologies, and made public the act of passing in ways that might have been uncomfortable for female viewers.

In a later study, Scott Paper Company reported that "60% of women had a positive response" to the ads.[25] Although it is unclear how this percentage was derived, it was enough to push the NAB to accept advertising for menstrual hygiene products at code stations beginning November 1, 1972. Only two products, however, took advantage of the changes at first: Confidets (Scott Paper Company) and Carefree Tampons (Johnson & Johnson). The money spent on Confidets was startling. During all of 1967, and the first nine months of 1968, Scott Paper Company spent $578,781 and $583,859, respectively, on magazine advertising.[26] Once the code was changed, it put all its advertising monies toward television. On the three major network stations—ABC, CBS, and NBC—Scott Paper Company spent $621,500 for the first ten months of 1971, $489,300 from January to October of 1972, and $500,00 in the November and December months alone. This included eight to ten "spots" per week during the daytime, with an average of about twelve with nighttime ads included. The "spots" were only run after 11:00 pm at night and during the so-called "housewife" times from 10:00 am to 4:00 pm on NBC, and 11:30 am to 3:30 pm on CBS.[27] One of the arguments for limiting the times was to protect children from exposure to the ads. However, it is difficult to believe that no children would see these ads if mothers were staying home to raise young infants and toddlers, thus this reasoning was fairly flimsy.

By 1979, many women felt that they and their children were not protected from exposure to the ads. The Canadian Radio-television and Telecommunications Commission (CRTC) received over 85,000 letters, notes, and names on petitions calling ads for sanitary napkins offensive and unsuitable for mixed audiences, especially men and children.[28] They believed the ads should remain in women's magazines. Newspaper columnist Nicole Parton, writing for the Vancouver *Province*, spearheaded the protest, instigating protest of the commercials and a write-in campaign to have them removed from Canadian airwaves. Incensed, Shirley Maddox conducted an impromptu door-to-door survey in her

Mississauga, Ontario neighborhood, and found only one of 275 who approved the ads. As she lamented, "[i]t forces mothers to explain this sort of thing to their four-year-olds."[29] This sort of "thing" included not just sanitary pads, but menstruation, maturity, and sexual development.

Feminism, Menstruation, and Menstrual Hygiene

Liberal and radical feminists from the early 1970s, on the other hand, were quick to criticize the feminized media image of women promulgated by advertisements, and the types of bodily conformity required by purchasing products, and I would argue, technologies. The National Organization of Women (NOW), a women's group interested in pressuring systems of governance to make them more democratic in terms of women's issues, unsuccessfully appealed the television code review board of the NAB to create stronger provisions limiting stereotypical, ultra-feminized, and sexist images of women on television.[30] Taking matters into their own hands, the Redstockings issued their own proclamations. The Redstockings, most renowned for the 1969 *Redstocking Manifesto*, minced no words in detailing men's sexual, reproductive, and domestic oppression of women. One means to get at this oppression was to critique the media, as addressed by a woman known as "A Redstocking Sister." She stated, "[t]he real evil of the media image of women is that it supports the sexist status quo. In a sense, fashion, cosmetics, and 'feminine hygiene' ads are aimed more at men than at women." Worse yet, the ads "encourage men to expect women to sport all the latest trappings of sexual slavery—expectations women must then fulfill if they are to survive." She lamented that "buying and wearing clothes and beauty aids is not so much consumption as work" where "clothes and make-up are tools of the trade."[31] Although she did not explicitly reference passing, sanitary napkins and tampons created the image of a clean, menstrual-free body, and one, presumably, appealing to heterosexual men. That the products were "tools of the trade" of exploitation speaks to how they can be viewed as technologies used in an oppressive way.

Gloria Steinem, who became a recognizable face of feminism, took a more tongue-in-cheek approach. She jostled embedded assumptions about menstruation in her pointed piece "If Men Could Menstruate." She mused that manufacturers would sell "Joe Namath Jock Shields—'For Those Light Bachelor Days,'" and that "Congress would fund a National Institute of Dysmenorrhea to help stamp out monthly discomforts." Intellectuals would argue that women as non-menstruators would be unable to "master any discipline that demanded a sense of time, space, mathematics, or measurement" because they lacked the "in-built gift for measuring the cycles of the moon and planets." Feminists would respond that women should "escape the bonds of menses envy" and develop alternative cultures.[32] Steinem turned the tables and exposed engrained menstrual assumptions so that they might be more easily dislodged with humor.

The radical feminists, in conjunction with more moderate or liberal feminists, not only questioned sexist representations of women in the media, but how sexist assumptions about women's health were literally killing thousands of women each year. One of the most profound developments came in the form of the Women's Health Movement, which has left a strong imprint on the way healthcare for women is delivered to this day, from challenging unnecessary hysterectomies, to advocating lumpectomy over mastectomy, encouraging natural forms of childbirth, and advocating safe and open access to abortion. The Women's Health Movement, including the National Women's Health Movement and the Black Women's Health Movement, sought to change the view of women's natural bodily processes from diseased to normal, and therefore offer services more in line with providing health care instead of disease care.

One approach was to by-pass the medical establishment and instead, through the collective, and provide health care to seekers who were not just patients-as-recipients but participants within the broader ideological movement. For those with like-minded political inclinations, self-administered treatments for yeast infections or diaphragm fittings were entirely in the purview of actions that women could take without the sanction of a physician. As such, with the experimental and inventive spirit of the health practitioners of the early 1970s, Carol Downer and Lorraine Rothman, members of NOW, devised a way to by-pass commercial menstrual hygiene through a practice known as menstrual extraction, or ME.[33] This process uses a cannula (a flexible tube inserted directly into the cervix), a syringe to provide suction, a one-way valve to prevent material flowing back into the uterus, and a jar to collect the menstrual blood. This device cannot be self-administered, but could quickly suction from the uterus all the menstrual blood in about three to five minutes, thus eliminating the need to use other menstrual hygiene technologies. Since technologies can be used in multiple ways, ME is no exception. It was sometimes called a "menstrual regulator" and designed as an alternative procedure to induce an abortion within the first few weeks of a missed period.[34] Many of the practitioners believed that this method was safer, less invasive, and legal since a woman may or may not be pregnant at the time of the procedure, so it gained some acceptance within the health collective. Its application to women outside of this health network was less clear, and it surely suffered from its association with illicit abortion. And, since it required assistance from someone knowledgeable, or a pricey fee of $30–$50 by a willing physician, it could not offer the kind of liberation and bodily independence that more mainstream menstrual hygiene technologies could.

Moving beyond the feminist networks to reach out to all woman to disseminate health information broadly was a cornerstone of the Boston Women's Health Book Collective, which produced the significant handbook *Our Bodies, Ourselves: A Book By and For Women*. Importantly, the book put women, not doctors, at the center of their own care, and encouraged women to be the experts concerning their bodies' special needs. Directed toward a lay audience, and one informed by a growing swell of feminism, the book had profound effects on the ways that women began to ask for and demand medical treatments, thus instigating social change in the perceptions of women's bodies. Besides bringing medical terminology to regular women to deploy at the doctor's office, the authors normalized the process of menstruation, and acknowledged women's feelings about their bodies during menstruation and their attitudes about menstrual hygiene, including some references to tampons. By acknowledging women's insecurities, they hoped to empower women with knowledge. One sidebar read: "The first month I was at college some of my friends were twittering about a girl down the hall. She was having a painful time trying to learn to put in a tampon. Finally, someone helped her and found she was trying to put it in her anus."[35] By recounting this uncomfortable story, it allowed others to empathize with the struggle of learning to use this technology, validated some women's feelings of insecurity, and thus demonstrated the importance of acquiring self-knowledge of the female body. Though the writers related that tampons were a "convenience" to many, they also promoted the use of the natural sponge, which absorbs menstrual fluid and is washed and reused. They also admitted, "[i]n a pinch, there are clean rags and toilet paper."[36] Like earlier proponents of tampons, they reassured women about their compatibility with the hymen. "If the hymen didn't have openings in it, the menstrual fluid couldn't come out. Most women have hymens with large enough openings to accommodate at least a small-sized tampon." By speaking frankly, albeit in a protective tone, the collective sought to reconceptualize menstruation as positive. "What we want to be sure to do is to tell both our daughters and sons about menstruation so that they can be comfortable with it and open about it in a way that we were not. We feel we can help our daughters to celebrate a new part of life."[37] The feminists of the early women's health movement recognized the trap of essentializing the body; regardless of women's accomplishments, menstruation was still a signifier of womanhood, but women could be responsible for how they incorporated it into their identity. The unanswered and lingering question raised by many feminists, however, was what constitutes womanhood—physiological, societal, and/or personal identities? Although the political ramifications for the answers to these questions carried significant consequences, there still remained the materiality of the female body and what to do with menses.

Redesigning Menstrual Hygiene Technologies

It is clear that women's wants and desires were not immediately incorporated into feminist design, although feminism was often stripped of its political overtones and used to sell new products. Yet, most corporations developing new menstrual hygiene technologies could not escape the political foment and changes wrought by the Civil Rights movement writ large, and what this meant in terms of profits. Innovators and corporate scientists within research and development questioned how to improve upon existing technologies or change the technological artifacts altogether, more often for monetary gain than any real desire for social change for women. Some were merely intrigued with "the problem." For instance, during the late 1950s and early 1960s, Karl Karnaky, a gynecologist and university researcher interested in treating endometriosis among other things, felt that neither sanitary pads nor tampons were very good, and "after seeing thousands of women during their menstrual flow with menstrual blood running down their legs and thighs, all over their perineum and even on their underclothing" he sought "to try to find out something that might be labeled at least a small advancement in the handling of the menstrual blood."[38] Karnaky proposed a radical technological solution: packing the vagina with powder, which, once contacted with blood, would render menstrual fluid into an inert salt that could be reabsorbed into the bloodstream. Due to the changes in pH in the vagina during menstruation, and the blood entering the vaginal canal, more bacteria were activated by these changes, thus contributing to the odor associated with decomposing blood. Thus, with blood absorbed by a salt, there would be no outward remnant of menstrual fluid to contend with.

Karnaky began measuring vaginal pH, which during menstruation becomes very basic—pH 7.2 to 8—as opposed to its non-menstrual state that is more acidic—pH 3.5 to 4. He collected information about vaginal pH from "virgins of all ages while they were in the charity hospital for non-gynecologic surgery."[39] As an aside, he became interested in vaginal pH when he noticed that pathogens grew more rapidly during the menstrual flow, as evidenced when he "experimentally inoculated *Trichomonas vaginalis* into the vagina of charity clinical patients" and they exhibited symptoms of this sexually transmitted disease during their menstrual flow.[40] Although he may have operated within the accepted medical ethics of his day and worked to create a treatment for Trich, it still is unsettling to imagine unsuspecting women and virgins leaving with a fresh STD distributed by the physician while being treated for something else entirely.

Through his experimentation on these "charity cases," as he referred to them, he learned that a non-toxic acidic powder inserted into the vagina with a glass or plastic plunger three times per application and up to three times per day would change menstrual blood "into a fine, dry, non-sticky, inert, non-toxic sterile powder which is apparently metabolized in the vagina by the enzymes into harmless chemicals which are reabsorbed into the general circulation."[41] He claimed that the adhesives in the powder prevented it from leaking. However, the application of the powder required some attention. The first application would cover the cervix and the next two would fill the vaginal cavity. The general ratio was one tablespoon of powder for ten teaspoons of menstrual fluid.

Then, between one and three low pH tablets, manufactured by Massengill—known for making douches—would be inserted into the powder itself. Finally, Karnaky recommended that women could also open up a sanitary napkin and layer powder into it, to really assure that there would be no leaks. He instructed over 200 of his private patients how to use the powder. He did not include their reactions toward or attitudes about the new product. However, he concluded "[t]here are now three ways in which a woman can dispose of her menstrual flow, external pad, internal tampon, and by using the new, low pH powder."[42]

It is not surprising that this powder did not catch on. Professionally, he was thought of as somewhat of a kook. Willard Allen, professor of obstetrics at the University of Maryland and associate dean of the medical school until 1982, writing to Frederick Zuspan on the editorial board at the *American Journal of Obstetrics & Gynecology*, referred to a letter to the editor written by Karnaky as a "typical Karnaky production" and "just another Karnaky 'throw-away.'" Yet, he admitted that Karnaky's "pleas for modern gynecologists to try medical management of endometriosis before rushing to the knife" made a lot of sense.[43] Zuspan responded to Willard's letter briefly. "What a sweet guy you are. I agree with your feeling about Karl. See you on the golf course in September."[44] Most likely, Karnaky did not share in this same kind of professional or personal familiarity or rapport. He certainly would have needed more support from other practitioners to go ahead with a chemical treatment of menstruation in the form of a period powder inserted vaginally. According to an archivist who knew Karnaky before he died in 1988, Karnaky "felt that his work had not been interpreted or used correctly by many physicians."[45] In this case, there are probably many reasons for this failed technology, among them his personality, the messy powder, and belief that tampons and sanitary napkins still worked pretty well. It does, however, highlight the fact that menstrual hygiene technologies were not taken for granted as fully developed or completed in their design.

A different change in sanitary napkin design came in the form of adhesives, which were being better formulated by scientists and engineers. Though cellophane tape had been developed at 3M by 1930, it was not until 1961 that Scotch brand introduced transparent tape, which was clear and non-yellowing.[46] By improving the vehicle for the adhesive through plastics, there were more opportunities for its application. Reconfiguring the machinery in the Johnson & Johnson plant to shorten the tabs and then apply adhesive to the pads resulted in a new application for the adhesives, and a new way for women to wear sanitary napkins. In terms of sanitary pads, there was not one particular adhesive used, and the patents generally do not specify an adhesive. By applying double-stick adhesive to the underside of the sanitary pad, the pad could adhere to dry underwear and be secured to a woman's underpants without much effort. They did not shift as much, and therefore caused less chafing. This meant no more laundering or replacement of frayed belts, and no more struggling with their correct positioning on the hips. However, they still did depend on careful placement; worn too high or low on the underpants guaranteed menstrual blood missing its mark.

Of course there are a wide variety of adhesives, but for sanitary pads, pressure sensitive adhesive proved to offer a technological improvement. Pressure sensitive adhesives are considered permanently tacky, can withstand some degree of heat and moisture, and need only a bit of force to adhere to a surface. Importantly, they are also removable, and in this case, do not impart residue on undergarments. Kimberly-Clark introduced the sanitary pad called New Freedom in 1972, on the heels of its competitor Johnson & Johnson who nationally marketed its own beltless version, Stayfree, composed of cellulose, rayon, and polyethylene, in 1971.[47] The significance of both companies vying once again for the same market demonstrated the power of improved technologies to win over consumers. And, just like the introduction of Kotex in the 1920s roughly correlating with women's right to vote, the new beltless pads emerged at the peak of the feminist movement in the early 1970s. It is no wonder that the companies capitalized upon the names New Freedom and Stayfree. They both offered material reminders of women's economic and political gains with women's liberation, and the advertisements, as before, incorporated cultural feminism without promoting its politically revolutionary elements. An ad for New Freedom claimed, "For peace of mind and body." The happy woman in the ad expressed "Free to be myself all of the time."[48] Thus, without the burden of old-fashioned belted pads, her pass in essence was more convincing, and she was free to be her non-menstrual self. Furthermore, the pad offered "no pins, no belts, no doubts." The ad assured that the pad "holds fast to a bikini panty," would not twist or lose shape, and that it could be flushed, which continued to be a dubious claim.

The Stayfree line by Johnson & Johnson had a mini pad as well, which was to be worn in rotation with the maxi pad, "[b]ecause you have two kinds of periods every month" both heavy and light.[49] To assure women that they would not need any "hardware" to keep the napkin in place, the ad compared adhesives to a lock, which would secure it to the underwear. To encourage wear of the smaller mini-pads, the ad suggested, "a remarkable number of women wear it every day of the month. Just to make sure their good panties and girdles are protected from everyday feminine discharge." The ad constructed the use of mini pads as contributing to feelings of femininity. With the mini pad, "you feel neater. Safer. Just a little bit more ladylike." Finally, the ad commented, "Don't be surprised if the mini-pad makes you forget you're having a period."[50] The ad promoted the idea of temporary amnesia, thus facilitating a successful pass.

Kimberly-Clark designer Charlotte Rickard patented a different kind of sanitary device in 1968 with a "wing" design: a disposable "sanitary shield designed to encircle the crotch portion of panty undergarment to protect against soilage."[51] Although this design did not immediately appear in consumer form, it challenged the rectangular shape of the standard pad. Since the angular shape of the pad did not conform to the curves of the leg or the pelvis, there was no reason to assume that the pad would fit well enough to catch all the menstrual fluid expelled. Inevitably, blood ended up on the underwear, which had often curled up and around the edges of the pad. Rickard noted that there were other methods to prevent these aberrant stains: a panty with a "plastic crotch piece which may be wiped clean if soilage occurs," and "padlets" or small pads much like the Stayfree mini-pad. Neither of these was preferable to wearing regular underwear with a comfortable pad of some sort. She proposed a shield, not quite as thick as a pad, which would encircle the crotch part of the underwear, and attach with pressure sensitive adhesive, snaps, or Velcro. In essence, it would serve as a guard, and could be used with other sanitary napkins or tampons. The shield required a variety of materials to serve its purpose. She referred to the shield as a "laminated sheet" with the bottom layer being a "moisture impervious material such a polyethylene or a similar plastic film." The top absorbent layer would be comprised of "cellulose wadding or non-woven sheet stock and may consist of one or multiple layers." Because its only purpose was to keep panties clean, another form of menstrual hygiene was used in conjunction with it, and it must have had limited appeal.

However, her clever idea of "wing-like portions" was not forgotten, and served as the basis for other patents filed for the now familiar "winged" sanitary pads that both absorb menstrual flow and shield panties from menstrual stains. By the time that winged pads such as Proctor & Gamble's Always sanitary napkins became readily available by the 1990s, many women thought they were a big improvement over the old. Faye, who discussed with me how she struggled with heavy flow until menopause, learned about the new pads from her daughters. With a smile on her face, she said that she thought they were "wonderful."[52] Other women were more skeptical about minor technological changes meant to seduce them to purchase a new and supposedly improved product. Wendy, who attended high school during the early 1970s, complained about the price of sanitary napkins, and stated "basically it's a box of compressed cotton, and they keep adding new and different features, like, we used to joke about ducks with wings, and pads with wings and this and that. What are they going to do? Fly away? It's like they keep adding new and new features just so they can raise the price, and women really don't have a choice."[53]

Even with all the bells and whistles added to the pads, tampons continually gained market share. By the 1970s, attitudes about sex were far more open than in the 1930s when Tampax was first introduced. Granddaughters and great-granddaughters of the women from Lillian Gilbreth's survey were now wearing tampons. In the early 1970s, Kimberly-Clark held 40% of the feminine hygiene market, with Kotex and then New Freedom holding ground. By 1976, Johnson & Johnson surpassed Kimberly-Clark with 46% of the sanitary pad market. Tambrands retained a respectable 25–30% of the market, which held fairly steady during the 1970s.[54] Some even claimed that upwards of 70% of all women wore tampons.[55] The most renowned product to challenge the domination of Tampax came from Proctor & Gamble in the late 1970s.[56] Proctor & Gamble aggressively marketed the newly designed tampons as Rely, and early results showed that women liked them. Despite its shape once it absorbed fluid, likened to an umbrella by one woman (which of course would be uncomfortable to remove), it still gained popularity.[57]

The tampon was comprised with entirely new materials, with researchers at Proctor & Gamble abandoning the traditional cotton fiber and instead designing a tampon of polyester foam cubes and chips of carboxymethylcellulose, an edible thickening agent used in puddings and ice cream, and known as "grass"— recognized as safe because it passes through the body without decomposing.[58] Encapsulated within a polyester teabag-like pouch, the tampon was unlike any other, and Proctor & Gamble marketed the new design as Rely, presumably because one could depend on it to absorb menstrual flow, and better yet, according to the packaging, "it even absorbs the worry."[59] Marketers blitzed mailboxes as early as 1975 with sample packets of Rely, and the tactic proved wildly successful. The numbers of packets distributed through the mail was impressive and aggressive: 45 million samples distributed, with the April 1980 campaign alone numbering 16,800,000 samples.[60] Early numbers indicated that women purchased Rely after using the sample, and if the trends continued, it had the potential to dislodge Tampax from its position of dominance in the tampon market. The company, however, began receiving calls from women who were concerned with uncomfortable side effects, such as fevers and chills, and they linked these symptoms to their menstrual periods and to using the new tampon. Unfortunately for some women who harbored the bacterial strain *Staphylococcus aureus*, the wearing of Rely promoted its uncontrolled growth. Some women experienced mild and uncomfortable flu-like symptoms. For those women whose immune systems could not thwart the bacteria, the toxins it released literally poisoned the body, with the worst-case scenario leading to a woman's death. After much difficulty in identifying and agreeing to the clinical terms of this disease path, the new ailment was dubbed Toxic Shock Syndrome (TSS). A case definition of TSS, according to the Centers for Disease Control, "requires four major criteria (fever, hypotension, rash and desquamation), involvement of three organ systems, and absence of evidence of other etiologies."[61] In 1980, there were 814 clinical cases of TSS, and 38 reported deaths. However, many more women likely developed cases of TSS, though they did not fit the strict criteria to be reported to the CDC. The company continued to send out free samples, to the tune of 2.5 million in July 1980, even after reports speculated a link between Rely and TSS.[62] Due to the increasing use of high-absorbent tampons, there were many women who exhibited some of the symptoms associated with a diagnosis of TSS but were not declared to have the disease. Some even had full-blown TSS but the link to tampon use was dismissed. Each manufacturer had been sued for product liability, including Tambrands, Playtex, and Johnson & Johnson, but the evidence mounted against Proctor & Gamble, with 71% of women who reported symptoms using Rely.[63] More than 1,100 lawsuits were filed against Proctor & Gamble, but the most successful case was tried by attorney Tom Riley on behalf of Patricia Kehm, a twenty-five-year-old mother of two who died within a week of using Rely tampons during her period in 1980.

An examination of the product liability lawsuit and trial in 1982 against Proctor & Gamble demonstrates the horrible unmasking of passing. This 3000-page transcript details the tribulations of Cedar Rapids, Iowa attorney Tom Riley taking on Proctor & Gamble, whose resources included a team of lawyers and corps of scientists and experts. In this court case, Michael Kehm sued on behalf of his wife, Patricia Kehm, who died from TSS linked to wearing Rely tampons. Urged by her sister to try the free samples, Patricia Kehm wore them for four days. As she began experiencing symptoms such as high fever, vomiting, and fatigue, she brushed off what she thought was a bad cold. Little did she know that her tampon would be a co-factor in her death on September 6, 1980. Though the Centers for Disease Control and Prevention in Atlanta was tracing cases of the syndrome, linking the menstrually associated cases of TSS to tampons and Rely proved to be more difficult. With the urging of the CDC and FDA, Proctor & Gamble removed Rely from store shelves on September 22, 1980 before a formal recall could be announced.

The trial revealed the extent to which Proctor & Gamble worked to muddy the association of tampons with TSS, to the degree that there is still uncertainty about the mechanics of how Rely could be implicated. On one level, many of the scientists and engineers who testified and had a hand in the development seemed genuinely perplexed that the tampon would cause such harm. Since sanitary pads and tampons were newly classified as medical devices by the FDA in 1976, Proctor & Gamble was required to conduct some product testing, although much was grandfathered in. However, researchers fed the carboxymethylcellulose chips to mice, and fabricated tiny tampons called pledgets for mice to wear during a two-year study.[64] Women also tested the product before the company marketed it, and the researchers found no signs of danger. However, since the *staphylococcus aureus* strain appeared in about 5–10% of women in the late 1970s and early 1980s and infection was linked to those women whose immune systems failed to expel the toxin, it is not surprising that the horrible consequences were not discovered in a small test group numbering about 1500 women. In description after description, Tom Riley could not budge the scientists into admitting any malfeasance on their part. Riley cross-examined Roscoe Carter, a Ph.D. chemist and safety expert at Proctor & Gamble, who among other things helped develop Crisco after World War II, and was retained especially for liability cases concerning Rely. The following exchange occurred between them:

> Riley: [W]ith all your knowledge, you are sitting here and you want this jury to believe you wouldn't tell a friend of yours to remove a tampon if she had those symptoms [of TSS], is that what you are telling the jury?

> Carter: That is correct. I would see a doctor as soon as you can and follow the doctor's directions. If he said to remove them, fine.[65]

What Carter's testimony made clear was that tampon technologies were not the problem. The tampons performed the way they were supposed to by helping a woman pass. Arguably, it was women's bodies that were at fault, with the tampons unfairly implicated.

The hubris of Carter galled Riley to no end. Riley's own expert, independent microbiologist Dr. Philip Tierno, entirely contradicted Carter's assertions in his testimony. As Tierno explained, he became curious about Rely's absorptive properties after his wife asked him why she did not come down with TSS when she wore Rely. He wondered about the efficacy of these new tampons, and in particular, what affect the vaginal flora had on the degradation of carboxymethylcellulose. In the Kehm trial, he testified that the chips degraded into their more basic element of glucose, which provided the perfect medium to promote the growth of more bacteria. As the external polyester pouch was impervious to phagocytes and their ability to eliminate bacteria, the staph continued to grow, thrive, and produce toxins. He testified that he was at loss as to why the Proctor & Gamble researchers did not conduct this test in the preliminary research phase, and why they were unable to repeat his findings.[66] Without a doubt, he believed that Rely was a co-factor in the production of TSS in those women who harbored the usually benign staph bacteria in their bodies.

The main arguments posed by Timothy White defending Proctor & Gamble were that Patricia Kehm did not use Rely and she did not contract TSS. Yet, her sister, Colleen Jones, testified that she encouraged Patricia to use the new tampons and switch from Playtex to Rely. While Kehm was pregnant with her daughter due in June, Jones "told her how absorbent they were and when it came time for her to start using tampons that she should try them." Jones had been bothering her about it since July when her period started, six weeks after the delivery. When asked how Jones knew that Kehm had started wearing Rely, she recalled it was September, because "I stopped over to her house one day, and she told me she was—wasn't feeling good, and then on top of that she had her period, and I said, 'Oh, have you tried Rely yet?' She says, 'I'm using them now.'"[67] Her mother, Jean Robinson, testified as well that Patricia had purchased and was wearing Rely. She remembered that Patricia had purchased them on a shopping trip because it was August 24, 1980, the day that Katie, the baby, had been baptized at St. Patrick's church. At the store she berated her daughter and asked, "so you are going to try those dumb things?" meaning Rely tampons, which she of course did.[68] In many ways, this example plays out the drama of the pass, with the women as the in-group having knowledge of her period and her technologies of passing, while her husband, Michael, the beneficiary of the pass, seemed to be the last to know. The defense lawyers asked: "I take it you and Patricia didn't sit down and systematically discuss what tampons she used or preferred?" Kehm replied: "That's correct. I don't think we ever discussed it."[69] He testified that Colleen Jones, his sister-in-law, told him that Patricia was having her period only after he described some of her symptoms and conveyed to her that one doctor speculated that it might be TSS. After she died and he returned home, he lamented "even though the doctors couldn't confirm that that happened to be it [TSS], I seen a box of Rely tampons, and I in a moment of anger and disgust, I threw them in the wastebasket."[70]

The defense repeatedly asked the emergency room physician and nurse why they removed the tampon, why they noted it was a Tampax and not Rely, and why it was not saved. The emergency room nurse, Lois Sterenchuk, forced to reveal her menstrual status under oath, testified that she was menopausal, and generically referred to all tampons as Tampax because she did not know of any other. Thus, in Kehm's medical record she entered "Tampax removed by L. Sterenchuk, RN."[71] The defense pounced upon this, and she testified that "I use the word 'Tampax' I guess as I might use the 'Kleenex' in place of facial tissue. Something like that."[72] In his redirect, Riley pointed to a box of Puffs facial tissue, manufactured by Proctor & Gamble, and questioned her.

> Riley: If this were sitting on the table and you needed one for a cold or something, what might you ask for?
>
> Sterenchuk: Kleenex.
>
> Riley: Despite the billions of dollars of advertising that has been spent by Proctor and Gamble, you would still refer to it as a Kleenex, because that was the original, isn't that right?
>
> Sterenchuk: Yes, sir.[73]

Though she may not have named it correctly, when asked to describe how the tampon looked she called it "mushroom shape" which clearly did not describe the elongated Tampax. After removing the tampon, she said there was no discussion. "I took it out. Just like I have every tampon in my thirty years of nursing. I have never saved one yet. Held it up, looked at it and disposed of it."[74] At that moment, it seemed to have little meaning.

Dr. John Jacobs, who was the attending physician in the emergency room on September 6, 1980 when Kehm was admitted, was not familiar with TSS, but learned about it that day. Even if he had known, Kehm's body had devolved into serious shock when she arrived at the hospital, and nothing could have been done to save her. The defense lawyer Timothy White read back the medical report to Jacobs, and pressed the issue concerning the reason why tampons were not mentioned.

White: Now, does that make any mention under diagnosis of tampons?

Jacobs: Well, of course, tampon is not a medical diagnosis.[75]

White continuously pressed Jacobs to admit fault, which ended up making him a sympathetic character, and not a bumbling physician. Asking a woman if she was wearing a tampon and then saving it for culturing were hardly standard ER procedures, let alone the basis of a diagnosis.

The defense worked to discredit the coroner's report, Kehm's medical record, and testimony of the hospital staff. They raised questions about TSS being caused by her IUD to implicate her body, and not the tampon, and therefore exonerate Proctor & Gamble. The case publicized Patricia Kehm's birth control decisions and menstrual habits in intimate and detailed ways, yet her husband at the time was clueless about these practices until the trial. His wife had been successfully passing, and he had the privilege of ignorance, and had no need to become educated about menstrual hygiene technologies. As a result of the trial, the jury found Proctor & Gamble negligent in the death of Patricia Kehm since it had knowledge about TSS in the summer preceding her death. The jury did not award punitive damages, intended to punish Proctor & Gamble for reckless disregard of rights, but it did award Michael Kehm $300,000 in compensatory damages in the liability case. As disappointing as the verdict was, it was successful in that it brought damages against Proctor & Gamble, and no other case was able to do that.[76] After Rely was discontinued just a few weeks after Kehm's death, and public health officials were able to get out the word about TSS, thousands of women stopped wearing tampons, and paper inserts concerning safety and use appeared in product boxes.

Alternative Menstrual Hygiene Choices

The irony of a product marketed to benefit women as salubrious and then proven to be dangerous at best and fatal at worst has not gone unnoticed. Women have reacted to these problematic menstrual hygiene technologies in different ways. First, there are women who still want to purchase and use menstrual hygiene technologies. They have continued buying and using the mainstream products and amended their habits, for example not wearing a tampon to bed. In essence, they have had to conform to the technology, and the technology has not changed for them. Next, there are women who have sought out alternative products, such as organic tampons or washable menstrual cups. Finally, many feminists who consider themselves part of the "third wave" have abandoned manufactured tampons altogether. They are concerned about design that presumes single-use and creates products destined for the landfill; health issues stemming from dioxin in bleached tampons; and the myth perpetuated by corporations that assumes the validity of a pathological female body. The result is that some feminists have imposed their own aesthetics and agency about menstruation onto the way products are defined and used. Influenced by the women's health movement, they have sought out alternative methods to trap menstrual flow. Readily available at health food stores are washable receptacles, some shaped in the form of a deep cup or shallow diaphragm, and worn in the vagina for up to twelve hours. Called menstrual cups, these devices are reusable and washable, and appeal to women who want to diminish their reliance upon disposable products. One woman with whom I spoke, Emma, a student at a small liberal arts college, proudly revealed that the menstrual fluid she saved from her cup, when mixed with water, promoted the growth of her plants when she used it as a fertilizer. She thought her plants never looked so good. She also happily claimed the honor of the "menstrual lady" bestowed upon her after she decided to educate women on her campus about menstrual hygiene alternatives such as the Diva Cup. She earned the name by initiating sewing bees in which women learned to make their own flannel pads. The women chose their fabric design, anything from the ironic plain red to Scooby Doo, and she instructed them how to sew in an absorptive layer, and where to put the Velcro. Emma said most women were amazed at how comfortable the pads were, and appreciated the benefits of washing the pads instead of tossing them out with the trash.[77] This practice takes us full circle, and back to women's customs before the sale of manufactured disposable menstrual hygiene products. Going beyond making pads, some women relinquished them altogether. There is a habit called free bleeding, in which women abandon technologies in total. Some exercise this only while sleeping, and find that by propping up the pelvis, or even sleeping on a towel, the vagina traps the blood that later can be expelled in the toilet. In this case, menstrual hygiene technologies are not necessary at all.

However, abandoning menstrual hygiene technologies altogether has proved too far-fetched, and most women have come to accept and even demand the practical element of managing, and even masking, the body with menstrual hygiene technologies. Instead of succumbing to the messages of producing a feminized and acceptable body, some women have redefined and appropriated the technology for their own means.[78] Gloria Nickerson, Major, United States Army Reserves (retired), remembered how she and the WACs started "a little feminist campaign" in the mid-1970s while on field duty. Issued small steel pots, used for a variety of things including a toilet, a cooking pan, and a wash-basin, they also were playfully worn on the head. An elastic band encircled the pot, and women usually secured and stored cigarettes along the band. However, the WACs began putting tampons in the band as a mark of pride. As Nickerson put it, "[t]he statement made was 'This is the only little instrument we need to deal with the biggest objection small minds have about women pulling field duty!' No one ever said shit about it!"[79] The technology, often signifying women's menstrual debility, became a symbol of women's power. Through this activity, they embraced the unique elements of being female to derive power from their bodies, through the sign of the female specific technology of tam-pons. More recently, my colleague Virginia Eubanks, who teaches in the De-partment of Women's Studies at the University at Albany, SUNY, developed a feminist electronic zine called *Brillo* while in graduate school. In characteristic interactive fashion, readers began offering homey advice to one another such as "leave a tampon on the dashboard of your car to deter auto theft."[80] As the cul-tural logic goes, a tampon would be so disgusting to a presumably male thief that it would not be worth the effort to steal or break into the car. Again, women's female specific technologies are re-appropriated and turned on their head. They are not about absorbing shameful menstrual blood, but empowering women to fight crime through their unique attributes as women.

The last part of the twentieth century has witnessed profound attitude shifts about menstruation and menstrual hygiene technologies, in part due to the spread of feminist health concerns. In addition, the four components—the narra-tives, pragmatics, agency engendered, and limitations—of technological passing clearly converged during this time period. Manufacturers and advertisers took up a cultural feminist narrative, making the claim over the years that tampons are liberating and freeing, thus allowing women to pursue rigorous physical ac-tivity. As an anecdote, Pat, who grew up in Tonawanda, New York during the 1950s, recounted a very sweet story about her neighbor, Eddie, who gave her a box of tampons for her seventh birthday. No doubt swayed by the marketing, he told her that she could "do all kinds of stuff with these things, like ride horses and swim." He got the message loud and clear about women's liberation, and was very excited that his friend might enjoy all the wonderful things promised by the advertising, though he clearly misunderstood the intended use of the ob-jects.[81] It is the very ubiquity of the advertising and the incorporation of freedom that has become normalized over the years. However, manufacturers' claims of liberation rang hollow when product safety was at stake. Feminists could not help but level criticism against Proctor & Gamble for foisting TSS onto untold numbers of women with Rely. Triggered in part by the distrust of business, many women began to conscientiously use or even abandon menstrual hygiene technologies to create their own woman-centered power sources.

How women have engaged feminist use of technology varies. Marketing has incorporated elements of feminism, yet by hooking a product into the notion of freedom, it ironically cheapens and diminishes that very idea as a true political aspiration by making it seemingly saleable. The consumer purchase of tampons does not bring improved citizenship rights for women, though arguably women do benefit in a pragmatic sort of way in the daily management of their bodies. The way that the products are advertised might be called commercial feminism, since the language of marketing hinges on democratic notions of freedom. Whether or not menstrual hygiene technologies can deliver political freedom is another question. The products embody the trappings of feminism, albeit in a consumerist venue. However, it is women's use of them, and how women choose to employ technologies of passing (or not), that redefines the technologies, knowledge, and practices.

Notes

1. Karl Karnaky, "A New Absorptive for Menstrual Hygiene," *Arizona Medicine* 16, no. 9 (September 1959): 605–608.

2. Memorandum, "Condensation of Presentation made September 29, 1964 with Reference to the Negro Market," by Daniel J. Edelman and Associates, Inc., 1964 Kimberly-Clark Corporation Archives, Catalog no. 09-03-01-001-0012, Box no. 9-172, The History Factory.

3. Robert E. Weems, Jr., "Consumerism and the Construction of Black Female Identity in Twentieth-Century America," *The Gender and Consumer Culture Reader*, ed. Jennifer Scanlon (New York: New York University Press, 2000), 166–178.

4. Memorandum, "Condensation of Presentation made September 29, 1964 with Reference to the Negro Market," by Daniel J. Edelman and Associates, Inc., 1964, Kimberly-Clark Corporation Archives, Catalog no. 09-03-01-001-0012, Box no. 9-172, The History Factory.

5. Memorandum regarding the teens' column "Very Personally Yours" for Negro newspaper and sample copies of columns from the Public Relations Department, December 11, 1964, Kimberly-Clark Corporation Archives, Catalog no. 09-03-01-008-0001, Box no. 9-180, The History Factory..

6. Memorandum, "Condensation of Presentation made September 29, 1964 with Reference to the Negro Market," by Daniel J. Edelman and Associates, Inc., 1964, Kimberly-Clark Corporation Archives, Catalog no. 09-03-01-001-0012, Box no. 9-172, The History Factory.

7. Report, "An Advertising Plan for Kimberly-Clark in the Negro Press," by Daniel J. Edelman and Associates, Inc., September 1967, 3, Kimberly-Clark Corporation Archives, Catalog no. 09-03-01-001-0014, Box no. 9-172, The History Factory.

8. "The Negro Family: The Case for National Action," Office of Policy Planning and Research United States Department of Labor (March 1965), http://www.dol.gov/asp/programs/history/webid-meynihan.htm (accessed June 7, 2005).

9. Report, "An Advertising Plan for Kimberly-Clark in the Negro Press," by Daniel J. Edelman and Associates, Inc., September 1967, 4, Kimberly-Clark Corporation Archives, Catalog no. 09-03-01-001-0014, Box no. 9-172, The History Factory.

10. Report, "An Advertising Plan for Kimberly-Clark in the Negro Press," by Daniel J. Edelman and Associates, Inc., September 1967, 4, Kimberly-Clark Corporation Archives, Catalog no. 09-03-01-001-0014, Box no. 9-172, The History Factory.

11. Memorandum regarding the teens' column "Very Personally Yours" for Negro newspaper and sample copies of columns from the Public Relations Department, December 11, 1964, Kimberly-Clark Corporation Archives, Catalog no. 09-03-01-008-0001, Box no. 9-180, The History Factory.

12. Report, "An Advertising Plan for Kimberly-Clark in the Negro Press," by Daniel J. Edelman and Associates, Inc., September 1967, 6, Kimberly-Clark Corporation Archives, Catalog no. 09-03-01-001-0014, Box no. 9-172, The History Factory. On the riots see "Detroit Riots 1967," http://www.67riots.rutgers.edu/d_index.htm (accessed September 27, 2005).

13. Report, "An Advertising Plan for Kimberly-Clark in the Negro Press," by Daniel J. Edelman and Associates, Inc., September 1967, 7, Kimberly-Clark Corporation Archives, Catalog no. 09-03-01-001-0014, Box no. 9-172, The History Factory.

14. Report, "An Advertising Plan for Kimberly-Clark in the Negro Press," by Daniel J. Edelman and Associates, Inc., September 1967, 10, Kimberly-Clark Corporation Archives, Catalog no. 09-03-01-001-0014, Box no. 9-172, The History Factory.

15. "Revised Code Flirts with Rich New Market," *Broadcasting* 76, no. 3 (January 1969): 25. See also Kathleen Kane, "Feminine Hygiene Commercials: A Political and Symbolic Economy" (Ph.D. Dissertation, Northwestern University, 1992).

16. Report, "An Advertising Plan for Kimberly-Clark in the Negro Press," by Daniel J. Edelman and Associates, Inc., September 1967, 5, Kimberly-Clark Corporation Archives, Catalog no. 09-03-01-001-0014, Box no. 9-172, The History Factory.

17. Letter regarding complaint that Kimberly-Clark is not adequately serving the Negro market through advertising, July 2, 1968, Kimberly-Clark Corporation Archives, Catalog no. 09-03-01-008-0001, Box no. 9-180, The History Factory.

18. "Proportioned What?" Kotex advertising copy for placement in *Ebony* magazine, November 1962, Kimberly-Clark Corporation Archives, Catalog no. 09-02-00-006-0014, Box no. 9-131, The History Factory.

19. "Proportioned What?" Kotex advertising copy for general magazine placement, November 1962, Kimberly-Clark Corporation Archives, Catalog no. 09-02-00-006-0014, Box no. 9-131, The History Factory.

20. "Revised Code Flirts with Rich New Market," *Broadcasting* 76, no. 3 (January 1969): 23.

21. "Group W Stations Quit Broadcasters TV Code, Citing Alleged Leniency," *Wall Street Journal*, February 2, 1969, in Professor Barrett Collection, Commercial Advertising Folder, University Archives, Washington University in St. Louis.

22. "Revised Code Flirts with Rich New Market," 23–24.

23. "30-Second Time Bomb," *Broadcasting* 78, no. 24 (June 1970): 5.

24. "Sanitary Napkins on Television?" *Broadcasting* 79, no. 1 (July 1970): 41.

25. "No Rush Through the Breach in Feminine-Product Advertising," *Broadcasting* 84, no. 1 (January 1973): 24.

26. "Revised Code Flirts with Rich New Market," 25.

27. "No Rush Through the Breach in Feminine-Product Advertising," *Broadcasting* 84, no. 1 (January 1973): 23–24.

28. Diane Francis, "The Promo that Launched a Thousand Protests," *Maclean's* 92 (January 1979): 39.

29. "The Promo that Launched a Thousand Protests," 39.

30. "TV Code Board Spells out More Ad Guidelines," *Broadcasting* 85, no. 17 (October 1973): 25.

31. A Redstocking Sister, "Consumerism and Women," in *Woman in Sexist Society: Studies in Power and Powerlessness*, eds. Vivian Gornick and Barbara K. Moran (New York: Basic Books, 1971), 662.

32. Gloria Steinem, "If Men Could Menstruate," *Ms. Magazine* (October 1978).

33. Feminist Women's Health Center, "Self Help Clinic Celebrates 25 Years," http://www.fwhc.org/selfhelp.htm (accessed April 2, 2007); Janice Delaney, Mary Jane Lupton and Emily Toth, *The Curse: A Cultural History of Menstruation* (Urbana: University of Illinois Press, 1988), 255–57.

34. "Unofficial Abortion," *Time Magazine* (September 11, 1972), http://www.time.com/time/magazine/article/0,9171,906342,00.html (accessed March 12, 2007).

35. The Boston Women's Health Collective, *Our Bodies, Ourselves: A Book By and For Women* (New York: Simon and Schuster, 2nd edition, 1976), 25.

36. *Our Bodies, Ourselves*, 34.

37. *Our Bodies, Ourselves*, 34.

38. Karnaky, 606.

39. Karnaky, 606.

40. Karnaky, 605.

41. Karnaky, 607.

42. Karnaky, 608.

43. Willard Allen to Frederick Zuspan (March 22, 1984). Papers of Edward G. Willard, Miner Library, University of Rochester Medical Center, New York, Box 10/4.

44. Frederick Zuspan to Willard Allen (April 13, 1984). Papers of Edward G. Willard, Miner Library, University of Rochester Medical Center, New York, Box 10/4.

45. Personal correspondence, Elizabeth White to author (February 24, 2005). John P. McGovern Historical Collection and Research Center, Houston Academy of Medicine-Texas Medical Center.

46. "Cellophane Tape," http://www.ideafinder.com/history/inventions /cellophanetape.htm (accessed October 4, 2005); "Scotch Tape and Richard Drew," http://inventors.about.com/library/inventors/blscotchtape.htm (accessed October 4, 2005).

47. For a detailed business history of Kimberly-Clark's slipping market share in sanitary napkins, see Thomas Heinrich and Bob Batchelor, *Kotex, Kleenex and Huggies: Kimberly-Clark and the Consumer Revolution in American Business* (Columbus: Ohio State University Press, 2004), 172–73.

48. "For Peace of Mind and Body," *McCall's* (June 1974): n.p.

49. "The Maxi Pad. The Mini Pad," *McCall's* (June 1972): n.p.

50. "The Maxi Pad. The Mini Pad," *McCall's* (June 1972): n.p.

51. United States Patent Office, #3,397,697 (August 20, 1968), Charlotte I. Rickard, "Disposable Sanitary Shield for Undergarments."

52. Faye, interview with the author (April 13, 2005).

53. Wendy, interview with Rebecca Moore (July 19, 2005).

54. *Kotex, Kleenex Huggies*, 172–75.

55. *Michael L. Kehm v. Proctor & Gamble*, United States Courthouse, Cedar Rapids, Iowa, April 5, 1982, 275.

56. For a detailed business history of Proctor & Gamble, including the marketing tactics used to sell Rely, see Alecia Swasy, *Soap Opera: The Inside Story of Proctor & Gamble* (New York: Times Books, 1993). For an autobiographical account of the trial against Proctor & Gamble, see Tom Riley, *The Price of a Life: One Woman's Death from Toxic Shock* (Bethesda: Adler and Adler Publishers, Inc., 1986). In addition, the women's health movement prompted publications concerning the dangers of tampons. See Nancy Friedman, *Everything You Must Know about Tampons* (New York: Berkley Books, 1981).

57. Swasy, *Soap Opera*, 138.

58. *Kehm v. Proctor & Gamble*, 2339.

59. "Rely Tampon: It Even Absorbs the Worry," n.d, n.p, Museum of Menstruation, http://www.mum.org/Rely.htm (accessed June 21, 2005).

60. *Kehm v. Proctor & Gamble*, 1334–35.

61. "Toxic Shock Syndrome—United States, 1970–1980," *Morbidity and Mortality Weekly Report* 30, no. 3 (January 1981): 25–28, 33.

62. *Kehm v. Proctor & Gamble*, 1335.

63. Friedman, *Everything You Must Know About Tampons*, 67–68.

64. *Kehm v. Proctor & Gamble*, 2261.

65. *Kehm v. Proctor & Gamble*, 2639–40.

66. *Kehm v. Proctor & Gamble*, 837–1007.

67. *Kehm v. Proctor & Gamble*, 1077–78.

68. *Kehm v. Proctor & Gamble*, 1120.

69. *Kehm v. Proctor & Gamble*, 1472.

70. *Kehm v. Proctor & Gamble*, 1441.

71. *Kehm v. Proctor & Gamble*, 784.

72. *Kehm v. Proctor & Gamble*, 786.

73. *Kehm v. Proctor & Gamble*, 824.

74. *Kehm v. Proctor & Gamble*, 816.

75. *Kehm v. Proctor & Gamble*, 642.

76. Tom Riley, *The Price of a Life*, 250–52.

77. Emma, interview with author (May 26, 2005).

78. Ron Eglash, et al., *Appropriating Technology: Vernacular Technology and Social Power* (Minneapolis: University of Minnesota Press, 2004).

79. Gloria Nickerson to H-MINERVA@H-NET.MSU.EDU, "Comment: Menstruation and Women in Combat" (August 14, 1998).

80. *Brillo Magazine*, "Tampon Tip," http://www.brillomag.net/No2/contents.htm (accessed May 22, 2006).

81. Pat, interview with author (May 3, 2006).

Chapter 8

Unveiling Menstrual Passing

[C]an we reasonably doubt that our present finely spun theories of menstruation will excite among medical historians of the future the same compassion which we now bestow upon the crude beliefs of our scientific forbears?[1]

—Emil Novak, 1916

In the course of telling people about the history of menstrual hygiene technologies during many years of research, I have received mostly enthusiastic reactions. On numerous occasions, women have excitedly told me that they want to read the book. Others have expressed to me the details of their first menstrual experiences. People have been intrigued with the history of menstruation and menstrual hygiene technologies, I believe because it is a unique topic and it resonates with their day-to-day lived experiences. On the other hand, I have received equally unkind remarks. One woman I approached for an oral history replied that the whole thing was "dumb" and could not believe anyone would stoop so low. When I wrote out a three-line bio for a recent article I published, the editor asked that I not include the title of the book; it simply would not "go over" with the readership.

More recently, I learned that the 1998 panel I organized for the American Historical Association, entitled *Talking Around Sex: Constructing Menstruation, Purification, and Sterilization Campaigns in Twentieth-Century America*, became evidence for the decline in standards for United States history. Specifically, Marc Trachtenberg wrote "The Past Under Siege" in the *Wall Street Journal* in which he announced the founding of a new group, the New Historical Society, which would reclaim "real" history.[2] Its goals are to reorient the "historical profession toward an accessible integrated history free from fragmentation, over-specialization, and political proscription."[3] In it, he calls current historical practices, of which I supposedly am a part, a "particular brand of history" based upon personal politics, not truth in history. My panel and specifically my paper were then referred to as "some of the more egregious examples of academic folly" by James Banner, who provided a retort to Trachtenberg that criticized the foundation of his new group. These impassioned reactions, both enthusiastic and dismissive, indicate to me that the politics of menstruation are alive and well, and discussing menstruation is a problem, often inappropriate and illegitimate.

The pressure that this tacit politics has put upon women is immense. An innocent question such as, "What is your book about?" often begins a conversation that breaks a long held silence about menstruation, and the women respond with stories they have never revealed before. So many women—some friends and some strangers—of all ages and backgrounds have told me things that I would have never thought to ask. Their memories and stories are incredible: the woman whose teacher handed out sanitary napkins after sex education class under the stage in the school cafeteria/auditorium, and how that made her feel dirty; the woman who remembered how as a teen, tampons were just too big, and the doctor told her she needed to start using a douche if she was ever going to have sex; the way "M" days at a suburban Chicago high school, where girls were still segregated during their periods even through the 1980s, made some of the boys feel uncomfortable; the teen who thought she was going to die from the uncontrollable bleeding coming from inside of her; the woman whose family vacation at the beach was ruined because she refused to wear a tampon instead of a sanitary napkin. The intimate, personal, and often traumatic stories were ones that they needed to tell, and finally had the opening to do so. Passing puts pressure on people to perform, and it takes a great amount of energy to do so. Many women get tired of the whole show, and I believe that my acknowledgement of their experiences opened the floodgates to discuss and validate their lives and identities.

One such instance captures this spirit. My research assistant, Rebecca Moore conducted an oral history with two women simultaneously. At first, they were a bit reluctant to open up, but gained confidence as the discussion proceeded. When Rebecca tried to conclude the interview, they refused, and one woman got very excited about continuing and asked Rebecca if she thought I would like her responses. She then requests, "ask me more!" with her friend Cindy chiming in, "Now you want to ask more?." Beverly talks for another twenty minutes.[4] I cannot help but smile when I think of this interview and witness Beverly's realization that her feelings and thoughts about menstruation and menstrual hygiene are important and that it is perfectly legitimate to talk about them.

This desire to keep talking about menstruation contradicts the prevailing medical trend to minimize its meaning. There is a new medical theory afoot that argues that monthly menstrual periods are not the "natural" state of women. Elsimar M. Coutinho, a Brazilian gynecologist and researcher on the first Depo Provera trials (a long-term contraceptive injection), and Sheldon J. Segal, a biochemist and former director of the Population Sciences Division of the Rockefeller Foundation, have written the book *Is Menstruation Obsolete?*.[5] Based on anthropological and historical studies of fertility patterns, they contend that women experienced fewer menstrual periods in the past due to multiple pregnancies and longer lactation times. They note that women today live longer, which also accounts for more periods on the whole. Their main conclusion is that modern women, excessively menstruating for years, develop more reproductive problems including endometriosis, anemia, and ovarian cancer. The doctors recommend that women suppress menstruation, potentially for years on end, and begin to menstruate only when they choose, if they want to become pregnant. Not surprisingly, this book appeared shortly before the FDA trials for a new birth control pill called "Seasonale," an eighty-four-day contraceptive pill regimen intended to suppress menstruation for four months at a time.[6] The goal is to eliminate menstrual cycles; the prevention of pregnancy is a side benefit. In this model, menstruation is a nuisance at best, pathological at worst, and void of any cultural meaning, further alienating women from their own bodies.

In addition, menstruation has also been reduced to a form of biological information relaying particulars of the body. Take for example the question of whether a woman is pregnant or not. Many women use a home pregnancy test to measure hormonal shifts that indicate a viable pregnancy.[7] However, if a woman's period is late, menstruation and not the test still proves to be the best information that she is not pregnant. In this case, it is rendered as data. Yet, menstruation is more than data because it is a bodily experience, and the practices around it display the political consequences of bleeding. That is why passing is so powerful. For many women it is empowering and allows them to sidestep the prejudice held against bleeding bodies. Yet, the prejudice remains. Using technologies of passing is a profound and ingrained way of existing, behaving, and shaping female identity. As multiple technologies alter and shape knowledge and behavior, individuals constantly sculpt and remake their own identities. These identities are "real" but only a partial truth and necessarily render material realities invisible. Just as women's bodies still menstruate, menstrual hygiene technologies mask the truth, and allow women to act and behave in a mode of denial.

So, what would menstruation look like without this reliance upon passing? As one colleague put the question to me, "When is menstruation considered to be a privilege?" After a long pause, I could think of no such contemporary instances related to power and privilege. When does a woman actually benefit—receive real, tangible, societal perks—from the very act of menstruating? In the early 1990s, Margie Profet won a MacArthur award in part because she argued that menstruation was protective, a biological defense against pathogens transported into the uterus by sperm.[8] This one benefit and pro-menstrual position received some media attention, most likely because the notion of "good" menstruation was radical and put forth as a feminist scientific interpretation of menstruation. Yet, it has been pretty well dismissed by most scientists.[9] So the question of privilege remains. If it were privileged, there would be less need for technological passing. Currently for most women menstruation is an inconvenience. But, if this is the best we can do, what ways of knowing does this attitude obscure, and what might we be missing by succumbing to the discomfort that hitting this cultural nerve precipitates?

As one woman interviewed for the book astutely commented, "to keep it hidden is expensive."[10] Certainly the cost of hiding menstruation with sanitary napkins and tampons is economic, but it is a psychological burden as well. The place of technologies of passing must be questioned and more thoughtfully critiqued, because the current United States culture is so invested in passing that the consequences of the simulation of reality, or simulacrum, equate to living with an artificial sense of reality. Though examples of cross-dressing or light-skinned slaves passing as white are more dramatic, likely because the political stakes seem higher, passing is far more ubiquitous than we have previously recognized. Cosmetic surgery allows one to pass as a beautiful person. Administering the prescription drug Ritalin to young boys masks hyper-activity and allows many to pass as calm or well behaved. Even an aspirin masks a headache without curing the cause of the pain, thus one may go about one's day as if everything were normal. In all these examples, the problem is not cured, only temporarily masked via technology. The pressure to conform to an ever-moving normative standard—however that standard is measured and in effect exceed it— exacts a social cost, and ultimately bankrupts the very quirks of uniquely human attributes. How privilege is garnered and maintained, and what role technologies of passing play in stabilizing systems of privilege must be recognized and in many cases contested. The examination of menstrual hygiene technologies provides an example of technologies of passing and is one means to discuss how managing the female body and performing temporarily as a non-menstruant reveal deeply embedded assumptions about women's identity in the United States. By recognizing the embedded politics in menstrual technologies, we may begin to challenge them as artifacts of control and instead use them as empowering tools of change.

Notes

1. Emil Novak, "The Superstition and Folklore of Menstruation," *Johns Hopkins Hospital Bulletin* 307 (September 1916): 274.

2. Marc Trachtenberg, "The Past Under Siege: A Historian Ponders the State of His Profession and What to Do about It," *Wall Street Journal,* July 17, 1998, on H-SHEAR, "H-NET Debate: Banner & Trachtenberg" (September 16, 1998).

3. The Historical Society, http://www.bu.edu/historic/ (accessed May 26, 2006).

4. Beverly and Cindy, interview with Rebecca Moore (August 13, 2005).

5. Elsimar M. Coutinho and Sheldon J. Segal, *Is Menstruation Obsolete?* (New York: Oxford, 1999); Liz Brody, "Could Your Period Give You Cancer?" *Glamour* (July 2000): 41–42, 44, 211.

6. Jennifer Aengst, "A Need to Bleed? Nature, Necessity, and Menstruation," (paper presented at the annual meeting of the Society for Social Studies of Science, Pasadena, CA, October 22, 2005).

7. Linda Layne, "Feminist Technologies: The Case of the Home Pregnancy Test," (paper presented at the annual meeting of the Society for Social Studies of Science, Pasadena, CA, October 22, 2005)..

8. Margie Profet, "Menstruation as a Defense Against Pathogens Transported by Sperm," *Quarterly Review of Biology* 68 (September 1993): 335–86.

9. John Travis, "Why Do Women Menstruate? Scientists Seek Reasons for this Feminine Phenomenon," *Science News* 151, no. 15 (April 1997): 230.

10. Cindy, interview with Rebecca Moore (August 13, 2005).

Index

About the Author

Sharra Vostral's research centers upon gender and women's bodies and the ways in which material artifacts and technology functioned historically in people's everyday lives. She has coedited a volume entitled *Feminist Technology*, a collection of essays that explore the possibilities of using feminist approaches to design new technologies. Her work also appears in edited volumes on the topics of menstruation and health and popular culture. Currently, she is an associate professor holding a joint appointment in gender and women's studies and history at the University of Illinois, Urbana-Champaign. Before arriving at Illinois, she was an assistant professor in science and technology studies at Rensselaer Polytechnic Institute. She received her Ph.D. and M.A. in history from Washington University in St. Louis, and holds an M.A. in American studies from St. Louis University. She completed her B.A. at the University of Michigan with honors in comparative religion.

DATE DUE

FEB 2 4 2012			